Juking

The

Masses

Fill Your Stoked Tank

A Surfer's Tale

By: Dave Boss

Dedication

This book and life could not have been without my family, Sammy, Jesse, Mom, Dad, The Carriage House Bed & Breakfast and our guests in Ocean Grove, NJ.

And my great old friends who have supported me along the way during my new healthier life path. Brett, Rick, Laddy, Chris, Gina, Sammy, Jesse and Katharine. You guys rule! Thanks dudes!

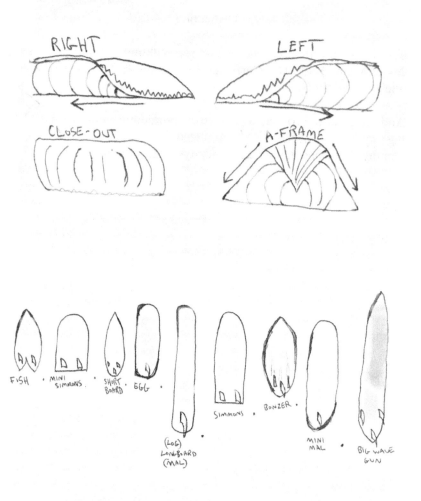

RIGHT

LEFT

CLOSE-OUT

A-FRAME

FISH

MINI SIMMONS

SHORT BOARD

EGG

(LOG) LONGBOARD (MAL)

SIMMONS

BONZER

MINI MAL

BIG WAVE GUN

4

Surfing is the fusion of flying and walking on water. Think about it!! Epic!!

Waves developing and breaking on the ocean's surface are a direct mirror image and scope of the physical contours on the ocean floor. The differences in these contours force the energy upward in shallower sections, causing them to develop into taller waves and break first, compared to deeper sections nearby. When watching waves break, they enlighten us with the secrets below, incapable of lying. They are transparent and have a direct relationship between stable and unique underwater nature (like reefs or temporary, always-changing sandbars) and moving swell energy, when combined, shapes the waves. Waves are a representation of the ocean floor, existing on the water's surface for us to see. This continues to blow my mind to this day. It's truly fascinating.

After decades of internal debate, I think The Velvet Underground is the best band in the world. Surfing is like The Velvet Underground. It's cool. I mean, really, cool. It's unique, it's crazy, it's honest, it can be chill, it can be hectic, but there's no denying it's radical energy.

Have you ever surfed in the rain? Paddling with your head just above the water's surface while looking out at the ocean in front of you. You see drops of water in every direction hitting the ocean's surface, thousands of them all around you, giving the illusion the drops are miraculously coming from the ocean and heading upward into the air, defying gravity. In windless conditions with an incredibly smooth ocean surface, it's quiet and natural. It's otherworldly.

Travel Is Everything

I want to document the last handful of years of my life, as I have a shit-ass memory, and a bunch of people have told me to, even though I feel what I do and how I live is not that important or impressive whatsoever. It's more for me to have some type of road map documented for at least part of my life. I have lived and traveled a lot in the last 17 years of adulthood, almost exclusively. At this point in my life, I'm extraordinarily bad at dates, years, and memories. For example, I couldn't tell you where I was in 2009, or where I was before or after. Being a traveling skateboarder/motorcycle rider/musician/surfer/outdoorsman/seeker of life, and general nomadic frolicker, I feel it's time to have a snapshot of when and where I was, at least for a little while.

I am documenting places I have been, experiences I have had, and relationships I have made through the scope of surfing. All of which have sculpted my life into who I am today. It's not meant to prove how cool or how much of some pro-shedding surfer I am. I'm not. I'm interested in documenting my travels, how I grew my surfing skills, unique things that happened while surfing, and how this made me the person I am today.

I've always had a subconscious interest in surfing; at the same time, being raised in Central New Jersey, I had no access to waves as a kid. The couple of days a summer that my dad took his boys to the beach was all we got. But we only body-surfed or boogie-boarded, having the most fun kids could have. I thought boogying was hokey fun as a kid, and I figured surfing was the same. I grew up snow-boarding from age eight or nine and skateboarding around age twelve. Surfing was always something I knew was out there, but I didn't exactly have a way to connect with it. I didn't relate to the Kelly Slater shortboarders, which was all I saw out there. I thought that was kind of lame back in the day. I was born and raised in the uninteresting, central New Jersey suburbia, where daily skateboard-ing and weekend Pocono snowboarding trips were options but surf-ing really wasn't on my radar. Over the years as an adult, I saw the sun-kissed, surf-bum type dude and was confused yet intrigued. Eventually, I became this.

Surfing saved or ruined my life, depending on how you think about it. Truthfully it doesn't matter either way, but it did turn me hard off course from anything else I may have been doing. I just live for it, so I guess it's a great thing that makes me stoked and smile.

In my mid-20's, I lived with my girlfriend (now ex) in Denver, Colorado for about six months, which is about as long as I last any-where. I convinced her to take an extended backpacking trip to Nica-ragua. I had an acquaintance/buddy named Chris, who I knew briefly through the skateboard scene in the mid-western USA, and I heard he spent some time in San Juan Del Sur, Nicaragua. This inspired us to go down there after I had saved up around $10,000 and quit my job. I was looking forward to trying out the activity of surfing but honestly had no expectation that it would even be cool. I put riding a surfboard in the same category as riding a shitty old boogie board from deep in the garage down at the Jersey Shore. I had no sem-blance at all that it was a vehicle for self-expression, meditation, high-intensity focus, coolness, etc....

When we landed in Nicaragua, I forced us to take a chicken bus as a mode of transport to save fifty bucks instead of a safer shuttle ride from Managua, the sketchy capital airport city in Nicaragua. Chicken buses were janky, old, yellow, elementary school buses that anything could happen in at any time – they were chaos but less than one dollar a ride. After almost getting my rucksack stolen off one of those buses and chasing the Nicaraguan man down in the street to get it back, we reached San Juan Del Sur. San Juan Del Sur is a funny surf town because there isn't any surf there. It's more of a convenient town to stay and go surf nearby. There are amazing surf spots and beaches to the north and south, which we eventually became savvy to and hitched a Jeep ride with a surf hostel to. Here, I rented a board to try surfing for the first time in Playa Madera sometime in 2012.

I was way too arrogant and prideful to take a surf lesson after being a halfway sponsored and traveling skateboarder for some years.

"Surf lessons are for nerds. How hard can it be right?" I thought.

I paddled out at Madera having absolutely zero clue what the hell I was doing, and I tried to figure it out on my own. I paddled out to where it seemed like other surfers were waiting and attempted to paddle into waves that other surfers seemed to be paddling for, but I wasn't grasping the concept one bit. I looked over to my left while trying to stay balanced sitting on my rented longboard and noticed a surf lesson. They were with the hostel that I turned down the lesson from. They were giving instructions within earshot from me. I eavesdropped, or poached free lesson advice from the group, yet pretended I wanted nothing to do with them. What a jerk I was, really, an asshole. I should go back and give a hundred bucks to that hostel now and thank them. This was before I grew modesty and honesty in my modern person. Since that period in my life, surfing, traveling, and experiencing different cultures has taught me better values.

After listening long enough next to the surf lesson, I gathered that I needed to paddle for a wave and sort of stand up on the board and ride what was left of it. For a beginner, it's whitewash or the whitewater of the broken wave that's left after a wave has broken. I went for it. My girlfriend was patiently watching me from the sand for an hour as I made a fool of myself. I rode some of that whitewater straight at her into shore. I caught my first whitewater beginner wave!

After hanging out for over a week, we talked about what it would be like to stay in San Juan Del Sur permanently. We both quit our jobs before we left, but we still had our apartment in Denver. We looked online and walked around town for a few days, searching for places to rent. We checked apartments that were in the range from super-shithole to semi-shithole until we stumbled on a one-bedroom apartment right off the beach on the first floor, and we almost said yes. My girlfriend wasn't super keen on my newfound gravity for staying more permanently or for my surfing desires that I just discovered. Inevitably, we did not end up taking the apartment. I still look back on that place thinking I should have rented it. The price was $150 a month USD! This could have been a lifetime opportunity, seeing that the older I get, low rent prices exist less and less.

I had only tried surfing that one time as we became indecisive about staying in San Juan Del Sur. We traveled inland, bouncing around the island of Ometepe within huge Lake Nicaragua. We hiked Volcán Concepcion, an active smoking volcano, and stayed in Grenada, an old historic town. I remembered talking with a couple from the surf hostel on the beach in San Juan Del Sur about other cool places around, and they mentioned a place called El Tunco, El Salvador – they had just come from there and loved it. With my newfound desire to catch more waves, I convinced my girlfriend to bus it over to El Salvador and check the scene there.

We arrived in El Tunco

"Now this…. is a surf town!" We said to each other.

There was surf surrounding my new, green, novice, frothing, surfer eyes. There were also babes and surfer dudes everywhere! I was not used to this. There was even a badass concrete mini skateboarding bowl I found as icing on the cake! The general attitude of the town was bohemian, truly. Not what people say today about a bohemian-styled interior design concept, but the town's vibe was saying, "To hell with the rest of the world's complicated lives, we need nothing but what's here."

It was my first time being in a place like that, and I was obsessed. We stayed a week, and I surfed almost every day. I caught my first real wave in El Tunco, El Salvador. The difference from my surfing experience in Nicaragua was that in El Tunco, I had managed to catch my first open wave, the way real surfers ride waves. It was a successful feat that took the entire week. I officially rode the open face of the wave instead of just the whitewater after a wave finished.

It took another few days of practicing but eventually, for a short time, I rode an open wave. My mind exploded. My life changed. I needed more of this daily. I was horrible at it, but still, the sensation of riding water was wild. Then to boost my low surfer-confidence, I came back to land and borrowed a skateboard from the hostel where the concrete mini bowl was. I shredded the way I already knew how, sweating as I had never sweat before in the Central American heat. We stayed about a week but continued our journey to southern Mexico to experience some ruins before we eventually flew back to Colorado… pulling me away from Mother Ocean.

San Francisco Is A Crazy Place

The day I got back to Colorado from Central America, it was on. The quest to convince my girlfriend to move to California officially began. With much time spent as a traveling skateboarder, I had friends all over the country. Some of my best friends had already moved to San Francisco from Phoenix, where we lived and skated together for years before that. My girlfriend and I talked with my friends over video chat, and they begged us to come out. They had a spare bedroom that was affordable for us. It was $900 a month, which was super cheap in San Francisco for one person to pay, and she and I would split it, which made it an insane deal. Straight away, my friend Brett was able to get my girlfriend a lucrative bartending job in the restaurant that he bartended at. She finally said yes! I had done it again, dragged her along somewhere else I didn't think twice about going. I just knew I needed to be there. To surf.

Even though I had taken some skateboarding trips to Los Angeles before, I had never been to San Francisco. I figured it was in California, so it must be palm trees and sunny weather. Wrong. San Francisco is one of the mildest places in the United States, and based on averages of the year, the coldest! I moved to the Excelsior neighborhood, which was high in the hills outside the busy downtown area, but still within San Francisco city limits. It can also be labeled as one of the coldest microclimates out of the many that exist in San Francisco. Regardless, I was dying to surf. I orchestrated this massive move, over a thousand miles, in my girlfriend's crappy old Ford Ranger with my Harley-Davidson motorcycle loaded in the truck bed. I did some research and found a surf town called Pacifica twelve miles south of San Francisco on Highway 1, or the Pacific Coast Highway. Pacifica has a beach, Linda Mar, known to be a beginner surf spot. After I drove from Colorado to California and moved into the house of friends, the next morning, I was on my way to Pacifica. I drove the truck down and rented a board at the NorCal Surf Shop to paddle out with.

"You need a wetsuit rental too?" The surf shop dude asked.

"Wetsuit? Like… The water is cold?" I thought.

Once I found out the bad news, I rented the wetsuit, too. A little different from Nicaragua and El Salvador. For the first time, I paddled into water that was 52 degrees Fahrenheit (11 degrees Celsius) and felt like crying. This wasn't in my surf plans!

When I got to San Francisco and showed a quick obvious interest in surfing, my great old friend Rick had something for me.

"Hey, when I took over the lease of my motorcycle shop, the last guy left a bunch of stuff, including a surfboard. It's always just been sitting in the back corner against the wall, but you're free to use it if you want." He generously offered.

This was an amazing gift because I didn't have very much money after our move from Colorado to San Francisco. I needed to work for a few months before I would be on top financially again.

My first board and suit rental in Pacifica made me realize that I needed to acquire my own gear quickly. Rental prices in California were much different than in Central America. I could not afford to pay over $40 every time I wanted to surf (every day)! I went to Rick's motorcycle warehouse in Hunter's Point straight after that first surf session to have a look at the board he was offering me. He opened his sea-air-rusted metal door that he welded together for extra security because Hunter's Point is one of the sketchiest areas of San Francisco. I beelined it to the back, dodging old Harley-Davidsons on motorcycle lifts, rusty parts sitting everywhere semi-packrat style, some beer cans, put-out cigarettes, and other things left over from the night before. I found the board propped up against the wall way in the back. I noticed immediately that it had the Bic of Bic lighters insignia printed in big lettering front smack in the center.

"What the hell is this?" I thought.

I picked up the board and took immediate note that this was not a real surfboard. It was a piece of plastic that seemed like it had been made for promotional reasons only and not to be surfed in real life. It had a seam of melted/beaded plastic at the center of the rail (the surfboard's edge) around the entire board. The kind of seam that if you picked at it enough, it would probably fall apart, and one area was sharp enough to cut your skin with. Picture the plastic seam of a Wiffle Ball bat. Now I was super disappointed because I thought I was being gifted a real surfboard and instead was holding this kid's toy thing or prop from the Daytona 500 for the NASCAR cigarette smoking fans. I was sure to be made fun of with it. Rick convinced me it would at the very least float, and why the hell not just try it out? It was free! Rick is from Indiana, also a landlocked state (lakes don't count), and even though he had many talented years on a skateboard, he had close to zero experience on a surfboard, so I wasn't very trusting of his surf advice. But I decided to try it out. After all, it was cheaper than renting a board. On top of that, his shop-mate, Jarrod, was a big-time shortboard-shredding surfer who had an old wetsuit with holes in it for me, too! Which, come to think of it, I don't even think I washed that wetsuit, I just put it right on and never looked back... (And we all know what we surfers do in wet-suits... We pee! Constantly! Like infant children! As if we never learned how to hold it. The moment we have to, pee party!) So just like that, because of great friends, I had a janky, makeshift, plastic board and a tattered, hand-me-down wetsuit. I was ready.

I don't think the surfboard was intended to be mine, but at the time, we all lived together in this tiny two-bedroom apartment. Even though I used the board every single day, it stayed in Rick's life. And he was cool with it. Thanks again dude! You helped this become re-al!

This two-bedroom in-law apartment that we all lived in was out of control. The common area was a bedroom, San Francisco style, to make crazy-expensive rent cheaper. Rick slept for a few months on the couch, and Brett had his legitimate queen size mattress on the floor in the corner of the same living room adjacent to Rick's couch. My girlfriend and I had a bedroom, and our other great old friend Doug had the second bedroom.

We called that apartment "The Perk," as in "park," but with a Canadian accent, as we were all obsessed with The Trailer Park Boys, a Canadian TV show. We lived a parallel lifestyle in our in-law, ground-level apartment with five people minimum. Our usable "living room" was the garage with our motorcycles, which in San Francisco we were lucky to have. We had no kitchen, but we built a horribly crappy kitchenette we installed in the corner of Brett and Rick's room with a small refrigerator, toaster, coffee maker, and hot plate. We made it a normal occurrence to cook dinner on the electric hot plate in their bedroom, the actual living room of the apartment. How I miss being 26.

I started surfing the Bic board. I surfed it every day. I would wax that plastic piece of garbage and paddle out. It had a three-fin setup. They were all the same size and not real fins either, again, just plastic, permanently in there. Most modern surfboards have fin boxes with slots for interchanging fins. I started surfing it, day after day until after a few weeks and months, I could rip that thing better than other surfers riding real boards in the lineup. It was amazing! It was 7'10". Not quite a longboard. It was narrower too, but long enough to provide some good volume for my novice arms to paddle on. I surfed that board almost every single day at Pacifica Beach for almost six months straight.

I had been working as a freelance audio engineer setting up shows all over the Bay Area and, after a few months, saved up enough money for a real, used longboard. I had been checking Craigslist classifieds for boards and was watching people getting rid of shitty longboards for around $350. That much money I could afford, but I didn't have much more expendable cash beyond that... Until I scrolled passed this one board. It was beautiful. It was THE ONE but a little out of my price range at $450.

"I have to have it." I told myself.

It was a sleek, stylish, classic, vintage-looking, single fin Noserider (a type of classic longboard shape) in a light, lime-green color, and on it said, "Owl, by Mark Andreini."

I had no idea who this man was, they were just words on a beautiful surfboard. I contacted the sellers and went down to Pacifica of all places, where I already surfed daily. I drove the pickup truck to a house in the hills and met this engineer husband and his surfer wife, Patty. The board was hers and the husband had the board shaped specifically for her. He even had Marc Andreini inscribe her name under the glass (the clear protective outside layer) down by the fin box where the board's dimensions were penciled in at the stringer (a long, thin string of wood under the glass, from nose to tail for board strength).

I was poor. I told him I wanted it but asked if he could do $400. I think he felt bad for me and wanted his wife's board to have a good home. He must have seen the stoke in my eyes absolutely needing this piece of art between my feet and Mother Ocean.

"Sure, we can do that." He replied, kindly giving in.

He gave me a leash, a Greenough fin, and a 10' board protector sock. At the time, I also had no idea who George Greenough was or anything about his fins. Turns out, the man had been inventing and building board shapes and fin shapes since the 1960s that tons of surfers still ride today. It also turned out that $400 was a deal of a lifetime for all this. Looking back, I'm sure he paid $1300 or $1500 for that new board for his wife, plus over $100 for the fin, and it didn't have a ding on it when it got into my possession. I changed that real quick, but then again, I got good at repairing my boards, too – a necessary skill for a true surfer.

I'm not super savvy on surf history. All I know is that in my surf life, George Greenough is king and influenced me directly and indirectly for some years. I know that surfing came from Hawai'i and was brought to California way earlier than I realized, like the 1880s in Santa Cruz from a Hawai'ian Prince. Then there was Duke Kahanamoku who brought surfing around the world in the early decades of the 1900s. In terms of what has impacted my life directly, I am relatively obsessed with older, classic things from the 1960s-1970s in most aspects of my life. Music, rock 'n' roll, motorcycles, cars, surfing, clothing styles... I seem to gravitate towards everything from those decades.

Watch *Crystal Voyager*, seriously. It's an Australian surf film from 1973 that is a documentary of George Greenough's life and his surfing. He was an out-there surfer and an innovator who changed surfing and surfing style with his board and fin designs. Greenough is from Santa Barbara, California, and so is Marc Andreini, the shaper of my Noserider. They were the ones shaping boards in that town with Greenough's board designs back in the 1960s and 1970s. I did some research after I became the proud owner of this board, and my mind was blown from what I discovered about Andreini and Greenough. They immediately became legendary to me. They were the first of their kind, true legends. I gravitated to this board by aesthetics alone, before I knew who these guys were and their contributions to surfing history. After I was aware of them it was an honor to rip that board every day. I still can't believe Patty wanted to sell it!

I rode that board every single day, regardless of conditions, for over a year. In storms, in horrible soupy, washing-machine-like conditions, and in conditions too big for a longboard, like those big winter swells that would light up Mavericks, the big wave spot down south. Pacifica wasn't a big wave spot but would still be much overhead and aggressive in the winter. Especially for a rookie longboarder like me. Somehow, I would manage to paddle out on my log (longboard) after getting clobbered by big breaking waves to drop-in on big on close-outs. A close-out occurs when an entire wave's lip breaks at the same time without any transition left open for the surfer to ride.

I eventually built up a bit of a fear riding in bigger surf. Usually, as waves get bigger, a surfer's board length would get smaller for more control and speed on the bigger waves, but I only had one board. A smaller board can also duck dive under larger breaking waves to miss a lot of that energy that would blow a surfer away on a longboard. But I continued to ride my very buoyant longboard in bigger surf and developed a panic paddle, paddling as hard as I could to make it safely over the cresting waves before they broke. I was unable to duck dive the huge board, and if I couldn't make it over the wave I would get destroyed. Simple. Most surfers have a quiver, or a surfboard arsenal, with multiple boards of varying sizes, and they choose an appropriate board size and shape for the conditions of that day. I just kept riding old faithful, that same 9'6" log, every day until eventually a year and a half later it was stolen off my car's wax covered roof in the Mission District when I was visiting a friend. I cried and mourned for weeks.

One early afternoon, before my Andreini Owl log was stolen, I was surfing Pacifica's Linda Mar Beach for the 1000th time. It was a Saturday, around noon, and sunny. Linda Mar is one big C-shaped cove, and there must have been 200 surfers spread out around the whole beach. There are roughly six main breaks, so divide 200 surfers by six peaks, and let's say there were over 30 surfers per main peak. It was busy. I was in the water a little north of the Taco Bell that's on the beach there. Yes, there is a Taco Bell actually constructed on the sand, and some locals refer to Linda Mar as "Taco Bell beach."

I was the deepest longboarder out in the water, waiting for a bomb. A bomb is the largest wave in its set. Waves often come in sets of three to six per set on stronger, more organized swells. Back then, I was always positioned the deepest, looking for the early stages of the developing bigger set waves. It's also the safest place to be as that area is deeper than the impact zone, where the waves crashed, and where I was afraid to be.

I was sitting with my longboard between my legs, looking west and waiting for incoming waves, as was everyone else. There were over 30 surfers around my peak, but they were positioned a little farther inside (closer to shore) than me. Everyone was waiting, also looking west. The ocean was temporarily flat. The next thing I knew, I saw a huge 8' gray fish completely breach out of the water in front of my eyes. The fish's upside-down T-shaped tail was a few feet above the ocean's surface, and the rest of the fish was vertically above. It had a large, few foot long fish in its mouth. It flailed around awkwardly in the air for half a second until it fell with its dead weight back into the ocean with a big splash.

I was the closest surfer to it, only a soft rock's throw away. It was close. Like, unbelievably close. I studied it in my mind over and over after it happened.

"Ok, what was that? Was it a dolphin? No... A swordfish? No... A marlin? No... A shark? Yes." I asked myself repeatedly, finally realizing the reality I was in.

"I mean, it must have been something else, right? It couldn't have possibly been a shark. Sharks are only in the movies, aren't they?" I tried telling myself.

Nope. After about ten seconds, I heard a guy in his fifties talking to the other older guys around him.

"So that was a shark, right?" One old longboarder said behind me.

"Yep. Sure was." They responded.

I turned around to see who was talking. I saw all the longboards and shortboards and every board shape in between turn the nose of their boards 180 degrees, from facing west, out to sea, toward land, and all paddled in like hell. Everyone was spooked, for it was a Great White Shark. I sat there on my board, just watching. For some reason, I didn't have the urge to flee like the rest. I just didn't feel threatened. I have relatively keen senses that I think work properly, and I never felt like I was in any danger. My primal instinct wasn't alerting me to run like I was about to become a shark's lunch. Or were my instincts just dumb and lazy for never needing to use them in the wild before? Was I about to be the sharks next bite?

Out of the big pack we started with, only one other surfer stayed out there with me. He looked like he was about eighteen years old.

"What do you think?" He said as he looked over at me, also noticing that we were alone.

"Well... it didn't mess with us before, and it clearly existed in the water here before we saw it. Now the shark is less hungry after eating that big fish, so we're good, right?" I replied.

The kid agreed with me. We stayed out there together, never once seeing a fin around us or feeling threatened by anything. We had the entire peak to ourselves for the next forty-five minutes, catching every wave we wanted until new surfers paddled out sometime after.

I was surfed-out, pooped. Since it was just one other surfer and me, I caught lots of waves, then paddled in. I was supposed to meet my buddy Rick out there, but he never showed up. Once I paddled in and got out of the water, I saw him walking up on the beach with his longboard and wetsuit on.

"You're late!" I said.

"Yea, I know, I got held up in the shop." He responded.

I told him about the shark encounter and how everyone else got out, but this other kid and I stayed and caught all the waves for a while. His Indiana-made eyes opened wide.

"No thanks. Nope. I'm out of here, you're crazy." He said, spooked.

He turned around and walked back to the parking lot with me. He tossed his longboard into the bed of his flat black-colored El Camino and took off. He refused to surf for a week.

One week in San Francisco, our Chicago friends showed up to stay at our already over maximum capacity, tiny apartment, The Perk. There were a few girls from Chicago who were all best friends with my girlfriend and planned to sleep wherever, including our bed. This meant I was kicked off and slept on the floor somewhere during their stay. The visiting friends were excited Chicagoans, with only a lake for a beach at best, so we planned to head to the coast for a beach day. We woke up in the morning and packed some food, drinks, blankets, beers, and everything for an afternoon at San Francisco's Ocean Beach.

Ocean Beach is almost never warm due to San Francisco's Mediterranean mildness, but our Chicago friends were still stoked regardless, even with flannels, beanies, and jeans on. Rick and I decided to take our longboards with us to surf while the rest of the crew hung out on blankets on the sand. Rick had been surfing with me for the better part of a year and bought his own longboard after a few sessions. We got to the beach and paddled out as our sand-dwelling friends set up beach camp.

As we paddled out, we realized it was a bigger Ocean Beach day. There were stronger waves than we were used to down south in Pacifica. Ocean Beach, San Francisco is a three-mile surfable stretch of west-facing, sand-bottom beach with beach breaks all along it. A beach break is a surfable wave that forms from underwater sandbars on the ocean floor. Due to strong currents, swells, and storms, sandbars are formed by sand piling up in certain areas, then waves break off these sand piles.

Ocean Beach is extremely exposed to all directions of swell and gets very deep quickly. So deep that there were massive container ships we called "slow boats to China" always passing by as they went under the Golden Gate Bridge to the Oakland port. Due to the coastline being completely exposed to all swell directions, and how deep it is there, Ocean Beach tends to have very strong currents.

One day I paddled out solo at Sloat Ave., the road that T-bones the south end of Ocean Beach perpendicularly. I knowingly caught left after left (the direction a surfer takes on a wave) and with the southern current pushing north, I ended up at the north end of Ocean Beach near Kelly's Cove – nearly three miles away from where I parked my car. I had to walk my 9'6" Andreini Owl log back three miles in the sand. The currents are no joke!

Also, since it's super deep nearby, there's big sea life close to the surf. It's common in the right season to see whales breaching not much farther than the surf lineup. Scarier than whales or dolphins, San Francisco is bullseye centered in the middle of the red triangle, the most densely populated area of Great White Sharks in the world. The triangle is drawn from Santa Cruz, passing San Francisco going north to Mendocino, and out thirty miles west into the Pacific Ocean to the Farallon Islands. This triangle is where a huge population of seals live, especially out on the Farallons. Seals are predominantly what Great White Sharks eat, and Great Whites have their babies nearby too, so they are all over. This is a wild thing to mentally deal with for surfers. Most surfers try not to acknowledge it. We can't dwell on some lightning bolt occurrence all the time, it'll ruin the fun! After I saw the Great White breach out of the water at Linda Mar in Pacifica, I knew they were nearby. There were times I over-reacted way too quickly and dramatically to random splashes in the water near me, too. Spooked. So I can't say I never thought about them being around while out there…

Back at Ocean Beach, where Rick and I were surfing head high to overhead-sized waves while the rest of the party from Chicago was on the beach, I caught a bigger wave that I wore out my welcome on. It barreled and threw me over the falls (crashing lips of barreling waves – not a good place to be while wiping out, but if you're on your board inside a barrel, then an awesome place to be!). The force of the wave pushing down held me under the water five or ten feet down as I had on a ten-foot leash. If my board was at the surface, I could have been ten feet underwater. If I was upside down, my head could have been another five feet deeper than that because the leash was attached to my ankle.

The wave's energy was so strong I felt it dragging my board forward with me attached. The energy above me didn't let up for much longer than usual, which normally was just a few seconds before I could swim up again. I started struggling. Hard. I realize, in hindsight, I was supposed to stay uber-calm in that situation, but this felt different, and I reacted to fear in a frenzied panic. I attempted to swim up as hard as possible but wasn't allowed by the wave's force. I immediately started trying to breathe underwater. I guess that's what bodies do in a severe physical struggle. I started inhaling gulp after gulp into my lungs.

I left my body. That's right. You read correctly. I was no longer in my body. In a blink of an eye, like a switch was flipped, I was standing (or hovering) above the water on the surface, looking down at my own body struggling. I realize this sounds insanely wild or fantastic, like some made-up thing, but it happened to me. I no longer felt fear, no adrenaline, no emotion really, just chill, Zen, peace. I looked up to the left, and a football field's distance away on the beach, I saw my friends. I could clearly see them. I looked back down once more and saw myself underwater, trying to swim up.

Just as fast as the switch flipped for me to leave my body, the switch flicked back, and I once again was looking through my eyes, in my body, underwater.

"Well, I might as well try," I vividly remember thinking to myself with doubt that I would be successful.

I think some of that peacefulness from outside my body stayed with me after I returned. I didn't feel stressed or panicked anymore, even in my struggling swim how I initially felt before I left.

I swam higher and higher with all my might. I could see the surface getting closer, as I was still inhaling sea water, the energy holding me down subsided. I stabbed my head through the water's surface with strength I no longer thought I had. I took one deep gasping inhale only to have the same rodeo happen to me again three times more, minus the out-of-body trip. I had caught the first set wave of which there are usually three or more per set. Every wave got a little easier but was still nerve-rackingly difficult after the stress that had been put on my body from the first wave.

After the set had passed, I wrangled my surfboard, boogie-boarded myself to shore, and collapsed on the sand. I threw up fountains of seawater many times and was coughing like mad, deep from within my lungs. Rick saw what happened and came out to check on me as he was an EMT/Firefighter with CPR skills. Thankfully, I didn't need any of his help, but the support was comforting.

"Damn, that was crazy." He told me.

We slowly walked back over to the friends' beach camp and told them what happened. I passed out on a blanket for over an hour, which was super unlike me. I awoke with the thought that if I don't go back out there right now, I probably will never surf again. I felt fear, distaste, and some trauma. My favorite activity in the world just severely hurt me, and I needed to mend my relationship with it. I apologized to Mother Ocean on my way out.

"I didn't appreciate your power, and I took you for granted. Never again." I said to the sea before stepping into her to paddle out again.

I told Rick, and he paddled back out with me just so I could catch about three more waves. I had some crazy emotions, like fear, but the kind where I felt I was up against something larger than myself. Fear that I could not conquer, but had to hold on to, that maybe

I was the dumbest human being in the world for willingly putting myself back into those conditions again. I was a sensitive creature in a rugged, merciless environment. I managed to put those feelings aside and just surf. I caught three good-sized, hefty, stronger waves and I got the hell out of there. I thanked Mother Nature for the utmost humbling experience of my entire life. I gave Ocean Beach the middle finger, and I didn't surf there again for years.

I used to bartend in a handful of bars around the Mission District in San Francisco. I was twenty-nine and got a third bartending job (the San Francisco hustle, always working, trying to afford it) at an infamous punk venue/dive bar/restaurant called Thee Parkside. Rick got me the job, as he'd been working there for years.

"You have to meet this old San Francisco shaper (surfboard maker) who's a legend around this town and comes into the bar every so often. His board shaping studio is right around the corner." I remember him telling me.

One day I was working behind the bar and Rick was there hanging out as the legend walked in. To this day I don't remember his name, but Rick introduced us, and we shook hands. Rick explained that he and I had been surfing every day for a year or two together, and he mentioned I was a pretty good surfer. The legend stopped Rick mid-sentence.

"So, you've been to the Rodeo? You're not a surfer unless you have." He said looking sternly at us.

"What's the Rodeo?" We asked.

"It's when the ocean takes you and doesn't give you back for a while... That's what Ocean Beach will do to you when it's double or triple overhead. Where you're a straight-up ragdoll on a bucking bronco only in all directions, upside-down and all." The legend responded sternly.

This was before my Ocean Beach incident and both of us just kind of looked down as if we were not worthy or didn't hold that badge of honor. After I went through my out-of-body situation out there, even though the waves weren't nearly as big as he mentioned, I had a better understanding of what that guy was talking about. Before that, I was fearless, I would catch any wave around me with no second guesses. Blind faith. Afterward, I grew in ways that only a surfer of many years can grow – extra patience, awareness of one's own skill set, and the risks involved with having something to prove. I could surf most waves before, but I lacked true respect for the ocean's great power, which only came over time. I'm still not the surfer I will be in five, ten, or fifteen years. Either way, kind of a jerky thing for the legend to say, attempting to haze us instead of supporting. But I eventually named my Australian cattle dog "Rodeo" after all that. She reminds me of Mother Nature's great power all the time and helps to keep me humble.

As all things must come to an end, my girlfriend and I ended up breaking up. This was much overdue, but after more than five years together, I was excited to take on the next chapter of my life. Because I had not been single in years, I was confused about who I was and tried to channel my independent life back. We shared the same friend group, and I decided to back away from a lot of our San Francisco social circle and distanced some great friends for a while. I moved out of The Perk, and through San Francisco's word of mouth, got a place on the other side of the neighborhood with a radical, eccentric, older skateboarder and writer dude named Rod.

I only stayed at this new apartment when I had to close the bar late, otherwise I was camping near the surf somewhere in my old 1986 Toyota Van, the type with the flat front that belongs in a 1980's movie, or the ones that are background props in the T.V. show *Stranger Things*.

I did a half-assed job of building a futon in the back of the van after gutting the seats and putting in some fake wood paneling and floorboards. Turning this thirty-year-old van into a full-blown, bitchin', surf-adventure-camping-rig! I only had basic hand tools and had to build on the street in front of my apartment building on Dolores Street.

Once I had this van up and running, almost every night out of the week I was out of town camping. I would hunt for hot springs somewhere in California, or I would be cliffside camping, waking up at sunrise to surf. I ended up finding a well-hidden California secret, a town called Bolinas. I have read other writers who have written or published photos of the place, so I don't feel that bad about talking about it now.

Long story short, Bolinas is an unincorporated hippie town but not with the Dead Head hippie types as much as a bunch of drunken poets and extreme eccentrics that came together in the 1950s -1970s and built the town. Some like-minded hippies wanted to leave the city, some after the summer of love in San Francisco, but wanted their visions and ideals to stay the same. The town outlawed new water meters by the early 1970s, making it impossible to build homes or commercial businesses, forcing the town to literally stay the same for decades. It is a beautiful place. Where Northern California forests meet the cliffs at the ocean. I have noticed in my travels that Eucalyptus trees seem to only grow in special areas of extreme beauty and a particular climate. It only makes sense that Eucalyptus groves exist in magical Bolinas.

Every home in Bolinas is completely unique and one of a kind. They're all some type of DIY cabin. The plants and flowers are something from Dr. Suess, and I swear that the golden hour there is different than anywhere else in the world. Half the town is dirt roads, like a simple European village, and it's a place where dogs roam free even though they all have homes. Some of the most interesting and mentally insane people I have ever met reside there, making it even more mythical or fantastic. A place where everyone kind of drank the Kool-Aid, but the Kool-Aid was a pretty rad flavor.

I ended up loving the small, chill, longboard friendly surf so much in Bolinas that after my bar shifts, I would drive up over the Golden Gate Bridge and thirty miles over Mt. Tamalpais on-and-off the Pacific Coast Highway 1, just to camp in town. I needed to be there early for a surf every morning I could. Also, unlike most California surf towns, Bolinas, at the time, did not care about people camping in town. In front of houses on the main street or out on the cliffs. I was camping most nights there. It was calm, but some nights I wasn't the only one. I feel like that has probably changed now for the busier.

For about a year, more than half the week, if not the entire week, I lived in my van somewhere in that town and surfed multiple times a day. I became kind of a regular and made some friends in town. I was exclusively a single fin longboarder. I identified with it. My style reflected it. It was retro, it was stylish, it was cool, and it was what almost everyone else there did too, as the pointbreak wave at

The Patch was almost always too mellow for anything besides a longboard. No one cared about high performance. None of the waves there were critical or heavy. This went along well with the town's general attitude.

This type of surfing back then was super fun every day. It was like autopilot surfing. Easy, relaxed, and low stress. In hindsight, it put a huge pause on the progress of my surfing because it was such an easy, beginner wave. The only fear at The Patch was that my larger single fin could clip one of about three boulders at a lower tide on the inside section. After leaving Bolinas, I had to relearn how to surf in bigger waves and for the first time learn how to surf shorter boards.

After much time invested in town, I finally sub-leased a studio forest cabin from a girl in Bolinas, who was a biologist and shipped away to do six months of research on a tiny, far away Hawai'ian Island near Japan. I lived in her little cabin-beach shack for six months with my dog Rodeo, hidden from the world. Besides rolling the van over the hill (Mt Tamalpais) to San Francisco to make some money, I avoided the city like the plague.

The cabin was full of the biologist's things. Her beach finds, sea glass, driftwood collection, and books on every sea animal in existence. It was a studio with a side kitchenette consisting of a hotplate, mini-fridge, and toaster oven. There was a toilet closet with nothing more than a toilet inside, and the door wouldn't close when I sat on the toilet. My feet would stick out into the room forcing the door ajar. There was only an outdoor shower, and the shower head was hidden in a rose bush that grew up the side of the cabin with roses everywhere. The outdoor shower had a wooden standing platform that was in a calla lily garden with big white lily flowers all around. The shower had no door or walls. It was an open view for me to shower with the wildflower hill, lily-padded-frog-pond, and horse pasture in front of me as I showered naked in nature.

Before I moved into the cabin, I camped in my van with Rodeo, often in our spot at the cliffs. There was room for four vehicles on the opposite side of the road from what the locals called "The Lookout," a bend in the road at the top of a hundred-foot cliff overlooking the Bolinas Bay. I camped up there at the lookout when I could, or just in front of someone's house on the street. It just depended on if there were any cliff spots available or not when I showed up.

1-The Groin surf spot. Bolinas, CA. 35MM

1-Six-Month-Old Surfing Rodeo. Bolinas. 35MM

Rodeo would usually hang out on the beach free to roam, but on small days at The Patch, I would take her out with me on my 9'6" single fin Noserider. We attempted to catch waves tandem style with her on the nose of the board. We always caught waves together, even though she never seemed to enjoy it. After a few rides, she would jump off and go run on the sand like there was a fire behind her, sprinting like a lunatic.

Bolinas Bay only accepts swells from southern directions, and it was rare for a strong south swell to maintain that far north. Since south swells are generated from way south and hit Mexico and San Diego, they oftentimes don't make it north of Santa Barbara with significant power. Therefore, San Francisco is always flat in summer, after strong winter swells from the north cease, but Southern California receives south swell waves all summer long.

One chilly morning, Rodeo and I walked to the beach together and I paddled out at The Patch, the righthand point break over a boulder/rock reef. This was the smallest, easiest wave I predominantly surfed for two years, stunting my growth in surfing. After riding this spot almost daily for those years, I think only one time the surf was head high, and we thought it was massive. I surfed for a couple of hours and was the only one out that early riding the righthand, tiny ankle biters (waves so small they are only as big as your ankles when standing on your board).

I came in for coffee and breakfast. I dried off back at my van on the top of the cliff with Rodeo. When I surfed, Rodeo would be free to do as she pleased nearby. She would sniff around, hang out on the sand, make friends with other people or dogs, and only once did I have to go looking for her in town. She was like a mountain goat and would run up the eroding sand cliffside that was so steep people couldn't walk up it. But she could! She had a buddy, another Blue Heeler dog friend who lived at the top of the cliff. She would find him to play when I went surfing. This doggie freedom was easily possible in Bolinas. Everyone in town thought the same way, so dogs would just be wandering around on the streets but wasn't a big deal. The speed limit in town was about 15MPH to watch out for our four-legged furry friends. Even part of Bolinas, or maybe it's technically the next town over, is called Dogtown.

After surfing, I boiled some water on my camp stove, a little single burner that was attached to a tiny propane canister. I drank my coffee and ate a banana. We went back down to the beach and walked around for a while. Rodeo and I liked to walk the beach in Bolinas farther than the surf. There was almost no one ever there, and it was one of the wilder places near the ocean I had been. The beaches were so rugged. Every few steps brought me amazing new sights I had never seen before. Huge driftwood in the sand and towering cliffs eroding onto the beach with tree roots sticking out the sides. Over time, the trees would fall down the cliffsides when the cliffs eroded enough, putting a new massive tree on the beach. There were huge boulders and rock reefs. As the tide went out, it all became exposed, bringing the coolest tide pools to life. A tide pool for those not near the ocean, is an ecosystem living in little crevasses and deeper holes in the reef as the low tide pulls back. When the water completely pulls back the only water left is in pockets of the reef holding fish, sea anemones, clams, plants, etc…

We walked the tide pools and noticed the spitting clams. They made me feel crazy at first, walking around the exposed reef tide pools. I would see something move in my peripheral and be confused about what was happening! It was the spitting clams, shooting filtered seawater five feet into the air in single spurts. But there were so many clams around that it happened once every few seconds.

It was foggy. Like always. And dreary. But not the type of drear that existed on the East Coast in winter, more like a Pacific Northwest melancholy-ness. A fantastic dreariness. Where life didn't quite stop, it just slowed down with a fire in the wood-burning stove. I always referred to Northern California as a fantastic place. It seemed like fantasy, not reality, as it had a type of beauty that did not exist back east. We continued to walk in the chilly, dreary, foggy, hazy, cloudy, fantastic morning, just exploring the beach like usual.

We found driftwood all over and played fetch with each one until I found a new, cooler, more unique looking driftwood piece, and that would become the new toy. Rodeo and I saw something in the close distance that didn't look like it belonged. It was a massive white rock or blob sitting on the beach, three car lengths long. We walked over to it. I had no idea what I was looking at. It looked like it was biological, not a rock but organic. I touched it. It felt swollen but squishy. It wasn't as tall as me but almost five feet off the ground and long as hell. I walked along the length of it to the backside and stopped abruptly. I saw a tail. This was a whale. This was a massive, dead, white whale.

There was no one else around. I wondered what I could do. It wasn't breathing. I saw a perfect one-foot square that looked like it had been cut out of its side, clean. I walked back to the head of the greatest mammal on Earth and tried to make out the mouth and an eye to get a sense of its head and face – they were ambiguous. It was difficult for me to decipher. There were many textured lines in beautiful patterns separating different parts of the neck and head but confusing to tell what position it was in. As I walked around it many times, I deduced that it was lying upside down. I saw, what was a butthole facing the sky, two-thirds down the whale closer to the tail, the size of my fist. It had its mouth open with its gigantic tongue unraveled, resting on the ground.

My emotions went from looking down at psychedelic sea anemones and spitting clams, alone with my dog, to stumbling upon a freshly dead, beached whale. I was in shock. I felt sadness and sorrow in my gut, like I wanted to puke. I felt like I had witnessed the fall of something great, greater than me. Even though it was not present in spirit any longer, I still had a few minutes of connection with the body of this massive, epic, kind creature.

I felt guilt. I had tears in my eyes from feeling overwhelmed with the death of true, honest beauty. Too much stimulation and abrupt mental input. I looked over and saw other primal instincts taking course in my Blue Heeler. Rodeo was biting the one-foot wide, open square of the whale's side flesh and blood. Pulling it like in a tug-of-war with a beef jerky stick. She was trying to rip off a piece of the whale to eat!

"Ey! Stop it!" I yelled at her.

"This is beautiful and tragic Rodeo! Can we respect it please?! All you can think about is eating it!?!?" I yelled more at her.

I shooed her away from the whale, but she found the perfect square puzzle piece that was cut out of the whale on the ground and started licking and chewing it.

I always brought my 35MM film camera down to the beach to shoot some beautiful nature at low tide, on the cliffs, or some good waves. On this particular day, I set up my camera on a rock with the analog timer set. I walked over to the great, wise, beautiful animal and, touching it with compassion, took a picture.

Biologists came and told me the square cut out of the whale's side was them taking samples to see if they could determine how it died. The Pacific Northwest is a wild place. I'd imagine it only got more intense the farther north you went, and Northern California was the very beginning…

II-Mourning A Beached White Whale. Bolinas, CA. Analogue Timer, 35MM

III-Whale's Rib Bone. Agate Beach, Bolinas. 35MM

<>>>>>><>>>>>>>><>>>>>

During bouts of no surf, I became a hot spring hunter on my days off from the bar. I fell in love with California in yet another way. One day off from work, I drove into the mountains in the Tahoe vicinity to do some hiking and thought to look up directions to a free, natural hot spring. I found directions to a place called Travertine Hot Springs and drove there from Tahoe in about an hour.

The last bit of directions took me off the beaten path. I was entering a type of government land, similar to National Forest land, off the paved road and onto dirt rolling over a few hills. I noticed the kind of vehicles I enjoyed being around. Old shitty 4x4s, camper vans, Sprinter vans, and pickup trucks with top tents. They were all spread out in their camping zones off this dirt road in the high desert.

I kept driving another mile until I got to a dead end. I parked, and Rodeo and I jumped out of the van. I was so excited. I ran over with Rodeo chasing me down the dirt path to search for the springs. I hadn't been to any hot springs in my life yet, but I found some of the most epic hot springs in existence. Travertine hot springs have a natural thermal spring that shoots straight out of the earth, and the spring was so old that all the sediment and minerals that came out with the water over time made a ten-foot high, hundred-foot long, berm hill.

It looked like a sleeping dinosaur. The spring's pressure pushed the water up and on an eroded track down the ridge of the spine on top of this berm. It fed four pools at the end of the long berm where the water dripped down. It looked like it belonged on Mars. I couldn't believe this was natural and free! I was around a few other natural hippies. Some people naked, some others in a bathing suit or underwear. Everyone was just relaxing in the high mineral, thermal, sulfur water.

I stayed there for hours. Afterward, Rodeo and I walked around the area on an easy hike and found four more springs, all single pools, spread out from each other in the wild. One was kind of daunting to get into as it was just a hole in the ground without visibility of the bottom. Was there a creature in there waiting for me to enter its trap? Was it fifty feet deep? Would something pull me in? Someone else had this same idea and dragged a thick tree branch over that was much longer than the hole. It was placed across the hole to use as something to hold onto in case it was deep or a trap! Of course, I had to get in and test them all…

Over the next five years, I hunted for hot springs when the surf was bad. I had a method of finding the hot springs I never told anyone until right now. I did some extensive research. I tried to find out more information online about where more of these springs were located. California sits on a Faultline near old volcanoes. There is more thermal activity in this area than the rest of the country to the east. I was obsessed with tracking more down.

Maybe this site is common knowledge, but after lots of research, I found a NOAA website (The National Oceanic and Atmospheric Administration) that had a country-wide map of every natural spring in the entire United States with temperatures and GPS coordinates. I cross-checked the GPS locations with Google to see if there was anything written on the map about it. If not, I would take the coordinates and plop them into Google Maps and get the closest driving directions possible to the spring and hike the rest of the way. I would drive for hours and hike for hours, only to find out that half of the time the springs were dried up or had become a residential development now. But sometimes I scored, and I found a secret hot spring!!!

When I was living in Bolinas, I was randomly driving the van near Ocean Beach, San Francisco, and a friend of mine, who was on a surf group text with me, put out a text.

"Anyone around who wants to surf Ocean Beach right now? I'm about to paddle out." My friend said.

I was nearby but had not surfed Ocean Beach since my out-of-body experience when I almost drowned two years earlier.

"This is the perfect time to go back out with a buddy, and it's not a big day, only a couple of feet, it should be great." I told myself.

I met up with her and we paddled out together. We caught a few waves for thirty minutes until one wave I caught swallowed me in the falls of the barreling wave. I felt a pain in my bicep as I got twisted around underwater, and my board pulled my leash tight. Just like that, instant release. My board was not pulling anymore, the leash broke with the wave energy, and my board shot all the way to the beach like a missile, which was about a football field away. The pain in my arm got more intense. As I was floating now in the water without a board, I looked at my bicep that hurt, and my wetsuit was still intact, but I couldn't see anything else through the suit. While I was treading water, I heard my friend from about twenty meters away.

"Shark fin!! I just saw a shark fin!! For sure!! Shark!!" She screamed at the top of her lungs.

I quickly turned around and faced the beach. I started swimming as I was startled by what she was screaming about, and I noticed that while flailing my arms around between treading water and starting to swim, I had blood running out of my wetsuit arm down at the opening at my wrist. I knew it was from my bicep pain. My fin must have hit my arm with so much force that it popped my skin open from under the wetsuit but didn't cut the suit open itself. It made no sense. I was in another shit-ass position AGAIN at Ocean Beach, submerged and bleeding in shark-infested water, without a board.

So, I swam. I swam like I was Poseidon himself with the fear of God in him. I didn't stop. I didn't think. I didn't pause. I just swam as fast as my body was capable, without thoughts. Until I hit the sandy bottom with my feet and still didn't stop. I ran out of that ocean, terrified. My board was nearby, beached in the sand. I got out of every inch of that water and collapsed in the sand.

"Seriously screw this place!!!!!" I yelled as loud as I could.

There was a very common saying that surfers and locals used around the Bay Area. "If you can paddle out at Ocean Beach, you can paddle out anywhere."

It was REALLY starting to sink in. My friend made it out fine, too, and we laughed about how sketchy it was there, but I can say I have not surfed there again. Honestly, I have nothing to prove anymore.

When I lived anywhere around Northern California, I used to surf Santa Cruz almost once a week. I surfed Pleasure Point almost exclusively. Steamer Lane was always a super aggro spot, so I tended to head to Pleasure Point or The Hook, which were both more chill. The pro surf tour went through Steamer Lane, making the place a crazy surf destination. All the local groms (young surfers) who thought they were the next superstar surfer surfed there daily, regulating hard.

Santa Cruz was filled with a culture of the meanest, aggressive, angry, jerky surfers I've ever been around out of any country I've ever been to. Anywhere I go in Santa Cruz, I get yelled at. So will you. I guarantee, after surfing some of the best waves all over the world, if I ever went back to Santa Cruz and surfed, the same way all other surfers do around the world, the Santa Cruz locals would still talk smack. It's like a rite of passage for them. Really, they're just spreading negative energy around. Because they were yelled at in the water growing up, it became normal behavior to scold the next younger surfer or the surfer less skilled, giving a sense of false power in the water. Like hazing almost. Even when surfing Cowell's, The Hook, or Pleasure Point, which are all known to be more chill, easy, mellow longboard waves, it still occurred there often. It's super annoying. So, Santa Cruz, maybe travel somewhere else and realize you exist in California with millions of people, and that's enough. Chill. If a Santa Cruz local went to Bali, their minds would implode from overwhelming aggro energy combusting in their skulls from the amount of international rookie surfers there that don't know proper etiquette. But it's okay. Honestly. It forces you to grow patience, a great quality to have in life!

All that being said, no one needs to be a pro surfer to paddle out, but everyone should know the etiquette of the water and how to navigate their board. Especially in bigger and more crowded surf. Then there should be no need for aggro behavior!

IV-Rules of the water. The Hook in Capitola, California. 35MM

I do love Pleasure Point though. What a fun wave when it was not surfer soup with hundreds of people out. I surfed it all the time on my Andreini 9'2" single fin log, and after a while, my 8'2" single fin Fineline. Pleasure Point is generally a righthander, which is my backhand, Australian for backside, where your back is facing the wave and your eyes are looking at the beach. Occasionally there was a lefthander that worked on the inside too.

Directions in California were funny sometimes to a non-native. I would be in Santa Cruz, Malibu, or Santa Barbara and driving on the Pacific Coast Highway east or west in reality, but the roads were named north and south. Kind of confusing at first. The coastline was completely horizontal before it turned north or south again. This is the main reason those areas have such amazing surf. Kelp beds, reefs, and other contributors are there too, but the coastline jetting in like that offers a filter from direct exposure to swells, which organizes energy.

When I was living in Bolinas, I drove down to Santa Cruz and Capitola to surf Pleasure Point. It was a fun-sized day, nothing too big. Some days I surfed Pleasure Point and there were well-overhead waves, some of the biggest waves I had been in at the time. I surfed it all on my longboards, which in hindsight, was nuts. The water in that zone is a few degrees warmer than the San Francisco area, but not by much. I put on my winter hand-me-down wetsuit that had holes all over it. The biggest hole allowing my knee to completely stick out. I surfed Pleasure Point for a few hours that day, had a blast, and caught a bunch of waves mid-day when most of the world was working or in school. After some hours, I paddled in, walked up the cliffs, and back toward my van. I had my single fin longboard on my hip, walking a few blocks on the cliffside path that overlooked the waves. Someone I passed gave me a funny look. I ignored it and walked past. I kept walking to my van. I passed someone else, and they, too, looked at me weirdly. The aggression only happened in the water, so I was quite confused.

"What do these people seem so angry at me for? What the hell?" I thought.

Eventually, I looked down and saw something bright pink on my suit. It didn't register for about three seconds that my used, piece-of-shit wetsuit had ripped in the crotch enough that I was walking down the busy walking path, cliffside in Capitola, showing everyone my penis.

"Ahh Shit!!" I loudly whisper-shouted and covered the hole with my left hand that was free.

"Are you kidding me!!" I yelled under my breath.

I held my crotch with my hand for about three more blocks until I got to my van and changed. I don't really get embarrassed, but I should have. I just felt like an asshole. It was hilarious, and I wish I wasn't alone to have shared that moment with a friend to make fun of me forever.

I threw out the suit right there in the garbage can on the cliffs. I wasn't about to have that be a recurring problem. I still wondered how long I had been surfing with my penis out! I wonder if I had caught rides that others could see while I was standing on my long-board, thinking, "I'm doing something cool." In retrospect, I was swinging my dick around in the wind on the ocean's stage for every-one to see. Also, most waves there are righthanders, so I was flashing the entire beach and cliffs where people sat and watched all the surf-ers, too. As it was my backhand, so my back was to the wave and my face and genitals were to the beach and cliffs in front of me for easy spectator viewing.

You may think, well, it's a bit far away to see something like that, but seriously, pink on black really pops harder than any other colors! When I noticed it on the walking path, it was like a bright glowing pink highlighter marker! Oh well. What can I do? I laughed hard at myself and immediately drove straight to my favorite store, Blow Out Wetsuit Repair, a used wetsuit repair shop on the main road around the corner from Pleasure Point. I asked them if they had another suit for me. I told the old married owners what just hap-pened, and they laughed hysterically and gave me a discount on an-other suit for fifty bucks. They are so sweet, and their shop is great. I luckily never had that problem again. Phew!

My Life In A Nutshell

The lifestyle I live might be normal for some, or impossible for others. I have been in many situations before where people say how lucky I am, or how they could never travel or adventure like I do. I want to explain that the point of this writing is to instill motivation and inspiration into people who are not stoked or need more out of life than they're currently getting. It is possible for many people to live how I do. I really am not that special. I just designed my life around doing what I love. I'd say it took six years, constant focus, and resisting things I really didn't want to do. Also, I quit drinking and smoking, too.

I worked jobs that I either quit or worked seasonally to allow myself the time for travel. I used to bartend in San Francisco for years, and the perk of bartending is making a lot of cash in a less than an eight-hour day, and the ability to take days off whenever you want.

I used to work about thirty days straight, every night of the week, working my own shifts and covering any shift that became available, which in SF was tons. At the time, everyone there was super lazy and just wanted to party, or they were working on their own passions like music or art and needed time for that. This would allow me to then take a few weeks or a month off after saving up money. In that city, like many cities across the USA, bartenders make between $150-$500 per night. The weekends were always more lucrative. Say, on average, I made $200-$300 a night. Now multiply that by thirty days. That was $6,000-$9,000, minus some taxes. My rent was always around $1000, so I would pay for the month that I worked and the month I took off. So that was $2,000, but the rest was up for saving, really.

If you buy groceries, prepare meals to eat at work, don't drink, don't smoke or do drugs or have any other expensive shopping habits, that money is there for saving and traveling. Plus, don't give in to social pressures of needing to buy bullshit constantly. Whenever I was back in SF working, I acted as though I was at summer camp or something, with a goal of being cheap and saving money. When I wasn't working, I would be surfing, hiking, cooking at home, playing guitar, reading, playing with my dog, walking around the city, doing any activity I could that was free. Also, I'm a minimalist so I don't really NEED anything (which I'm not a hardcore minimalist, I just don't have anything, but I do get off a little bit on not having anything...). No one really NEEDS anything material. I buy surfboards. Used. Sometimes. Or, when my wetsuit got so shredded that my penis popped out or wasn't helping me stay warm in the ocean, then maybe I'd buy a new one, off season when it was cheaper or used.

On the same note, I haven't had one sip of alcohol in about five years. I used to live a super negative lifestyle. I bartended late nights, drank every night of the week, did drugs recreationally, smoked cigarettes, stayed out all night, and slept in all day. I was hung over a lot. I was sleep deprived often. I was the healthiest young kid ever, and over time, I developed anxieties and sleeping problems with my unhealthy habits. My life was slowly spiraling out of control, and I wasn't even sure who I was anymore or what was wrong with me.

One summer five years ago I was visiting my Dad in New Jersey feeling down.

"You are built just like me, and whenever I am feeling down, I go exercise, and I immediately feel better. You need to go move your body." He said to me.

I took his advice. I had previously tried everything under the sun negative for me, but I refused to try to help myself in a positive way. It was the only thing left, so I went for it. I went to the gym a few times in Jersey with him, then I drove across the country a few days later and moved into a house in Oakland with friends. The entire solo road trip I listened to podcasts that taught me about weightlifting and nutrition for lifting. After forty hours of information. I was excited to apply my knowledge to my body. I had a goal.

Within a few weeks or less, I became addicted and obsessed with exercise. My body always loved to exercise, only now I made it a priority with a goal to do so. The positive feeling I got after lifting made me feel incredible. It exhausted me to the point that I slept like a rock every night and became more calm, focused, and sharp in my days. Along with positive mental health and attitude came pride and confidence that I never had before. I was proud to be me, and I was confident to be me, without fear of judgment. I became a real person again. This goes hand in hand with being sober, being healthy, and being a minimalist. My living room has been the ocean, the gym, or the mountain trail. I'm never bored, yet I'm never wasting money either.

After you buy a board, surfing is free. The gym requires a monthly membership, but the more often you go, the cheaper it gets. I also like to justify positive ways of spending money, like a gym membership, by asking myself how much I used to spend on a bar tab almost every night that I never thought twice about paying.

After I had this new lifestyle, I was actively trying to be somewhere new all the time, and I stopped spending money when I was back working. Eventually, I had to leave San Francisco and city life behind to pursue a better quality of life for myself. This was when I moved to Maui with friends. I bartended out there right away and took trips to the other islands and to Vancouver's surrounding areas.

Now, I work seasonally at my family's hotel on the beach in New Jersey as a manager in the summer season. This funds my minimalist, modest surf travel for the rest of the year. I think it's important as a minimalist to let go of things mentally, including social pressures. Minimalism is not only material items, but also ditching mental baggage as well. Like insecurities, doubts, or hang-ups that people drink, do drugs, or impulsively shop to cover up; or the fear of being alone. After I refined my life without drinking and drugs and bettered myself with exercise, I didn't need any of those other things. I was content. I have this "Dream Life," some people call it, because I don't have a dream. I don't have the American Dream mentality that I need to be successful with a fancy job title, six-figure salary, fancy cars, and a big house. This lacks modesty. To me, all of that is a prison. Your things end up owning you.

Most people in America live on credit and don't own their houses or cars. I'm not in debt one dollar unless I used my credit card that month and didn't pay it off yet. I don't have any debt because I don't feel the need to have mountains of material things. I need to explore and experience cultures that are not my own. To grasp a larger sense of the world we live in. To further accept and appreciate others. To grow. To be a better person. To be a better me. To exude, expel, and explode positivity from my body in every way I can, and to live in the real world of love, truth, honesty with genuineness, which seems to have dissolved through the cracks of our modern society. To me, having nothing or very little in the world by choice is truly the most freeing thing I can think of. I get anxious when I feel like I have a few too many items on a trip and my rucksack is hard to zipper closed. I have been living out of my rucksack for over three years straight now, and I wouldn't have it any other way.

Since I started down this path, I can now enjoy a lot of the smaller things in my life. I cook all the time. And I love it. I cook for nutrition for my active lifestyle, and I eat about six meals a day. I enjoy cooking all my meals because it's cheaper, healthier, and I think of it as paying myself the money I would be paying someone else to make it for me. When I'm traveling, I splurge more on my adventures, but that's ok, because for me, it is what life is all about. I don't have a wife, kids, a career, a mortgage, a car payment, or health insurance.

Yvon Chouinard is my inspiration. He created the clothing company, Patagonia, at first, so he could afford his surfing and climbing trips. He started a company, so he DIDN'T HAVE TO WORK, but instead live his passions. This man recently gave his multi-billion-dollar company away entirely to a trust, to help fund the studying of climate change and prevention. Also, to help the environment in general. This man thrives to be a dirtbag, and so do I. I live life to experience and explore, and I want others to know that it's easy if you want it to be. All you need to do is stop caring about what other people think of you. The moment you really stop caring about judgments, the more free you are. Those people who might judge you negatively for changing your lifestyle significantly probably aren't the right people to be around in the first place. Cut the fat off of your life and make a change for simple happiness. I'm no preacher. I don't know anything. I'm just a guy, who found something special, who would like to motivate anyone looking for some similar stoke.

Ozzzzzzzzzzz

I had a newfound respect for the world outside of the USA. It was really the kick-off, eye-opening point for throwing in the towel of an average career or nine-to-five-till-I-die kind of lifestyle. I was always a traveler inside of the United States. From age eighteen, every few months to a year I would move somewhere new, but I didn't ever grasp the idea that I could go *anywhere* I wanted. Or that I could save up money for half the year and travel the other half. Now at age thirty-five, having lived that way, I much prefer this type of lifestyle!

I was camping in my van in Bolinas at the beach most days back then, a few years after my long-term relationship ended. I had met a girl who was friends-of-friends of mine that also lived in Bolinas. She was a Kiwi, from New Zealand. She lived in the city, but most long weekends she would come up and rent a little back house from a friend who I would hang out with a bunch, too. We started dating fast for about a month or two, and I really enjoyed her Kiwi banter. It was different than anything I knew at that point. My infant-level traveler brain was just beginning to expand with curiosity. It was fun to be around. It kept me on my toes and using my brain more than an American autopilot brain, like most of us without witty banter.

Once again, all things come to an end, and she took off back to New Zealand, and I never heard from her again. This was a bummer for about a week, but after that, I started thinking I should go somewhere over there (down under) and see what that part of the world was all about.

When I was a little down those first few days, I called up my great buddy, Brett, who I lived with in San Francisco. He was living in Australia doing the work-visa thing, that I was already too old for, otherwise, I would have, too!

"Brett! Can I come sleep on your couch for a few weeks and check out Australia? It's a bit of a bummer over here in the rainy-ass Northern California winter." I asked, already knowing the answer.

"Totally, just let me know, anytime. I have a bar job, but it doesn't make a difference." He responded over the phone.

"I bought a ticket. I leave tomorrow. I'll be there in four days. Staying for two weeks." I texted him ten minutes later.

I'd have been there sooner, but it took three days of travel to get there!

My flight was from Oakland to LAX, LAX to Sydney, and Sydney to Melbourne. Over thirty hours of travel, and three calendar days. Craziness. I had Rodeo, my Australian cattle dog stay with my roommate Jean, who was obsessed with Rodeo, for a couple of weeks.

I landed in Melbourne. My body and mind were both disheveled. I went to pick up the car rental that I booked online, and they required a five-thousand-dollar deposit for the vehicle. I wanted to go berserk but didn't have the mental capacity after the flight.

"Ok cool, whatever." I responded to the rental car counter person.

I went to the parking lot to match the key chain number with the parking space number where my car was sitting. I found the car. I opened the door, got in, and closed the door. I look down.

"Hmm..." I said with a confused tone.

I noticed there was no steering wheel in front of me... It was next to me in the passenger seat. I took a deep breath, transferred my crazy flight emotions into my past, and smiled. I smiled really wide, like a total idiot, and laughed. I got out of the car, walked completely around, and got in on the other side. I was about to learn how to drive on the wrong side of the car, on the wrong side of the road. I was officially in Australia, and I realized it. Hell yea! This was going to be awesome! Trial by fire! I tried driving out of the parking garage, and I hit the curb a few times where the toll booth prevented you from stealing their cars. Then I was free!

I got an Australian sim card in the airport for ten bucks and fired up the shitty cracked phone to get directions to Torquay, a surf town on the south coast of Victoria, a southern state in Australia. It was about an hour and a half drive, and I seemed to be doing alright driving. The car was a manual transmission on top of being backward to what I was used to. It was more difficult that not *everything* was reversed. The shifter was in my left hand – opposite of what I knew – but the gears were all in the positions same as back home. Meaning first is top left, second is bottom left, third is top and to the right of first, fourth is down and to the right of second, etc. The foot pedals are also the same as what I was used to. There was a learning curve for sure, but I'm easily adaptable.

I drove down the highway with the radio on, and AC/DC came on, the song "TNT." I never gave it much thought that AC/DC was an Australian band, but if there was one thing about Australians I learned while being there, it's that Australians love everything Australian. Especially Australian things that are known worldwide. I finally pulled up the driveway where Brett's house was, and he came out and gave me a big ol' hug.

Brett brought me inside, gave me a tour, and took me upstairs to show me the room he was renting.

"Here we are, you get the top bunk." He said.

He had a bunk bed set up that looked like it was designed as a child's room, but a bed is a bed. I thought I was going to be sleeping on the couch or floor, so this was a big win!

We hadn't seen each other in about a year. At that point, we had been great friends for over a decade and even had tattoos of our names on each of our legs that we did ourselves. Way back when, we tattooed each other's names on one another after only knowing each other for a few weeks... I believe that's called friendship-love at first sight.

We had some beers out on his back deck and caught up. This was before I stopped drinking. He did a year working visa in New Zealand first. Their maximum age restriction for a work visa is a year earlier than Australia's, and I couldn't do that either. Brett is six months younger than me, so he was able to apply for both, just in time.

The next morning, my first morning in Australia, I went hunting for a board. We jumped in my rental car and drove around to a few surf shops in Torquay, the town Brett was staying, then down the beginning of the Great Ocean Road to Anglesea.

First, Brett had me stop at Bells Beach, one of the most famous surf spots in Australia. This was also where the final scene in the movie *Point Break*, with Keanu Reeves, supposedly took place. We checked the surf for a while, then moseyed on to the surf shop in Anglesea. I looked around in a few shops at this point, and figured my options were:

#1 Spend an exorbitant amount of money on a sick single fin log, around $800.

#2 Hold out for days or weeks looking for a deal, missing out on surf.

#3 Rent boards daily, a real pain in the ass and gets expensive.

#4 Buy this not-very-cool longboard that was cheap, $250, and not worry about a board for my trip.

I chose the latter. It was way more my style to have spent $800 on a used stylish retro Noserider and wasted all my money, but I just really wanted to surf.

I bought this, who knows what you even call it, 9'-ish longboard with a thruster setup (three fins instead of one), gross. On a short-board, a thruster setup is crucial, as it's a higher-performance board, but on an inherently lower-performance longboard, pretending like a thruster will do much of anything to improve your performance is hilarious to me.

It was ugly, but it worked just fine. I had a soft travel rack with me, the kind that's meant for putting your boards on the roof of a car that has no roof rack. It strapped through the car and onto the roof with little pads and straps to cinch down the board. This travel rack came in handy in times like these when I had the car rental company holding my $5k hostage until I brought the car back looking the way I got it. This was a difficult task for me, to keep the perfect car perfect.

We threw the board up on the roof, strapped it down, and took off. Brett was learning how to surf back then and was borrowing his roommate's longboard, which was perfect for us to longboard togeth-er. We went down the Great Ocean Road looking for some chill, fun surf. We turned down a little road for signs to Point Roadknight. We got out and checked the surf. It was a small, friendly longboard wave that was maybe waist high with righthanders breaking off the rocky point, and lefthanders breaking from the center of the bay toward the point. They were mellow, long, peeling, beautiful waves. Super chill! I was so excited to surf in Australia. I could care less that I was on some ugly longboard. It looked like the perfect first spot to jump in-to. We surfed for a few hours and had a blast. Brett caught some good ones, too! There were some unique rock structures at the point that we monkeyed around in after the surf, before we headed back to my rental car. Point Roadknight became a joke between us that it was our favorite spot around, even though it had the tiniest beginner waves.

After we surfed Point Roadknight, we drove back to Torquay and went to say hi to one of Brett's Aussie friends.

"This is it. Brode's place." Brett said as we parked the car with our boards on the roof.

We walked in like Brett lived there, no knock on the door or any-thing, when we entered the ranch-style house.

"Broooodes!" Brett yelled.

His full name was Broden. This thick, long blond-haired, dread-ed hippie dude popped out of a bedroom. He didn't really look like the surfer type at all.

"Mates! How you going?? Brett, who have you got here with ya??" Brodes asked with his very thick Australian accent.

We introduced ourselves, gave each other massive hugs, and I immediately loved him like a hilarious Australian teddy bear.

They explained to me how they met working together, running a bar/venue in Wānaka, a ski/snowboard town on the South Island of New Zealand. After Brett's New Zealand working visa expired and Brodes was also planning on returning to Australia (Aussies and Ki-wis can travel and work between their countries without needing vi-sas), he told Brett he could get him a bartending job in Torquay at this restaurant he planned on working at himself. That was how Brett landed in Torquay. After we chatted for a bit, Brodes invited us to a barbeque that he and his mates were throwing the next day. He was even planning to install a brand-new expensive grill on his back deck for it.

This was the most Australian thing I heard anyone say so far. An Aussie throwing a BBQ and buying a new grill for it! We said we were down and would be there for sure.

We awoke the next morning and had some instant coffee and eggs with toast.

"A lot of Australians use instant coffee, and it's cheap, so I do too." Brett informed me of the local ways.

We drank instant coffee together and planned our day. We decided to go into Torquay town and check the local Torquay Beach wave.

Torquay is a surf hub. The difference between surf town and surf hub is that I could get anything I needed in Torquay. All the board shops are there. Rip Curl was founded and is headquartered there, which also says something about the town (like there's probably quality surf nearby). A surf hub is like a surf town on steroids. The town thinks about surfing all day every day, like Santa Cruz, San Clemente, Encinitas, Byron Bay, or the North Shore of O'ahu. Those towns live, eat, sleep, and work around the surf. A regular surf town might have some decent surf, one surf shop (if any), and might be difficult to find other surf necessities or might not alter their lives around the surf every day.

We drove around Torquay, and Brett showed me the cute little downtown strip until we drove around the traffic circle to the beach. The surf conditions were glassy and smooth with swell. Awesome!!

"People claim it's bad here a lot, but this looks pretty sick right now." Said Brett, surprised.

We took our boards off the car, put on our wetsuits, which were needed all year round in southern Australia, and paddled out. This place was more of a cove surrounded by cliffs with beach break type surf mixed with a few rock-reef peaks too. I found some nice lefthanders running toward the cliff on the west side, and they had a bit of size to them that day, too!

After we got out, we dried off and took a walk to the southside cliffs and stood on the sightseeing deck. There was a sign mounted on the deck. It read: "Antarctica 6000KM."

I thought that was so unique and had never seen a place or signage telling its proximity to Antarctica before. I was far from what I knew, and I loved every minute of it!

The next day was my first Aussie barbeque, and I was excited. I figured, since stereotypically they were known for barbeques, an average Aussie barbeque must be more like a barbeque in the USA on steroids, like on July 4th or something.

We showed up around noon and helped Brodes set up the large barbecue grill once we got it up his deck stairs. After he installed it in-place around his other deck counter space, it was time to fire it up!

Brodes had already bought all the necessities, so we each popped a beer and started preparing the shish kabobs with veggies, shrimp, and meat. I don't eat meat, only eat fish, so I made a few special skewers without the meat. Brodes also had steaks, corn on the cob, and a seafood medley, which seemed way overkill for us, but I hadn't realized that this was about to be a full-fledged party.

As it was a Saturday, his roommates, who were also his close friends, started popping up out of their rooms from a previous late night. More friends started arriving, and the barbeque was becoming full-on. People were eating and drinking, with more and more friends arriving. Vans full of people were pouring in until sunset when everyone was full and flushed with alcohol.

I figured a barbeque was more of a social day activity, but no one left. Everyone kept indulging more and more, later and later, until it was after midnight. We came up with the great idea to tattoo each other with some packaged legitimate tattoo needles a girl had stashed in her van for situations just like these. Everyone got their own clean tattoo needle, of course.

Brodes and I decided to trade names on each other. I think I may have been a little less inebriated and gave Brodes a halfway decent "Davo" on his knee, stick-n-poke style, meaning one jab at a time. My name in Australia also became Davo because of Brodes. From the first time we met, he only called me that. Must be an Aussie thing... Australians love shortening words and tossing a vowel at the end. For example, service station, they would say "servo," for restaurant they would say "resto," and Dave, they apparently go for "Davo," even if Davo isn't actually any shorter – it's longer (syllables)!

Brodes attempted to tattoo "Brodes" on my shin after I gave him a close to flawless "Davo." In actuality, he gave me something that is a word, technically, but is not quite decipherable in the sense that it's a name or even his name, but I love it. It couldn't have been done any better by any better of a bloke that I just met and wanted to remember forever!

I also met another Aussie dude, who I immediately had a man-crush on, named Stew. I believe the crush was mutual. We got a little matching dot tattoo on our wrists to remember the night. Stew was awesome. Another super carefree dude that was all about laughs and good times. He was tall and skinny with long scraggly brown hair and a gristly short beard. He looked more like a musician than a surfer. He was both. I'm drawn to the friend-type that doesn't take life too seriously, or serious at all for that matter, as I am the same.

A few nights later, there was a rare lunar eclipse that was called the "Super Blood Wolf Moon Eclipse." The most metal name for an eclipse ever. After discussing it at length, Brett, Stew, and I decided to paddle out on our surfboards somewhere under it around 11 p.m. when it was meant to take place. Stew was a chef. Brett and I waited at his work for him to get out of the kitchen by around 10:30 p.m. so we could jam over to the beach. We decided on Whites Beach, right across the street from the restaurant Brett and Brodes worked at, called Señiors.

It was generally flat there (without waves), and if there were waves, they were super small. We figured that was a good place to paddle out and watch the moon from Mother Ocean. Sure enough, Stew ran out of work a little after 10 p.m., and we drove over to the beach. We had a beer on the sand watching the moon and the water as we put on our wetsuits and decided it was a good idea to cram an unopened beer into our suits for when we got out there. There were no waves to surf, so why not?

Super Blood Wolf Moon Eclipse. That's a wild name. "Super" means the moon was really close to Earth and was a percentage bigger and brighter than usual. "Blood" refers to the dark red shadow the moon becomes when in its eclipse. The red is made from refracting light as the sun's light rays travel through the Earth's atmosphere, giving the light a red tint. January's full moon is called the "Full Wolf Moon." Traditionally, wolves were heard howling more in the cold winter months because of a shortage in food supply, so January's full moon was deemed the "Wolf Moon." This was a once-in-a-lifetime event! The moon's close proximity to Earth, appearing larger in the sky, with the eclipse happening at that exact time. We were going to do something about it.

We paddled out. We made it about a hundred feet out and stopped, looking up at the spectacle. The moon was so bright that it lit up the ocean to where we could see our surroundings quite well. At that very moment, the wind shifted, lightly blowing offshore, and knee to waist size surf started coming out of nowhere. The waves were very organized, as if we were given this little gift from the surf Gods in a place that, as far as I saw, rarely ever had surf or good surf to boot! It was incredible! We didn't even get to pop our beers in our wetsuits, we just started surfing under the bright Super Blood Wolf Moon Eclipse, on the south coast of Australia, 6000 KM north of Antarctica. It was unbelievable.

We surfed for a solid two hours. Wave after wave. We could barely paddle back out after catching a wave to turn around and paddle into another. We had Super Blood Wolf Moon Eclipse party waves, where we were all on the same wave at once, screaming. Stew even pulled his beer out of the neck of his wetsuit, popped it, took a sip, handed it to me while riding right beside him, I sipped it, and I passed it to Brett who also sipped it – all on the same freaking wave!!! They were long!! It was a killer session!! It was an unbelievable rare gem of an experience that I couldn't have hoped for in my wildest imagination. And we were living it. The three of us jokers, had one of the best, most unique surf experiences of our entire lives. In the dark. Under the Super Blood Wolf Moon Eclipse in Torquay, Australia.

We got out finally around 1:30 a.m. hollering into the night, absolutely stoked, and collapsed on the sand on shore just gazing up at this magical moment that we knew would never happen in our lives again. It was beautiful. We were maniacs. I wouldn't have it any other way.

Brett and I wanted to take a trip together farther than the South Coast. I kept looking at the map of Australia, and I was fascinated with Tasmania. It seemed too surreal that it was even an option, and I needed to go there. Also, domestic flights around Australia seemed to be cheaper than the United States. Flying most places was under $100 a flight. I took advantage of this. Brett was up for Tasmania, or "Tassie," (sounds like Tazy) as the Aussies say it.

We bought flights. I bought mine for the following morning and Brett was going to leave a few days later, after his work week. We booked an accommodation for a few nights when Brett landed in Hobart. Hobart is the biggest city in Tassie, it's a super rad, small, clean city, where the airport is located. When I got to Tassie a few days before Brett, I rented a car, and for two nights, I camped in my tent as far southwest as the roads took me on the island. I went so far south that the road turned to dirt, and I kept driving further. I drove until the dirt road ended. I was completely in the middle of nowhere with pristine beaches, and virtually no one.

I hiked around, read my book, cooked over the campfire, and chilled alone for two and a half days. It was incredible and very introverted of me. I was as far south as a car would take me in all of Australia. I was even closer to Antarctica than the 6000KM sign I saw in Torquay. After those two nights, I drove back up, picked up Brett from the Hobart airport, and we checked into our accommodation. This was great because I was in dire need of a shower. I can only rinse off in the ocean for so long. We met up with a few of Brett's traveler friends he knew from his time in New Zealand who were living in Hobart.

We all went out together and had some laughs. They crashed on our couches in our rental flat. The following day, Brett and I headed to Cradle Mountain National Park, a few-hours' drive away from the city. We hiked a trail on Cradle Mountain that took us up to a 5,069' peak, a solid five-hour hike. On the way back down, I almost stepped on the biggest snake I had ever seen in my entire life that was basking across the trail. I thought it was a log until it moved as I was walking over its thick black body. Nearly shot me ten feet in the air with surprise!

On our last day in Tassie together, we took a ferry to the MONA, the Museum of Old and New Art, that was owned by a private billionaire. Its theme: sex and death. This sounded too tempting, we had to go. It turned out to be the most unique, modern, connective, museum I had ever been to. There was a wall of one-hundred ceramic vaginas and a robotic intestine track that would get fed and literally take a dump every hour. There were visceral rooms of sound art and crazy neon lights, a room full of crude oil, and a mountain of broken glass that museumgoers create. The purpose of most of the exhibits was to push taboos. Our experience was even more enjoyable with the tab of LSD we split that an Aussie mate gave us at the barbeque in Torquay. Australians truly party hard.

We flew back to Melbourne and got back to our hunt for surf. The next few days we surfed Torquay, Jan Juc, Point Addis, Point Roadknight, and Lorne. I love Lorne. Lorne is an all-around hippie surf town with stunning nature. It seemed more tropical than Torquay where Brett was living, even though neither place was in the tropics. Lorne's surf is sick. The righthand point break off the rock slab on the west side of town was loads of fun, and even the beach break in town was easy, mellow fun when we were there. We also went to a beautiful waterfall that we needed to walk down a million wooden stairs to witness. Brett needed to work, so I drove him back up the Great Ocean Road an hour just to drop him off, turn around, and drive right back to Lorne. I was obsessed. I camped in my driver seat at the cliff edge overlooking the ocean that night. The next morning, after waking up all kinds of mangled in my seat, I drove all the way to Cape Otway, hours further, and passed another hippie town, Apollo Bay, just to see me a koala, and I did! I also hiked the rainforest at night on this elevated wooden platform path looking for glow worms, but I never saw one. I got way too spooked and sprinted out of there back to my car and drove back to my campground.

I was getting ready to move-on in my Australian trip to Byron Bay. I said goodbye, for now, to Brett, Brodes, Stew, and the boys. I caught a flight to Gold Coast Airport from Melbourne and rented another car. This time when I arrived in Byron Bay, I decided to go the hostel route. I rented a private room in a hostel for a few nights, and they had super-sick, stylish single fin logs for hire that I rented a week at a time. These were the types of boards I was looking for around Torquay with Brett but couldn't find. I also left my ugly longboard at Brett's house, I couldn't bring it on the plane, nor did I want to.

I forgot to mention until this point that I was supposed to be on a flight back to Oakland right about… yesterday. I totally didn't get on it. This place was far too fascinating, and I knew there was more to be done in Australia, so I didn't even bother booking another ticket back to California. I just existed in Oz for a while. It was exhilarating.

I decided it was time to take my stylish, single fin longboard out to The Pass. The Pass was Byron Bay's local surf break. It was an amazing point break that has at least four different peaks in the same general area. I had the choice of the wave far outside the rocks that can barrel or the three-ish peaks on the inside of the rocks for mellower longboarding. The further inside, the smaller it got but was some of the best longboarding ever. All the peaks were righthanders. I was riding on my backside the entire time, which was not ideal, but I couldn't complain one iota.

I moved from the more expensive private hostel room, that was about $100 a night, to a cheaper beach campground called Clarkes, which was practically at The Pass. A campsite here was only $35 a night. I had a tent. They had showers. All was good!

Clarkes campground sat on the back side of some sand dunes from the main Byron Bay beach. It was also about a fifteen-minute walk from Byron's downtown strip.

I was traveling there alone, 8,000 miles from my own country, and stoked to check out Australia's surf town culture and nightlife. Byron Bay has a nightlife scene for a surf town. Some surf towns are considered sleepy, where after sunset very little happens. Byron has a bunch of bars, a venue, events, and it seemed like a pretty happening place. I was starved for social interaction, which is common when traveling solo. After so many hours of the day alone – surfing alone, eating alone, and being in my accommodation alone – it was much needed to strike up a conversation with a stranger or even make a new friend.

Almost every night that I was in Byron I walked from the hostel or the campground to the downtown strip for dinner and some drinks. I also discovered the espresso martini here. I was not much of a classy martini kind of drinker, but I saw them on the cocktail list at the place Brett worked at in Torquay and decided to give one a try. Think, strong, cold, espresso with a touch of an alcohol bite at the end. They were also garnished with a few espresso beans. This was my favorite part; I'd chomp the beans down whenever I decided to save them for – the beginning or the end. Also, after a whole day of surfing in the sun, it was a nice pick-me-up to get in the mood to be more social when my body was telling me to collapse from exhaustion. I bounced around from a few bar/pub/restaurants every night before walking back to my hostel or my campground tent to call it a night.

I made plans to fly back to Tasmania in a couple of days. I did more research about the island and really wanted to explore more open natural beauty. I also realized that when I was in Tassie last, I did not surf. I really wanted to, even for nothing more than just to say I had. Surfing was added to the trip docket.

I learned that the northwestern point of Tasmania is a location of the world, reported by a science research facility there, to have the cleanest air on the entire planet. It's called Cape Grim, and supposedly they bottle their air and water and ship it to places of heavy pollution throughout the world. The air in Cape Grim has traveled thousands of miles over open ocean, getting filtered, before hitting the northwest of Tassie, as the first bit of land the winds see since South America. Since Tassie sits on a latitude farther south than the tip of

South Africa, the strong ocean winds blow from Argentina with nothing in its way until Tassie. On the other side of the world. There are no pollutants left after this pure ocean distance. I was obsessed with the idea to fly back to Tassie to drive across the entire island just to breathe. Am I nuts?

I flew back to Tassie. I rented a car. I started driving. Even though Tassie, in comparison with mainland Australia, looked tiny, it's not that small of an island. I couldn't drive across it in one day. I tried and made it somewhere in the center, in an old mining town, after hours of driving. I pulled off and had some food at a local pub. I sat down and ordered dinner at the bar before realizing that this might not have been the friendliest of places, but I had already ordered. It was too late. Just from talking with the bartender when I ordered my meal, some of the local patrons overheard my accent.

The next thing I knew, while sitting on my bar stool, I felt something on my back. It was a man, well, a man's massive gut. Some local pushed his gut up onto my back and held it there.

"Sup Yank." He said as he leaned up on me.

"Sorry?" I responded.

"You a Yankee ain't-cha?" He said in his crazy thick Australian accent.

At this point in my life, I had never heard of an American called that, but I mean, I guess it made sense. There's a baseball team called the Yankees, and that's what we are, I guess, from the USA? I'm also not sure if it's derogatory, but it sure sounded like it.

"Yep." I responded.

I turned my head to see that this man was huge. Well over six foot and as wide as an ox. He must have weighed 300 pounds. He had on blue jean overalls, a red tattered cap, and had a patchy brown, gingery beard.

"So, you like Trump?" He said while his gut still pushing on my back.

I wasn't sure what to say, as he seemed upset with Trump, but he was clearly a blue-collar worker from a minoring town, which in my American brain meant conservative who would like Trump. I couldn't make up my mind on how to navigate this conversation.

"Where are you from boy?" He asked me in a real curious kind way that was clearly judgmental.

"San Francisco, California." I said.

Even though that's not where I was born. California is shinier to foreigners than New Jersey, so I stuck with it, and it was where I *actually came from* on this trip, so I wasn't really lying.

"California, huh? You must not like Trump then?" He asked me, trying to put words in my mouth to call me on whatever opinion he had about Trump.

I didn't say anything, just nodded my head to show I was listening and maybe barely agreeing with him. He took his gut off my back finally, took another crack at a "Yank" joke, and went back to his pint with his friends.

"Frigg'n hell." I thought.

I barely skirted myself out of that one. I didn't understand it but ate my food quietly and took off. Better than getting in a fight with the local hillbilly miners and having them tie me up in their truck or something crazy.

I drove outside of that town to a place, where apparently people put dead cars in piles, in an open dirt field, and passed out in my car till morning.

At sunrise, I got up, brushed my teeth, spit on the ground and hit the road for Cape Grim. I was a few hours away and got there by mid-morning. Well, by got there, I mean I got to a dirt road with a fence that said: "DO NOT PASS, No Trespassing, Employees and Government Officials Only."

The fence was on the side of the dirt road, not blocking the entrance, so I could keep driving in, and I did. I was a little spooked, between the place being named Grim and that miner guy from the night before. Who knows what would have happened if I got caught here? I found out later, that fat miner in the pub was what people in Australia call a Bogan. Bogans are very nationalistic Australians who would be considered a redneck in the USA. I was also later informed by my surf buddies that Bogans also sport the Southern Cross stars on the Australian flag as tattoos.

As I drove in, there was no sign of anyone around on this scientific government property, but there were bunkers and storage houses and research towers in all directions. I drove around like secret agent 007, did a lap, and when I saw a few people walking on the premises, I decided to get out of there. I didn't really want to have to explain myself.

54

"Hi, my name is Dave Boss, I am from the USA, and I am here to breathe." I would sound like a complete alien cyborg and wasn't looking forward to that conversation, especially if detained.

I went back to the fence, which was the end of my road, and took some pictures with the no trespassing Cape Grim sign as a keepsake. I then sat on the dirt ground for a while, closed my eyes, and breathed. I was hoping to do this on a cliff overlooking the ocean or somewhere more picturesque, but I was right there, and that air was just as good as a few hundred feet further. I breathed deeply to try and hold on to some of that air in my body, saving it for after I left. I felt peaceful and ridiculous but what the hell.

I turned around and drove six-hours back to Hobart. Actually, a little beyond Hobart to the southeast coast. I had one more thing to do. I rented a soft top (a type of foam longboard for beginners, it was all they had, and I'm not above it if it means I can surf!) just to paddle out and catch a few below-average waves in Tasmania, Australia. After my short session, I went back to the airport and flew back to Byron Bay. I had officially caught some choppy, short, close-out waves on a beginner board in Tasmania!

I returned to Byron Bay and stayed in the private hostel room again, mainly to rent one of their stylish longboards for another week. It was discounted if I stayed with them. I surfed The Pass again. The conditions were so consistently good there. It was beautiful, fun, chill longboarding in friendly surf. It was an all-around good time.

I did some research and found a hippie-dippy, right up-my-alley kind of destination called the Crystal Castle. Just outside of Byron, up a little mountain. This place is a Zen Garden, mixed with a botanical garden, mixed with a massive crystal collection, mixed with a yoga/meditation/peaceful sanctuary. I had to go. I drove up a steep windy road to get there and parked.

I walked in after paying an entrance fee and started walking the path. There were statues of Buddha everywhere and different nature scenes every so often. I walked by beautiful lily ponds, bamboo forests, mountain views, and amazing flowers everywhere. There was also a life-size walking labyrinth, a circular maze of stone on the ground that you are supposed to walk its path one person at a time in complete silence. There was a sign that said it took twenty minutes per person to complete the path.

"No way it looks so small I'll do it in three minutes." I thought to myself.

Twenty minutes later, I finished. I couldn't believe it. The intricacy of the maze was difficult to see from the outside. The Crystal Castle also had massive chunks of crystal for photo ops, one holding the record for the largest pieces of amethyst in the world. They were standing tall like something out of *Lord of the Rings*, and I stood between them hoping for some of their energy to leave with me.

"There must be a strong energy field between these suckers." I thought, amazed.

When this place couldn't get any cooler, I walked up to a Tibetan prayer temple. There were Tibetan prayer flags everywhere. As I walked closer, I saw spinnable blocks on bars with prayer writings all over them, called prayer wheels, surrounding the temple. It explained how to spin the prayer wheels with your hands while walking completely around the square temple. Spinning the blocks column after column on all sides and praying until they all stopped. I did some research on these afterward, and the spinning prayer wheels are called Mani Wheels. They are used to collect wisdom and purify bad Karma. Each wheel is decorated with a mantra, written in a clockwise direction, the same movement as the sun across the sky. Radical!

One of my favorites was the reflexology walk. They asked guests to remove their shoes and walk on stones that were purposely raised when cemented in the ground to put pressure on your feet in a certain way. I walked across this path, which in turn, was supposed to help my entire body. I walked it again, and again. Just in case it needed more than one round to work. Reflexology is a traditional eastern medical practice with a theory that every part of your body, and organs in your body, are connected to a different region of the bottom of your foot. By massaging your feet in a certain way, you can help different parts of your body. I had so much fun.

As I was leaving, I noticed a small group of strangers around each other, and I inquired. There was a guided meditation class starting and everyone was invited to enter. Yes! I was stoked! I had never experienced guided meditation before. There was incense burning, softly spoken loose instruction, and lots of silence. When I left, I felt extra grounded and slow. As in, mentally slow in a good way. I wasn't all scatterbrained and A.D.D.-brain like I can be. It was beneficial for my internal calmness and Zen level. I understood why meditation is such an important tool that we often overlook in our daily lives to control our emotions, fears, anxieties and to live presently.

The next day, I started branching out my surfing and went to a place called Tallows. I was groggy, I wasn't quite in the mood to surf yet, and hadn't had much coffee. I checked this spot, with a fresh coffee in hand, just to have a look and hang by the beach. I walked down the path through the brush foliage and had a look. I stopped dead in my tracks. Five seconds of straight awe. I turned around and ran back to my car for my board. It was incredible!

"OH MY GOD OH MY GOD OH MY GOD!!!" I kept repeating as I ran.

I grabbed my board from my car, ran back, and paddled out as fast as my slow morning body allowed.

Tallows has a cliff to the north side of the beach where there was a very consistent lefthand barreling wave, but I was not up to par at that time, and it was already occupied by a bunch of sunrise-session shortboarders. I had a longboard, and I was looking for long cruising rides, not huge pitching aggressive barrels.

I decided to go out in the middle of the beach to catch some beach break waves that were looking seriously magical and were what I saw initially that made me run back for my board. The waves were big for me then. Not overwhelming but big – it was still fun as hell, but when the set waves came, it got a little dicey. I caught a screamer. I rode it ridiculously long for a beach break when, usually, beach breaks are shorter rides. I caught another. And another. My face must have looked insane with the goofiest grin of all time, as I wasn't even awake yet! Was this a dream?

I ended up drifting (by total accident, I swear) right near this girl who was someone I could literally never take my eyes off for the rest of my life. A pure angel. A goddess. Long blond hair, blue eyes, and she started talking to me.

"Looks like I'm on the wrong board. This thing's too short. I have my longboard in the car. I want to catch these like you." She said to me in a European accent.

I almost fainted in the water right there. She came back a few minutes later with a longboard and paddled straight for me. We talked a little more, and she caught a wave with her longboard. Then I caught the next wave in that set. I dropped in. The lip was pitching up, but I felt like I was in a good position, deep in the pocket, right where the wave was about to break.

    57

The next thing I knew, the lip pitched over me, and I was long-boarding through a barrel! I made it out and kept riding the wave farther! The girl of my dreams saw the entire thing as she was paddling back out from her ride and saw it up close! She gave me props, and I couldn't believe myself. That was the first barrel I had ever truly been surfing in – versus wiping out in – and the first barrel that I made it out of successfully. It was a monument in my surfing career. To ever be remembered, my first barrel at Tallows Beach, New South Wales, Australia.

I paddled back out. She and I were sitting on our boards a couple meters from each other, when out of nowhere, as we were waiting for a set to come in, a pack of little bottlenose dolphins swam all around us and even dove under us!

"Can I buy you lunch?" I asked with all the luck momentarily on my side.

"Yes, totally." She said laughing hard.

After our surf session ended, she drove her car to town, and I followed to her favorite café. I found out she was from Belgium and was living in Byron working as a wedding planner's assistant. I told her, up until that point, this was my favorite day of my life. I wasn't lying.

I ended up finding out a few days later from a friend that a man got killed by a Great White Shark attack at Tallows Beach less than a week earlier. When I find things out like that it really makes me feel lucky, or maybe we do have a certain amount of time here on planet Earth, and his was up but mine wasn't. I was spared by the sharks and Ocean Gods, day after day. Or a shark was just starving and decided to choose him because he was closest, and it's all random. Who knows. It's spooky either way. I was a little hesitant to paddle back out right away at Tallows after that. I figured because I had such a good time there I was for sure overdue and would be next for the sharks because the balance, you know?

The following day, I checked out the next beach south called Suffolk Park. Suffolk is a tiny, hippy, sleepy beach town south of Byron Bay that has a long stretch of beach and beach break surf, touching Tallows beach to the south. I met up with the dolphin girl from Belgium there and we went for another surf together. I remember the waves being so clean I was mesmerized.

I came from California, and especially up north around San Francisco, it was consistently choppy or blown out. From time to time, I'd score an offshore sunset session or something, but it seemed common for Byron to have amazing conditions. Hence, why it's such a special place. It's also possible that I happened to score on one of the better days of the year, but I doubt it.

I didn't use to enjoy an average beach break because, in my experiences in the past, they were messy, unorganized, aggressive, or just closeouts. I would surf a Suffolk beach break every day of my life. My pretty friend from Belgium was leaving on her next journey to South Africa in a few days, and I was driving up north to meet Brodes in Noosa Heads. We would not see each other again, and it stung a little. It was hard to walk away, but our futures were not aligned. I still had a few amazing surfs and a memory of my first barrel together.

I wanted to stay in Australia forever. I stayed for six weeks in total. Four weeks without having a return ticket after skipping out on my flight home on day 15. I felt like it was time to go back and reclaim ownership of my dog. My roommate Jean was still watching her for me in Oakland. The last month I spent in Australia, after I missed my first return ticket, I had been getting my bartending shifts covered weekly. When I didn't make a ticket yet after a weekend, come Monday, I would send out a group text asking all my coworker bartending buddies who wanted to pick up more shifts that week. I managed to cover every single shift I had for the six weeks of traveling in Australia. I was sure I wasn't going to have a job when I got back because of these logistics, but I ended up making it work, from another continent, for a month and a half! Hell yea! I still had a job after all!

While in Torquay, Brodes invited me to his family's house he would be visiting with his friends in Noosa Heads. Noosa Heads is an upscale hippie town nowhere near Torquay, many states away on an entirely different coast of Australia. Byron Bay is in the Gold Coast region of Australia's east coast, and Noosa Heads is in the Sunshine Coast region of Australia's east coast farther north. It's about a four-hour drive between the towns. Brodes would fly there from Melbourne, but I decided to drive to meet them. Noosa has a famous surf break called Tea Trees and seemed like a cool laid back hippie vibe. This seemed like a surf town that I needed to visit. I planned my trip to Noosa Heads from Byron as my last stop and bought a plane ticket back to the States out of Brisbane airport for the day after arriving in Noosa.

It was great to have one more night with my new Australian buddies before I left. I wish Brett could have been there too, to see me off, but he had to stay back in Torquay and work. I made it to Brodes' address. It was a super nice house right on the canal of a man-made river to the ocean. I knocked on the door and Brodes and his Torquay roommates, who I knew pretty well at this point, greeted me with hugs and gave me a tour of the house. Brodes pointed to a bedroom that was where I would be sleeping so I tossed my bag and quickly walked back to the group to see what the plan was for my last night.

"Well, it's *your* going away party, of course!" Brodes said with excitement.

It was still early in the day, so I rented a board in town and headed out to Tea Trees. Once I got there, it took a minute to figure out what was going on. In the corner of Noosa, there was a road that took me to Noosa National Park. From here, I parked and walked on a trail for twenty minutes to Tea Tree Bay, a bit of a hike when carrying a longboard. It was crazy beautiful. Tropical. I had spent a lot of my time in temperate parts of Australia, like Tassie, Torquay, the Great Ocean Road/Surf Coast area of the south coast. They were all mild places. As I went north in Australia, I got closer and closer to the equator, and it got warmer and muggier at the coast. Byron was way warmer and more tropical than the Torquay area, and I noticed Noosa was even more.

I walked through Noosa National Park, carrying my rented longboard. My favorite part, these trees, that I think I have only seen in Hawai'i before, that, to me, defined the place as being exotic and tropical. They are called Pandanus trees or Screw pines. They look something like if a Joshua tree, a Palm tree, and a Mangrove tree all had a baby together. They have narrow, green, long Palm-type leaves with pointed ends, but their trunks resemble a Joshua tree how they all look different, almost like they were dancing awkwardly, each having their own distinct personality. Then, they had these exposed root systems, or many lower mini trunks, the same way a Mangrove tree does. With all these unique looks, as an American at least, I knew I was somewhere special. I finally got a glimpse of Tea Trees Bay as I turned a corner on the trail from a higher vantage point, and it was stunning. The wind and surf were not great, but there was a wave, and this was my last full day in Australia, so I was going to surf it either way!

I paddled out and caught a bunch of these surprisingly longer choppy righthanders. Considering the less-than-ideal conditions, it was a blast. The wave still held up more than I expected from the bad winds, and I had a bunch of long righthand rides. I got out, hung out on the beach a while, and hiked my board back out of there. Time to go meet up with the Aussie buddies for my last night.

I got back to Brodes' house and showered off. We were planning on going to dinner and hitting a few bars in town afterward. I was the fifth wheel with Brodes, his girlfriend, his roommate, and the room-mate's girlfriend too. We had so many laughs that night I couldn't count if I tried. We had a delicious meal, hung out at this outdoor cyclist-themed bar, and made it back to the house. There, we took out kayaks on the canal, and I think there may have even been some skinny dipping off the dock at one point. I was really going to miss my new friends.

It seemed I had left the United States to find something different, to find a different attitude on life, a different energy, and I had found it. I wasn't looking forward to San Francisco, to the place I wanted to run from, but at the same time the Aussies had changed my life and taught me a few things that I felt I could share in my own way with the people around me where I was heading back to. I spent a month and a half nowhere near a city in Australia and felt like that was one of the beautiful things about my trip – constantly being around peaceful nature. I was no longer a city person. It was inevitable, only a matter of time until I left San Francisco.

I had loads of fun in Australia. Loads. Every single day was a new, genuine heartfelt experience. Since I was a solo traveler and was generally looking to be social a lot of the time, I went out almost every night for the entire six weeks I was in Australia. I was a little tired, but I was also tired of drinking and having that unhealthy side of traveling. I decided to leave drinking and smoking behind in the place where I enjoyed it the most, with the Aussies who love a good party! Now, as I write this, it has been over five years, and it was a phenomenal decision for my life. I have more time, mental energy, money, and health to focus on more trips, more surfing, more adven-ture, and more personal growth. I love you, Australia. Thank you.

Aloha

"We wish we could stay here forever! We want to live here!" Brett and I kept complaining to our Australian friends.

"Mates, you're stupid, you flew OVER Hawai'i to get here. Hawai'i is part of your country. You can live there whenever you want! Us Australians can't do that!" Said Brodes one night, tired of hearing us complain.

He was right. The grass was always greener. We were ignoring a ridiculously beautiful surf hub that we *did* have the ability to live in if we chose, and we didn't even consider it. Brett and I looked at each other, as his year-long work visa in Australia was nearly half over already, and we agreed to do it. We planned that in six months, after his Australian work visa expired and my sublease in Bolinas expired, we would move to Hawai'i together. It was on!

During my six-month sublet in my forest-beach-shack-cabin dwelling in Bolinas, I commuted to the Mission District in San Francisco almost every single day. I worked at one of the three bars I was employed by daily to sock money away to move to Hawai'i with. I worked, surfed, slept, ate, and exercised. That's about it. My life was cheap. I covered bartending shifts for coworkers who wanted a day off every single time one came up. I cooked almost all my meals at home and would bring prepared food to work. I just stayed focused on saving money. I continued to keep alcohol out of my lifestyle, so my focus remained, and my wallet stayed full.

Brett and I decided on moving to Maui. We had a couple of great friends out there already who did the same move – Maui after Australia. My great friends, Chris and Gina. It was an incredible advantage having them out there as a resource to help, which they were super willing to do because they wanted more friends around, too. Maui was a slow place.

About a month before I moved, I flew out there with a surfboard bag and duffel bag with my things that I stashed at their place. I would be returning with my dog, Rodeo, and wouldn't be able to have as many checked bags and surfboard bags with me then. While I was out on that trip, I was in negotiation with a hippie woman for her 1989 rust-bucket color Volkswagen Vanagon that had been sitting in the jungle in Haiku (north shore/upcountry jungle town), Maui for who knows how long. Years. It did run quite well. It was just old and slow, but it had a convertible bed in the back and plenty of room for friends and boards. I ended up settling with her for $3500 and paid $100 to store it at a local storage facility (someone's vacant land) for the month that I wouldn't be there.

Things were starting to come together, and I could envision myself living there. I had some things, a bag of boards, and a sweet van on Maui now. I just needed my body, my dog's body, a place to live, and, eventually, a job.

As time passed in California, I was saving more and more money, but I had new hurdles to jump through to get my dog to the islands with me. I found out that there was no rabies on any of the Islands of Hawai'i, so they were very strict about letting dogs from the mainland over. I needed tons of paperwork, vaccinations, and proof of rabies tests within a few months. When it was time to go, I also needed a health certificate for Rodeo, saying she was healthy enough to fly. I also needed to be in contact with the State of Agriculture of Hawai'i and pay them for my dog to be accepted into Hawai'i. This all cost quite a bit of money and countless hours of research, paperwork, vet visits, and energy.

After I had brought my four surfboards to Maui in a ten-foot coffin-style roller bag, the only board I had left to ride in California was my pig. This board was shaped in 1957, a 9'2" Gordon & Smith pig-style longboard, with a glassed-in D fin (non-removable wooden D-shaped, old, retro single fin, under the polyester resin that the whole board is coated with). The board weighs about 32lbs. I still have it in my brother's garage in Pasadena. It's for sale. It doesn't have a leash plug, so I surfed it with no leash. It was a crazy workout trying to get it from my yard to the roof of my Subaru, to the surf, and back.

One day in Bolinas, my forest-beach-cabin-shack dwelling neighbor, a woman in her fifties who was usually doing hippie things in Todos Santos, Mexico, asked me if I could take her out surfing. I told her that I would love to, and we went out the next day in Bolinas to The Patch, a point break in town. We paddled out together. I was on my only board still in California, my old pig, and I caught a few waves while she was building her surf courage to go for one herself.

After I had just caught a wave and was in waist-deep water, I started paddling back out again. A larger shore-break wave appeared, and I paddled into it. I attempted to pierce through it— duck-dive-style— as the wave broke over me. Normally, when I duck dive on any length of board, my board and I pierce through the wave as one entity and pop out through the back of the wave together. Well, for whatever reason on this unusual day, with the heaviest old board in the world, it didn't work out that way. I held onto the board as the board and I both pierced through the wave, only this time it was as if we were independent of each other, and the energy of the wave caused me to literally headbang (like at a metal concert) my board, hard. When I popped through the wave, I saw stars and was con-fused. I was on the verge of having been completely knocked out. I kept paddling to move my body and concentrate on something to stay awake and present, so I didn't pass out in the ocean. I made it back to my hippie neighbor in the water.

"Dave, your nose is bleeding pretty good, what happened?" She asked.

I told her what just happened, and I didn't feel much better, so I paddled in to shore and laid on the beach for a while until my head stopped buzzing. She caught a few fun waves, and we went back to our cabins afterward.

I woke up in the morning. When I awoke, I went into the bath-room, I had a headache and wanted to look at my head to see if there was a cut or anything from the board smacking it. When I looked in the mirror, I saw the reflection of a raccoon person with two com-pletely swollen black eyes that developed overnight. I had to work that way for about ten days before they started going away.

I think I was moderately concussed, but I'm not really into doc-tors unless it's an absolute emergency and I'm dying, which I wasn't. I was fine. This sort of thing only happened one other time about a year prior, south in Pacifica, with my first Andreini Owl board. I didn't get a black eye from that one, but my nose was broken and a little crooked afterward. I just left it and had a crooked nose for a while. Well, as I was looking in my mirror with my black eyes after the head bang in Bolinas, I noticed that my nose was straight as an arrow again! So, thank you for fixing my face, Mother Ocean, the provider, right on!! I thoroughly appreciate it!!

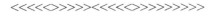

From working almost every single day for about six months between three bar jobs and a few odd jobs, I ended up saving around $25,000 for Maui. Luckily, my rent in the Bolinas beach-forest-shack-cabin dwelling was only $800 a month. This was an insane deal because the town had virtually nothing to rent. The biologist girl could have charged $4000 a month, and someone would've paid it. My life was cheap though. Surf, gym, work, eat, sleep, coffee, repeat. Just Rodeo and me. There was a grocery store in California called Grocery Outlet Bargain Market, or "Gross Out" as we called it, and that was where I exclusively shopped for my bargain groceries for more savings! There wasn't one anywhere near Bolinas' hippie beach forest, so I had to drive over a mountain to Petaluma if I wasn't going to the city for work. I would make a pit stop at the gym while I was there, too, and make a day of it.

Time got closer to the date when I told my work I was leaving, and my plane ticket to Maui was approaching. About a month away, I started realizing that it was going to be too difficult to fly directly to Maui with Rodeo. I was still without a permanent place to live on Maui. My good friend and old Oakland roommate Jean, the same roommate who watched Rodeo when I went to Australia, decided to watch her again for me while I figured it out on Maui. We planned for Jean to ship Rodeo on a flight once I was ready. Jean was a lifesaver. At this time, Brett and I had found a studio apartment to rent for the first month, but we needed to find something bigger and dog-friendly for long-term during that one-month sublet.

Finally, after six months, it was time to move to Maui! The bars I worked at had a little going away party for me there, which really was an excuse for everyone to drink except me, and I was done with

San Francisco! I loved that place so much but was excited to be somewhere tropical with better surf and great old friends!

I had a 2005 Subaru Outback that I had to sell before leaving. I hadn't incorporated any money from the sale into my savings numbers, so it was extra money. I also had a super close friend, Johnny, who I recorded a record with, whose last car just exploded somewhere in the Santa Cruz mountains on a trip, literally. I knew he recently moved to the city and didn't have much money. I told him if he took me to the airport in my Outback, for $500, it was his. It was probably worth around $2000 at the time. I bought it for $3500 about a year earlier, and it had over 200,000 miles on it. So after a $1500 taxi ride to the airport, I was off!

I landed at Kahului International Airport somewhere around the beginning of August. My friends Chris and Gina swooped me from the airport, and I had already left my boards and clothes with them in bags a month earlier, so I only had a little bag with me. I arrived on Maui a week before Brett rendezvoused from Australia to get our one-month studio rental. I had planned to stay with Chris and Gina for the week. We just hung out and surfed. They also weren't big partiers, so it was super easy and fun hanging with them, besides they're some of my best friends in the world.

I tried living on Maui once before, but it wasn't a real try. I was about twenty-one years old, and I was driving across the country. First to move to New York City, where my younger brother Jesse told me I could stay with him for a while in his crazy Brooklyn loft space. On my way across the country, I visited friends in Chicago. While my car was parked overnight, an intense hailstorm blew through with baseball-sized hail stones. My little, newer compact car had little dents all over it (not super noticeable, but they were there) and my insurance told me to go downtown and see an adjuster since this happened to many cars.

I went there and an hour later left with a check written to me for $6500 as a twenty-one-year-old kid! I was beyond stoked! I won the lottery! And I didn't plan on fixing the car, that was for sure. I got to NYC and told my brother the story.

"Let's move to Hawai'i!" I screamed!

My brother is three years younger than me and at the time, eighteen and broke, but I just found free money! I would support us until we figured it out. We left thirty days later from the moment my brother heard the idea. I love spontaneity. It's a driving force of energy, of being alive, it really is.

We were screaming when we bought plane tickets that night. I found an ad on Craigslist by a surfer mom who owned a duplex on some land in Haiku town on Maui. It was affordable at the time, sixteen years ago, at $800 a month. My brother and I would share it. Curveball, my brother got scabies while in NYC and flew them to Hawai'i, giving them to me once we moved into this apartment. We were freaks of nature for a couple of weeks, itching everywhere. After we recovered from loads of harmful chemical cream lathering, we realized we were in the middle of the jungle, with no car, no friends, nothing. The closest bus stop was seven miles away.

We hiked every day. Walked around everywhere. Tried hitchhiking. Went to Twin Falls every day, which is a pair of beautiful waterfalls that we cliff-jumped from. We found a secret avocado tree off one of the trails and would climb it higher and higher every day to pick more free avocados until a thin branch finally broke and Jesse fell from high up in the tree. His body horizontal in the air from high up, straight to a pile of leaves on the ground that saved him. We were bored. I tried to buy a car. It was a total piece of stinking garbage Honda Civic for $800 from a kid younger than us. I couldn't do it. We took the bus and hitchhiked all the way home.

"Dude, let's get out of here." I said.

He agreed. I bought us plane tickets to Phoenix, Arizona and spent the rest of my money on my first Harley-Davidson motorcycle. So now that I surf, am a decade older, have a van already, and had friends on the island, I wanted to try for round two.

◇<<<<<◇◇<<◇>>>>>

Brett landed on Maui! We swooped him from the airport, and all hung out at Chris and Gina's in central Maui (best strategy for surfing north and south coasts) for a couple of days until our studio was ready. We got the call and headed over to check it out. It was just a month-long sublet, but it was the only spot we found. It was hard to find anything on the islands, especially affordable. We were stoked.

We checked it out, and it was a no-frills, semi-dump, but it would do fine. We were used to that level of shithole. It even came with its own private jacked (buff), meth addict, sketch-ball tweaker who lived upstairs.

We met the owner of the house, a skinny Asian lady in her fifties, and gave her the money. We were in Waiehu town up on a relatively steep hill, overlooking the north shore and a surf break called Sandpiles. If I didn't preface this enough, we were SUPER stoked. We officially lived in Hawai'i!!! We both didn't have much, just a bag and a few surfboards each, but we moved in. The studio consisted of a bed, a couch, a bathroom, a simple kitchen, a TV, only one oscillating fan, and no air conditioning. All in one room. I offered up the bed and took the couch. I had my VW campervan and was planning on doing some serious beach camping in it often, so I wouldn't be around every night anyway. Just like that, we were living!

Every time I came home to our ground-level studio, if Brett was home, the WSL pro surf league was on the tube. Either a live contest somewhere in the world, surf videos, or commentators recapping after a contest ended. Brett got hooked on it in Australia, and we watched it all the time even though I never knew anyone in it.

We went surfing. We surfed Sandpiles beach often due to its proximity to our studio, and we could tell if it was good from the house. We just had to walk out our front door to the middle of the street and look left down the hill. Besides Sandpiles, and Pavilions at Ho'okipa, the only other surf breaks on the north shore we surfed were Kanaha near the airport and Tavares. There were waves at Paia Bay too, but I never liked that wave, so we would just hang out in Paia town but surf elsewhere. I visited Gina at work all the time in Paia. She was a clothing buyer and sold gifts and clothes to tourists at Biasa Rose boutique where I would hang out and drink their coffee. I think Brett surfed Paia a few times without me, which was totally fine.

Some of the biggest waves I had ever seen that were not at an official big wave spot, were at Ho'okipa in winter. I surfed Ho'okipa a handful of times, and it was super fun, but it always had the potential to be a little sketchy or super terrifying. It's known to be big there. Lots of locals park on the cliffs, set up camp, and just watch it. Sandpiles was always the most mellow and as a longboarder still, I preferred it. Sandpiles was always my safest bet when on the north shore of Maui.

Maui, at least to me, is sort of broken up into three quadrants of surf. North shore, south shore, and west side. The north shore of Maui, just like the famous North Shore of O'ahu, receives huge swells from around November/December through March/April, and the south shore generally gets its swell in the summer – the opposite months – so there was surf all year! My favorite surf was on the south side.

I used to surf Grandmas, 1000 Peaks, Launiupoko, Shark Pit, and Lahaina Breakwall. All of them, all the time. On special occasions, when it wasn't packed, we'd surf Olowalu. Shark Pit was one of my favorite waves on Maui. Thanks for that, Chris! I learned how to ride a shortboard on that wave. Well, my Marc Andreini 7'0" single fin, sharp, mini-gun-looking thing (a long, pointed board meant for riding larger waves). A 7'0" board isn't usually considered a shortboard, it's in the realm of mid-length, but the way this thing is shaped, it has characteristics made for surfing bigger waves, like more volume, but very narrow. It looks like a shortboard compared to other mid-lengths and it was my first step down to that world of shorter board.

In terms of getting my surfing to the next level, moving to Hawai'i was the best thing I could have done. Some of those Shark Pit or Lahaina Breakwall or Olowalu days were well overhead and terrifying to me back then, but I learned how to surf them. I eventually had to ditch my longboards and started riding my shorter boards most of the time. I had a 6' single fin vintage egg from the 1970s I would ride, or a 5'4" Mini-Simmons twin-fin I would ride, which was hilarious. A regular Simmons-style board is a retro design, around 7'- 8' with a twin-fin set up (two smaller more triangular fins often glassed in with the rest of the board). A Mini-Simmons is the same idea, only much shorter, 5'- 6', super thick, buoyant, and wide. It looks like a bar of soap with twin fins on the bottom. Essentially, if you stood a longboard up on its tail and cut it in half at its middle horizontally, you would take the top piece and attach twin fins to the bottom. That's a Mini-Simmons. To say the least, it was a low-performance, fun, strange, weird, silly design, that was the only board I brought with me when Brett and I took our North Shore, O'ahu trip (where there were the most HIGH-performance waves in the world... go figure), but I'll get to our O'ahu trip in a bit.

I had an old friend, nick-named Tall Kan, from Colorado who was already living on Maui in Lahaina town, the busiest little nightlife tourist town on Maui. I asked him if he could keep an ear out for me for any work he knew of. The next day he called me with a bartending job. His best friend was the bar manager of a kind of sports bar restaurant by day, club by night, kind of place. It was not my scene at all. The bars I worked at and managed in San Francisco were eclectic dive bars and venues that were musician-focused, but beggars can't be choosers.

"Hell yea!" I said to Tall Kan.

Thankfully for me, there was a high turnover rate on the Islands from the traveling nature of the population there. Just like that, I scored a relatively well-paying bartending job. I didn't care for the job, but it was great in the meantime to keep my savings that I thought I would need to use for a while to get on my feet. I was thankful.

Brett and I would surf Lahaina Breakwall, then I would go to work at the bar, and sleep in my van at the beach just outside of Lahaina. I did this a few times a week. After a few weeks of surfing, working, and house hunting, Brett and I found a cheap two-bedroom house on Craigslist up the volcano on the north side of the island, in an upcountry town called Makawao.

Makawao is a historic cowboy town 1600' up Haleakala, Maui's 10,000' volcano. We met the owner, who was a middle-aged blonde lady. We found out she was an old playboy bunny a few decades back who now settled down with kids and a real estate job. She and her family lived in a separate house on the property. She was extremely nice and explained how she had some riffraff-type of people living in there before, who she had to evict, and asked us if we were of similar kind.

"I don't even drink, and when I'm not working, I go to sleep between 8 - 9 p.m. to surf sunrise in the morning. You have nothing to worry about." I said while laughing.

She accepted and allowed us to move in. The rent was $2000 per month. I felt it was fair to pay a little more for Rodeo to be there, so we split the rent, $1100 for me, and $900 for Brett. Now, I could fly Rodeo out because we found a place to live!

Brett and I moved in. Luckily, the place was furnished because our vagabond asses had nothing. At the same time, we were a little concerned about the level of grossness the riffraff folks left behind. The place looked relatively clean, and my bedroom had a lanai (outdoor covered patio porch) that overlooked the entire center of Maui's north shore from Ho'okipa to Sandpiles. It was epic.

V-My view from my lanai of Maui's north shore. 35MM

We were in the Maui groove after living in our new spot for a few weeks. We surfed every day, worked some, watched the sunset every night from somewhere different, and repeat.

One day the four-pack, Chris, Gina, Brett and I, met up and drove over toward Lahaina to surf. Chris was all about Shark Pit, so we checked it, and it was amazing. Head high, thick, fast lefthanders breaking over coral reef. We had to go. On the other side of the channel that we used for paddling out, was another wave, a shorter ride, but a mirror image righthander. Gina was and will always and forever be a chiller. She totally rips longboarding but tapped out this day since it was bigger. She was just planning on hanging on the beach while we surfed.

The three of us paddled out using the deeper channel, near the one rusted metal rod sticking out of the water submerged in concrete below. We hung a left and paddled over to the lefthander that Chris and I wanted to surf, as we were both goofy and that's our frontside, sorry Brett! Shark Pit had its name for the tons of Blacktip Reef Sharks that lived in the area around all the coral. Reef sharks are smaller sharks, and the ones we had seen while in the water were only a few feet long, nothing to be too spooked over.

We surfed for three hours. An incredible session with only a few others, making the lineup easier to catch more waves. I took out my 7' single fin Andreini, my transitioning-to-shorter-boards board. That was around the time my shorter boards started to work for me. I always found riding shorter boards easier in bigger surf. It was much easier to downsize boards, as that's what shortboards are meant for (duh, Dave, bigger surf!). The power and speed of a wave really picked me up on a lighter, less buoyant board. When in smaller surf, there isn't that kind of power. After a while of catching these long lefts, Brett paddled over to the other side of the channel, over to the right-breaking wave. Chris and I were goofy-footed, and we prefer our frontside or taking waves to the left (surfers' perspective as they drop in, you have two choices, left or right), versus backside (our right), where the rider faces the beach with their back to the wave.

Goofy vs regular. Goofy stance on anything, a skateboard, snowboard, or surfboard means that your right foot is in the front and your left foot is in the back. This is my stance on a skateboard and a surfboard. Regular stance on any of those shred sticks, is left foot forward and right foot in the back. Somehow, this is my snowboarding stance. I must be ambidextrous in the skate/surf/snowboard world. I am regular-footed on a snowboard, but goofy-footed on a skateboard and surfboard. I don't quite understand why, but it's just how it is.

Surfing frontside on a wave gives a surfer a more intimate relationship with the wave. You're right there staring right at it. It's easier to see how the wave is behaving, where it's breaking, where the shoulder is, if you are going too fast or need to pump and speed up. These are easier to notice when facing the wave. Brett is regular footed, reversed from us goofy footers. He had been surfing our lefthander at Shark Pit backside this whole time just to hang with us, with his frontside wave just on the other side of the channel.

Now Brett was after the wave that would provide his better frontside rides. I paddled over with him. I wanted to try the right also as I had never surfed it before. Brett quickly caught a few, and I was more hesitant looking for a wave that I was more comfortable with. Not only do I prefer my frontside, but I am a bit more selective with my backside waves as I don't have the same gung-ho confidence. After being so choosy, I was positioned great for a bigger right, and I took it. I shot down the line, pumped some, took a turn, and a cut back. The wave ended and I jumped off my board. I collapsed into the water and kicked something that hurt the top of my foot, but I quickly lassoed my board, hopped back on, and paddled back to the lineup consisting only of Brett and me.

While I was sitting on my board waiting for more waves, I looked at my foot and it was cut badly, bleeding quite a bit of watered-down red. I continued to surf and eventually got out with Chris and Brett, meeting up with Gina on the beach, then heading back to their house. A few days went by, and I continued to do my normal things, surf, exercise, walk the beaches, whatever, but I noticed that the coral reef cut on my foot wasn't looking too good.

Every morning I woke up and checked the scabby cut, which seemed to have gotten larger and darker in color overnight. I also noticed separately that I seemed to have a strange cut inside one of my nostrils that kept growing and growing. I thought at first it was just like a hard dirt booger that kept returning, but over the course of five days, it consumed my nostril, and the scab started creeping out and showing on the outside of my nose.

"Oh, hell no!!" I said when I saw the scab on my nose in the mirror.

Between my foot and my nose, I ran to the emergency room. A local I worked with at the bar told me to go to the top of Kula, a town much higher on the volcano than Makawao where we lived. There was an empty, quiet emergency room there. I drove my old shitty VW van up there and saw an old surfer doctor in his sixties. He looked at my foot and my nose.

"Yep, you've got a staph infection on your foot and MRSA, the strong staph infection strain, in your nose." Said the doctor.

"AHHHHHHHHHHHHH!!!" I freaked in my head.

I heard a few rumors in my life that if you got a staph infection, it stayed with you for life, reappearing as wounds every so often. I asked the doctor about this in desperation, and he laughed at me.

"Where did you hear that? He asked smiling and continued to explain, "That's not true at all, nurses get these in their noses all the time from working in the hospital, and after a few of these shots and antibiotics you'll be fine in a week or two."

I was incredibly relieved. I thanked him very much and took off back down the hill. Thanks modern medicine, for curing my flesh-eating bacteria that would have left me looking like a zombie-mummy with no nose left on my face. Or worse, no face left on my head.

When Brett and I moved in, we made sure the place seemed like a good fit for a week, then I contacted Jean in Oakland about shipping Rodeo for me. She was ready. I already had all Rodeo's paperwork in order: the health pass, rabies test, Hawaiian Department of Agriculture paperwork, etc. I called the airline, and they told me if I was a passenger on the flight with Rodeo accompanying me, it would cost a few hundred dollars more to check Rodeo under the plane in a kennel. Since I was not a passenger, it became a freight cost, where the dimensions and weight have a particular price. This price was about $600. Although steep, it was my only option. I booked it.

A few days later, Jean took Rodeo to the Oakland International Airport at 4 a.m. and dropped her off in her kennel after feeding her a sedative I left from the vet. There was no direct flight from Oakland to Maui, so I had to fly on a little puddle jumper eight-seat plane to O'ahu from Kapalua Airport, a little tiny airport on the west side of Maui that is only meant for inter-island flights.

This was my first time on such a small plane as an adult, and it was such a fun experience to fly so much lower to the ground than larger commercial planes. We were only a thousand feet off the ground and over the ocean. We flew over the east side of Moloka'i, a smaller less populated Hawaiian Island, that had surreal views from the plane of massive cliffs, crystal clear blue water, massive waterfalls, and huge canyons as we flew by.

Thirty minutes later, I landed at O'ahu International Airport. I could quickly tell it was much busier of a place than Maui. I got off the little plane and went down the mobile staircase onto the tarmac, then headed to the State of Agriculture Office where Rodeo was being held. I walked in and saw her in her crate down the hall. When she saw me, she went nuts with excitement. The plastic travel box she was in bounced around off the ground. I filled out even more paperwork and, finally, I got her out.

I brought my skateboard so I could put Rodeo's empty travel crate on it, making it easier to carry by pushing it down the street while Rodeo was on a leash walking next to me. This was a great idea as it was about a mile between the office and the gate. I had a three-hour layover until we both caught the same flight back to Maui. The gate was a shipping container-size shoe box where the employees worked behind a desk, and the few other passengers and I waited outside.

Rodeo and I played in the grass for a while. It was our time to board the little plane. This was the first time she and I would fly together in the cabin! We boarded and took off. The flight wasn't full, there were only four other people on the flight, leaving the seat next to us open – more room for Rodeo. She was so scared she hid under my legs on the floor. But as a fifty-pound Australian Cattle Dog, it wasn't that easy for her to hide under me like she was a Chiwawa or something.

After we got up in the sky, I picked her up and put her in my lap, hugging her. I was in the window seat, and she turned her head and looked out the window. I watched my dog's mind explode. Her facial expressions went from confused, to processing, to understanding, to rejecting, to upset that she was in the sky and not on the ground where she belonged. She stared out that window, then dove her head into my armpit or neck in fear. It was adorable and she was a champ as always.

We flew lower into Kapalua, Maui, and I had the perfect vantage point to see the surf breaking on the coast about fifty seconds before we hit the tarmac. Waves caught my eye as we flew low that looked surfable with no one on them. I made a mental note approximately where I saw it in proximity to the airport. We walked off the plane, I unleashed Rodeo, and we ran to my rusty VW van parked in the parking lot. The Kapalua Airport is no international airport. It was more like a storefront, consisting of only two gates. As soon as I landed, I walked out the front door and was in the parking lot. So easy. I wish I could fly like that forever.

I had a board stashed in my van, and at sunset, Rodeo and I went hunting for the wave I saw from above on the plane. I was looking at the map on my phone trying to apply it to the view from the sky I had saved in my mind. From Kapalua, I drove the van straight to the ocean and took the little windy beach road around until I saw it. I'm not sure what the break was called or where I even was exactly. I was wave hunting. I parked the van near an apartment building's dumpster area, as "no parking" signs everywhere forced me to. I left Rodeo in the van with the windows cracked and paddled out having no idea about the spot.

I saw two other surfers. One a stand-up paddle boarder and one a longboarder, not surfing the main peak I was watching but a few other peaks farther down the beach. I figured I would try my luck at the main peak that was empty. I paddle out to it, got in position, waited a minute for a wave, and saw one coming. I turned around and started paddling to catch it. Out of nowhere, the suck-back from the wave, exposed its trough (every wave has a peak and a trough right before it) with a ton of black lava-rock reef that stuck up one foot out of the water. I was already paddling, had committed to the wave, and was about to pop up when I saw the reef in front of me. Since I was already committed, I popped up onto my board and rode the wave as high as I could, staying near the lip, away from the bottom of the wave. Once the peak's lip started to pitch as the wave was breaking, I jumped off my board over the back of the wave into safer water.

I was in a minefield with zero idea where the lava rock reef was hiding. I then realized why the other two guys were surfing farther away. Those waves were probably safer with deeper water. I tried paddling back into shore to get the hell out of that situation, but as I paddled in, I ended up basically becoming beached on the sharp black lava rock reef in the water. My board and fin were stuck sitting on top of the reef with me on it and waves kept crashing down. I got off my board, stood on the sharp, jagged lava rock, picked up my board and leaped backwards to where I came from in water a little deeper, allowing me to at least paddle. I remembered the route I took initially and followed that same path around to get back to shore safely. I dodged a bullet. I was relieved.

Sometimes surfing means putting myself into very stupid situations, which forces me to stay calm and think. I made it out with nothing more than a few scratches on my leg and a few scratches on the bottom of my board. A big win. I really could have been much more scathed. It was almost dark after a brilliant purple-red sunset sky. I walked back to the van, kissed Rodeo, and drove home up the volcano.

<<<<◇◇>◇>>◇>>>

A normal morning for me in my Makawao-volcano-mountain house was to wake up around sunrise and with a coffee on my lanai, watch the sunrise painted sky reminding me I was on a Pacific Island. Afterwards, I would eat eggs, oatmeal, and fruit, accompanied with the largest avocado of my life. We had an avocado tree in our backyard, but I wasn't even sure it was an avocado at first because of how large and morphed the fruits' shape was. I found out it was a special type of avocado that I had never seen in the continental United States, called a Bread Avocado. These suckers were the size and shape of gourds that I've seen at farms around Halloween or Thanksgiving. They must be five times the size of a regular Hass avo. They were as hard as a piece of wood when I picked them off the tree, and they needed to sit in a paper bag deep in a cupboard for two weeks before they finally softened. I developed a system with different avos on different shelves for different ripening times, so I always had some ready to eat. After breakfast, I would scoot my van down the volcano and start checking the surf.

One morning offered a strong winter swell on Maui's north shore, so Brett, Chris, Gina, and I decided to take a mission over to Honolua Bay. Honolua Bay is one of the most famous breaks on Maui. The pro tour makes a stop there every year, and it is one of the most insane waves when a good north swell comes through in winter.

The northwest coast of Maui is a beautiful place with huge vibrant green pine trees, rugged cliffs, and wild jungle. To get to Honolua Bay, I took the crazy windy Honoapiilani Highway. I pulled off onto the uneven, rocky, dirt road that took me to the top of the cliffs overlooking Honolua Bay. Everyone lined their cars on the cliffs up there, as it was a great spot to day camp and just hangout to watch the surfers below. Honolua Bay has something like four different peaks, and surfers can pick the wave depending on how crowded it is or what part of the wave they were after. It's a righthand point break, and when it's big, it all connects, leaving a super terrifying long ride if the pitching/barreling sections are beat down the line. Oftentimes, surfers can't make it the whole way fast enough before a section closed out, so there were spots to pick up the wave and take it after another surfer's ride ended. It was easy to see this from the cliffs above.

When it was time to surf, I left my van on top of the cliff and walked down a steep dirt trail with my board. This was the only way to the water, but there was no easy way to paddle out. Most surfers at some point fall on the hike down toward the water. It was that steep with crumbly loose gravel rock. It was inevitable. I've watched many people wipe out on the trail. The loose dirt/gravel just gives out below your feet. I fell once, close to the bottom of the trail and dinged my board on a rock, forcing me to walk back up the trail to the top of the cliff to switch my board for one without a ding in my van (good thing I had two boards with me).

Once I made it to the ocean the first time, I saw that there was no real straight forward way to paddle out. Most surf breaks in the world have an obvious beach, slab, or rocks, or jetty that I would enter the water on. Honolua Bay has a small beach tucked in on one side of the cliff, but at higher tides, it's completely gone. Also, from some experience, the beach was not a great place to paddle out from on bigger days, as it was next to impossible to get through the impact zone on a longer board.

Watching some locals gave me the secret paddle out maneuver. At sea level, they stood on a rock that stuck far into the ocean at the cliff point. They timed the waves perfectly, leaping off the rock into the ocean, and landed on their bellies on their boards into an immediate paddle on the backside of the wave. Now, my timing must be spot on if I didn't want to get washed up into the rocks. It wasn't that difficult, I just waited for a few waves to go by in the set and went for the next one. As the wave came up, it brought more water to the rock I planned on leaping off. When the water was high, I JUMPED! I paddled like hell because if I didn't, the rocks were at my back, and I could easily have been smashed. After about fifteen seconds of continuous paddling, I was good to go and continued to paddle out to a nice early section of the Honolua Bay wave.

VI- Smaller day. Honolua Bay, Maui. 35MM

Chris paddled all the way over to the north side around the corner of the cliffs. I could not see him from the main peak anymore, he disappeared. Brett and I were right out front of where we paddled out, about one third of the way through the wave if it all connected on a big day, which this day, it was.

We had a five-foot north swell with a stronger period (period or wave interval is a measurement in surf reports) Brett was on a Neck Beard, a model of an Al Merrick high performance shortboard. He was sitting on the inside barrel hunting. I'd watch him catch waves (on his frontside since Honolua Bay is a right and he's regular stance) and be high on the transition watching the lip. If it pitched over, he was ready to duck and get inside the barrel!

I, on the other hand, was on my 8' single fin Fineline (almost a longboard but not quite) and was sitting deeper catching the waves a little less developed for longer rides. After a fun session, I loosened up some and went after bigger waves and steeper sections. Even though I was surfing on my less desirable backside, I had some awesome rides. I flew down the line toward a more open part of the wave, made a wide slow turn, cut back, and continuing farther down the wave again, even on my longer mid-length board. I met up with

79

the walled up white water of the breaking wave and flew away from it again further down the wave. I made big turns or just sat high and tight and kept speed jamming down the wave that was taller than me by a lot and one of the thicker waves I had ever ridden. It was huge and scary, especially back then.

It was a blast until I got pinned under on a big set wave I chose to drop in on. I could see into the future, and I knew my ride was abruptly coming to an end, but I couldn't jump out the back of the wave into safety because it was much larger than me and already pitching to break. I jumped off my board in the barreling wave and entered the rodeo once again. I got spun in all directions for a while. I had no idea which way was up. The pressure of the wave's energy was still holding me down. I was trying to stay Zen about it, but my Zen underwater mantras were beginning to wear off. I recalled a conversation that Brett and I had earlier that week about how we always kept our eyes closed when under water in those situations and one time, he decided to open them. When he did, he realized he was near the ocean floor and used it as a launching pad to push himself up from. When this memory popped into my brain, my eyes immediately cracked open, and I found myself in the same situation Brett described. I was only a couple feet from the sand and rock bottom. I stopped struggling and allowed the energy that was pinning me down to push me lower to the floor. Within a second, I was standing on the ocean floor, crouched down, and sprung as hard as I could up towards the surface. It was enough force to pierce through. I popped up and gasped for air. I was in a set, so more of those waves were about to crash on me and start the rodeo over again.

I quickly jumped on my board and paddled into shallower water and avoided some of the initial impacts of these thick overhead waves, but the energy still pushed me toward the rocks and cliff face. I now saw that I was in new danger of the waves pushing me into a cave area that was within the rock face. For a few seconds, I had to ditch my board and push off the rock face at the entrance of the cave attempting to get away from it, like it was the side of a swimming pool as a child. I was worried that if I entered the cave, the ocean energy would keep me there and I could drown. I sprung off the side wall of the cave with my legs, and I swam away from the cliff as hard as I could, exhausted. I had to fight for way too long, and I felt like I was going to pass out.

The current was sweeping me south toward the cliffs, so I got back on my board and paddled and paddled and paddled. I was near the tucked-into-the-cliffs small beach, and if I just paddled a few more feet north, I would be able to access it after I cleared the large rock pile. I made it. I could barely breathe, and my arms felt like Jell-O. I sat on the sand for a minute to regain my composure. I skirted away from a potentially bad situation. Hell yea. I walked up the cliff trail and hung out with Gina on Chris' truck tailgate.

From the top of the cliff, the waves looked magical, but the danger was not translated in their beauty. Also, from the top of a cliff, waves generally looked smaller and more inviting. But really, it was a well-overhead break that once we got down to the sand, with a different perspective, we would form a different opinion.

"Oh shit, that's huge and terrifying!" Would be our new thought.

Honolua was another amazing day. Sometimes the challenge of escaping a dangerous situation was as much a positive, prideful, satisfying thing as a successful surf session, and it made for a stoked and peaceful rest of the day.

After living on Maui for a few months Brett and I decided we needed to know more about O'ahu. Both of us had never really been there, outside of the Honolulu airport, and we knew surfing on The North Shore was amazing, obviously. Plus, there was a city with 2.2 million people, things to do, and nightlife, all vastly different from Maui.

We hopped on our boards in Lahaina and started paddling to O'ahu. Psych (those are two different islands). We booked flights from Maui's main Kahului Airport and figured we would wing it on a place to stay. We brought our tents and sleeping bags just in case we could find a campground too. The day came and Chris lent me a shortboard travel bag that I put my thick, wide 5'4" Mini-Simmons board in. We landed on O'ahu, rented a car and hit the road for North Shore. During the hour drive we (super last minute) researched campgrounds, Airbnb's, hotels, and came up with nothing except out-of-our-budget expensive accommodations and a booked-up campground.

We thought about where we would sleep that night but decided to go surfing instead. We paddled out at an empty Laniakea (North Shore spot) for a couple hours and caught some fun waves on a bigger-for-us head high day. It was really the first time I tried to ride that Mini-Simmons board in sizable surf, and it was a silly, goofy, hilarious feeling ride. The board could catch everything. Most shortboards have much less volume, needing to be in the perfect spot of a wave, where the peak and lip are starting to pitch, but not the Mini-Simmons. It was so wide and thick, giving it a lot of volume. Because of its width and glassed-in twin fins, it was not very practical for fast turns or quick cutbacks, it was mostly just a chiller. Like a glider – soft turns and easy riding. Also, the board was shaped like a tombstone or a bar of soap. It doesn't have a sharp pointed nose, a pin tail, or a sleek single fin. It's nerdy. The bottom was literally squared off, and because it was so short, I felt like I was trying to surf a plastic, rectangular food tray from a fast-food joint or my high school lunchroom. This was cool for a bit but limiting. Either way I was just happy to have a board to ride in general, and alternative board shapes are always fun. It was too expensive and too much of a pain in the ass to take a longboard on a trip like this, so my Mini-Simmons was the only board I could fit in the bag that Chris lent me. We paddled back in and hung out on the beach.

After surfing, we went to an açai bowl shop, and as we were ordering, we asked the local counter girl, who was our age, if she knew of any free camping spots around. She said her and her friends had camped on a specific beach before without issues, so it got us thinking.

"We have nowhere to go, we have our camping stuff with us, and it's about to be sunset." I said to Brett.

"Let's renegade camp." Brett replied.

"What the hell is renegade camping?" I asked him.

"The kind that's not exactly legal." He alluded.

I was down for it. We had nowhere to go. We were both big-time tent campers with our own gear and were already on an empty little beach at sunset. We waited until after dark on a part of the beach that seemed less trafficked with big boulders and trees around for a little coverage that we set up our tents around.

After a while, we noticed there were other headlamp flashlights further out on this rock point from us. There were other people renegade camping, as well, about a football field away from us. This made us feel a little better that we were not the only ones breaking the law. At sunrise, we awoke and packed our tents away to hide the camping evidence in the car and surfed until a coffee shop opened. We repeated this move for the next two nights, also making sure we didn't leave a trace behind.

We surfed Chun's and a few other spots around Laniakea, as those breaks were a bit calmer compared to farther down the road near Waimea and Pipeline, which are NOT chill. Of course, we totally went down there to check them out, though. We stood on the beach looking out at Pipeline. At the time, it was barely breaking, tiny for there, but it was still amazing to watch. Standing somewhere legendary is always chilling. Where some of the most insane surfing in the world has happened. Legends made. Where others lost their lives doing what they loved. It was heavy, and we felt it.

VII-Walking down the Pipeline alley. Pūpūkea, Oahu. Digital

Brett and I both subscribe to having tattoos and enjoying the old, traditional, sailor-style tattoos. While we were on O'ahu, we had to at least attempt to get tattooed at the infamous Old Ironside, traditionally, Sailor Jerry's Tattoo shop. Sailor Jerry, for those who don't know, is one of the most famous and influential tattooers of all time. He tattooed from the late 1920s through the 1970s until he died, and he invented traditional designs of flowers, exotic animals, and military/naval imagery, all still used today.

We walked into the tiny tattoo shop in China town that was so small it barely allowed space for two workstations or the both of us in the lobby at the same time. There were two tattooers, and they were both available! We came up with ideas. Brett got an octopus originally drawn by Sailor Jerry on his arm, and I got a traditional buffalo head on my shin, the most painful tattoo I ever received. All on the bone. It felt like someone was electrifying my entire skeleton. I could feel the vibration throughout every bone in my body and I heard my skeleton vibrating between my ears in my head. The traditional tattoo required super fat lines via a 14-round needle with fourteen actual needles at the tip all jabbing me at once on the shin bone. Getting tattooed on bones always hurt worse than muscle. Especially bones that I have fractured over and over skateboarding and healed incorrectly (my shins).

"It sounds like you're being tattooed by a machine gun!" Brett yelled looking over from his massage table, laying on his stomach while getting his triceps tattooed.

"Sure feels like it!!" I yelled back.

The tattooer kept looking up at me and laughing.

"I'm so sorry, but you chose this spot, not me!" He kept repeating.

He wanted to put it on my ass, back, or stomach, and this spot seemed like the only realistic place for me, as I didn't have any room left anywhere else for something this size.

After three hours we were finished. It was absolute torture, but worth it in the end to have a keepsake from O'ahu and the legend, Sailor Jerry. I have been asked to count how many tattoos I have on my body, at the time of writing this, I have somewhere over 125. Counting isn't easy. And I don't care who you are, every single one I have ever received hurt like hell. There are different degrees of pain depending on the spot, but don't let anyone tell you otherwise! That shin was a special kind of pain though. After our tattoos on our last night on O'ahu, while still in Honolulu, Brett and I went out to a neat Tiki bar that had unique old antiquities everywhere, and Brett had a few Tiki cocktails while I had my soda waters. It was a good day and a great little trip with a great friend!

Sometimes surfing is hilarious. Other times, people are hilarious. At a break on the west side of Maui near Honolua Bay called Shitty's, it was both. Shitty's is a wonderfully accurate description of the break itself, and it was hysterical. The wave sucks. It's almost exclusively an overhead close-out. It shouldn't be, yet it was a real spot. And my friends love going there. Chris and Brett knew some other Lahaina guys, and they would all meet over at Shitty's for an afternoon of punishment. They would quickly paddle and pop up on shortboards into a perfectly horrible close-out wave. They would technically get barreled (this is when a surfer enters the open tube of water) over and over but never make it out knowingly as they entered. Every wave, wave after wave, for hours, they dropped in to big closing waves and took the punishment of a hard wipeout as the wave swallowed them. This doesn't exactly sound fun, which is why I never went out with them, but it took the right kind of jokers to have a blast in this type of surf. Now that I have shortboarded for a few years, I could be interested in giving it a go, especially with my buddies, but at the time I wasn't super keen on shortboarding taller, punchy surf. I had to outgrow that fear.

I made a friend while walking the north shore cliffs on Maui one day, a girl who lived on Lanai. Lanai is a very small Hawaiian island to the west of Maui with significantly less people. After talking with her for some days, I decided to go take a camping trip there and hopefully meet up with her. I had a few days off from working at the bar. I packed my rucksack with the normal change of clothes and toiletries travel bag, but also with a tent, sleeping bag, and dog food for Rodeo. I took my van down the volcano over to the Lahaina Harbor. There was a ferry that ran between Lahaina, Maui, and Manele Harbor on Lanai. It ran back and forth every few hours and was about $20 each way for about an hour-long trip. I parked my van in Lahaina in a place I thought I could leave it for a few days and walked over with Rodeo to the Marina. I bought my ticket and got on the big vessel.

The ferry had two decks for sitting, one inside on the first floor and one outside on the second floor. Rodeo seemed a little spooked. She wasn't used to walking with her sea legs, so I just sat inside at the window with her. The boat took off and we quickly were in the open ocean. I saw a bunch of dolphin fins come up close to the ferry on our ride. They were so close! I love being around wild nature! Modern society has taken us so far away from wild nature, from feeling alive. We only get a reminder once in a while if we seek it out.

Similar to when I picked up Rodeo from Honolulu and took the puddle jumper plane over the islands, I just got this spectacular view from a new angle of the islands that reminded me of their beauty. My appreciation for true wild nature accidentally dwindled from time to time, with the tunnel vision of my own life. We all need spark moments like this to wake us up!

I have a saying or mantra that I try to live by. I try to "keep my stoked tank full." I believe we all have a tank, or an inner receptacle meant for holding stoked, positive, childish, vibrant energy. By stoked I mean, smiling, energetic, silly, ecstatic, what I live for, can't-wait-for-the-next-day-to-come kind of behavior. Happy. Content. Being beside myself that I am living the life I want by being on that mountain peak, in that tropical surf, or in that different country. Where my passions lie. Fill your stoked tank where YOUR passions lie!

Smaller endeavors can fill my stoked tank too, like watching sunrise or sunset, drinking my favorite African coffee, being outside, playing music, exercising, etc. When my stoked reserves are depleted, at least with me, I'm lethargic, pessimistic, negative, more rude or more judgmental than normal, and grumpier, as if I have a dark cloud of frustration over me. In the past, when I reached this low level (it always snuck up on me), I ended up a flight risk. Once I realized it, I booked a ticket for the other side of the world, left, and told no one. As this wasn't the healthiest approach, now I am aware of my stoked level and feed it every day as if it's food, water, or an essential nutrient for my body and mind to operate on a positive, stable plane. It took some years to figure that one out too. But hey, we all live and learn. I have a tattoo that was inspired by my buddy Anthony's tattoo: *PMA*. It stands for *Positive Mental Attitude*, with an ocean wave as a "check the stoked tank level" reminder.

I saw the island of Maui behind me, Lanai in front of me, and Moloka'i to the north.

"Damn, I'm stoked right now, this is awesome!" I thought while on my little island-hopping adventure.

My new friend met us at the Lanai Harbor and drove us to the grocery store for camping provisions and then to this totally deserted beach that was on the east side of Lanai facing Maui and Moloka'i. We chatted, had a snack, and watched the sunset. She took off and let me and Rodeo camp. I remember laying on that empty beach staring at the stars for a few hours with my head sticking out of my tent. There was a lightning storm over the tall mountains on Maui that I watched in amazement for hours.

Every lightning bolt lit up the entire sky. It was like nothing I had ever seen before. The shoreline was just fifteen feet from my tent. Stoked tank beyond full, can't hold anymore stoke, can't compute the sheer beauty of this any longer, stoked tank overflowing and recharged! I WAS IN THE MIDDLE OF THE PACIFIC OCEAN! I passed out.

The next morning, I awoke and walked the beach for a while with Rodeo. There was a super-cool, abandoned, driftwood clubhouse that was built into the trees on the beach, made only with materials from what looked like had washed up on shore, like driftwood and trash. My friend came back with coffee and took us to the harbor where Rodeo and I took the ferry back to Maui. This time, while on the ferry, we saw a humpback whale. Are you kidding me!? Life is so cool.

After a month in the sublet near sandpiles and four months in Makawao, I started to think Maui wasn't the life for me anymore. I was all for adventure always, and I felt like I had built this little nest there that allowed me to relive this amazing day over-and-over again, sort of *Groundhog's Day* style. I watched the sunrise and sunset on a beach or from our volcano house. I would surf tropical beach breaks, go to the gym, and work some. It was the life. But that life never really changed, every day was identical to the last. After a while, I started to yearn for more social interaction or a different adventure altogether.

I planned my exit. I took off back to California with Rodeo and on to the next. To this day, I miss parking my rust bucket VW Vanagon in the dirt near the empty field in front of my house at night, on the volcano, getting out and just looking up. Sometimes I would lay on the roof of my van or lean up against it with my head awkwardly positioned up for way too long, stargazing. Most nights the milky way was so dense and vibrant with color that I couldn't take my eyes off it. I saw shooting stars every few seconds—as long as I looked up. I have not been to another place where the night sky was anything comparable. There was extra energy and power there, I could feel it, it was charged.

Good Research = More Scoring

In my years of surfing, I have taught more than a handful of people how to surf. One of the biggest mistakes I have seen in new surfers, whether old or young, isn't even in the water.

"I know how to surf already." Many beginner surfers have said to me during a surf lesson.

As if letting me know I don't need to start from the basics.

"Ok, before we go out, what's the surf report look like for today?" I would reply.

Their responses were always the same. They had bewildered looks on their faces like I had three heads, or they responded with something about how they don't understand all that science or numbers.

"Well, the surf forecasting app Magic Seaweed or Surfline rate it four stars today." Is another common one said by beginners.

My brain hurts when I hear these responses. I have tried many times to explain surf reports to people so that no one needs to rely on a surf app for its silly star rating. Hopefully, there is someone out there starting out that this can help!

To begin lightly, this is simple. Don't freak out because there are a couple of numbers involved. Surf reports and forecasts vastly depend on where in the world you are reading a report or forecast for. Different oceans, different continents, and different seasons, all have different features to them. There is no standard reference for good surf.

Now that's been said, let's get into it. Surf reports always have the same information broken down in the same way for you to interpret. All information on surf reports comes from data buoy readings. Data buoys are regular buoys (anchored floating markers in bodies of water), with sensors strapped to them, recording data and sending that data to companies who organize it for us to read. They record data like wind speed, ocean swell height, swell direction, and period. This information will then make it onto a surf report app or website, always written in the same way.

Here's an example: **4.5' @ 14s WNW 282°**. Let's break this down one at a time. **4.5'** is four and a half feet. This refers to the **ocean swell height**. Literally, the amount an ocean data buoy gets displaced from an ocean wave's trough to peak, a mile offshore in the ocean. It is NOT the surf height. The surf height, which is what you can ignore on the surf report once you can read reports on your own, is the app's interpretation of how large they think the height of the waves will be when you surf them. It's a guess at best, and it can be far from accurate. Tides, changing winds, and the relationship between the specific surf spot and swell direction are all factors that not all surf forecasting apps address. As they are normally regional guesses, every specific spot will be vastly different, so you're better off learning how to read the report yourself and applying your knowledge to reality. Waves can also be two times the size or more than a report's recorded swell height. Or vice versa, the swell height can be large, say 8' or more, and not have waves at your beach nearly as large. Learning how to read reports for yourself and gaining experience is very important to minimize your dependance on these vague rating systems for these reasons.

Now, the variable that will tell you how organized and powerful the waves will be (organization and power go hand in hand) is the next number in my **4.5' @ 14s WNW 282°** example, **14s**. The "s" after 14 stands for "seconds," and it's called the "wave interval" or "period," measured in seconds. This is a number that vastly depends on where you are in the world. A 10-second period in New Jersey is reasonably powerful, but a 10-second period in California or Hawai'i is pretty shit and might be completely flat. Like I said, different oceans, different sets of circumstances. Do research on your area.

As I said, the period indicator in the forecast tells you how powerful the surf will be. The more powerful the surf is, the more organized the energy inherently becomes. At Beacon's Beach in Encinitas, California, I have seen a 1.2' swell height— in reality— be well-overhead and powerful because of a 20-second period. It was a phenomenal day. Now, if the forecast was a 1.2' swell at 10 seconds, Beacon's would have been pancake flat. The period is extremely important, realistically more important than the swell's height.

Lastly, in my **4.5' @ 14s WNW 282°** surf report example, **WNW** means the swell is coming FROM the West-Northwest. This is telling you the general swell direction, and the **282°** is the degrees on a compass of exactly where that WNW swell is coming FROM, as "WNW" is vague. So, we have energy in the ocean that is moving toward a coastline, say California for instance, but that energy has a source of where it originated from. It could have come from many sources, a storm, a hurricane, Nor'easter, a typhoon, or an earthquake somewhere in the world. When the source of this energy lets energy loose, the energy moves in a particular direction or multiple directions. It is important to know where it is going because the direction will affect areas along the same coastline differently, depending on the exact angle the swell energy is moving in.

California is a good example of interesting coastline. It has so many nooks, crannies, coves, and unique coastline features that, depending on which direction-angle the swell comes from, will directly hit some areas, wrap around other areas, or completely miss areas that are deeply protected on the inside of coves or behind headlands.

Once you have decided that the combination of swell height, direction and period seem decent, good, or great, for a surf, you must look at the last two variables – wind direction and wind speed. Potential party crashers. These are very important because even if the swell height and period seem amazing, if the wind is pushing in a strong onshore direction, the conditions will still be garbage. For example, we'll say that the wind is 10KPH W 267°. This means that the wind speed is 10 knots per hour coming FROM the west at 267° (think compass) exactly. Knots per hour are similar to miles per hour. For every knot per hour, is 1.15 miles per hour, and for the sake of surfing, you can think of KPH and MPH as the same, for a general idea. The wind direction and swell direction are always described as where they are coming FROM. So, an east wind is FROM the east moving west, and a west swell is coming FROM the west moving east.

Now for the fun part. You have your swell height, period, swell direction, wind direction, and wind speed. Pull out a map, or mental map if you know surf breaks' land geography well and line up the swell direction's trajectory with your favorite surf breaks on the map. Check if it seems like your surf breaks are exposed to that exact swell direction's angle or not. If your break is going to receive that swell energy, because there is no land mass blocking it, then you must look at the map again for the wind direction to make sure your favorite surf break will not be blown to crap by a bad wind. If the wind speed is light, say under 15KPH, the surf should still have decent conditions. If the wind direction is not desirable and more than 15kph, the waves can get pretty textured or choppy conditions. Meaning, a choppy, shit-ass mess.

Wind directions are put into three main classifications. There is an **offshore wind**, which is generally the best wind direction. It blows from land out to the ocean, is great for grooming the surf nicely, and holding waves open longer before they break. This leaves more wave transition open for a surfer to ride longer.

Onshore wind occurs when the wind blows from ocean to land, which I mentioned earlier, is the worst wind direction for surfing as it makes the waves messy, choppy, ugly, and close-out or break sooner from the wind blowing the wave peeks down from behind.

Lastly, a **cross-shore** wind occurs when the wind blows horizontally from one side of the surf to the other in either direction. Whether the wind comes from one side or the other, it is not great for surfing, but often there will still be rideable waves in these conditions if the wind speed is not too strong.

I guess, technically, there is a fourth wind classification of no wind at all or calm. This is truly what every surfer desires. **No wind = true glass**. Glassy conditions are fully indescribable if you have never experienced them. While paddling, the water feels different between my fingers. It feels like it's a different medium entirely than the water I'm used to putting my hands through when paddling. It feels like it's not different enough from the air I'm in, maybe because of less friction and movement against my skin. It smells different, and the light reflects off it differently. It always makes me think I'm surfing on another planet, it's otherworldly. Epic. These conditions tend to only exist around sunrise or sunset – when we're lucky.

Wind is created by two different pressure systems colliding, and pressure systems are created by differences in solar radiation. This is why at midday, when the sun is its strongest, it tends to be the windiest time of day. When the sun is going away at sunset or when it was away all night at sunrise, winds tend to be calmer. But if a storm is sitting on top of you this does not apply, conditions will remain windy until the weather clears up.

The last part of this equation is the tide. Even if everything in the report is perfect with the wind, swell, size, and intensity, there are still many surf breaks in the world that are entirely dependent on a particular time within the tide for there to even be the potential for waves to exist at all. Other areas in the world are not as dependent on the tide. Again, you must do your research. Check what the tide swing is in your area. If there is a 15' difference from high tide to low tide, that spot will most likely be tide dependent. If there is a two-foot difference in water height between tides, then you can probably catch waves most times throughout the whole tidal cycle.

In Costa Rica for example, I surfed a break with an 8' tidal difference from low to high tide. Even if the break had overhead surf at high tide, at low tide, with 8' less water, there would be no wave at all. At low tide, there was an entire football field of a newly exposed sand beach that was underwater at high tide. Chances are, the wave you wanted to surf was in that football field of now newly exposed sand at low tide until the tide swings around and brings the water back.

Every beach in the world is positioned in its own way. Some face west, some face north, some face southeast, etc. You will have to put your new forecasting skills to work. Forecasting websites and apps are great for relaying the current conditions and letting you see the potential swells that might come a few days into the future. They also tend to be wrong, often, as weather changes and forecasting isn't always accurate. Reports tend to be regional as well. Two totally different surf breaks a few miles from each other with coasts facing different directions, one a beach break and one a point break, will sometimes still have the same exact forecast. How can this be? It can't. Go do your research for five minutes, figure out which break will more likely work better, and go score some waves. Wind forecasts are wrong a lot too. Wind is a fickle thing. A general rule of thumb is GO SURF EARLY. If there's good swell in the water, and it's not a horribly windy, stormy day, go surf at sunrise. It'll be sick.

What The Hell, I'll Try Los Angeles

This part is out of order. I technically lived in Los Angeles between living in San Francisco and Maui. Honestly, I was thinking of leaving LA out of the book. It wasn't my favorite or a radical destination, but in terms of recording my life, I did surf a lot there. Since I wrote this chronologically in my brain but left this out until now, I feel like it's cheating to sneak it back in after San Francisco when it was technically in the middle of San Francisco.

I initially moved to Los Angeles to escape the difficulties of living in the Bay Area. Most people that live in or around San Francisco might think the LA escape is like selling out or giving up, but everyone has thought about it at least once. Cheaper rents for bigger spaces, better weather, with similar opportunities. It's tempting for everyone, and eventually I jumped on the southbound train after living in the Bay for five years.

I had a couple friends that were renting a rad house in Santa Monica about ten blocks off the beach. Steve and Jon, both from Chicago. Steve the punk rock, motorcycle riding skateboarder, who was one of my closest friends for over a decade, and Jon a good friend I also met through the Chicago skateboarding scene. A travel nurse I didn't know, who lived there with them, was leaving for a four-month contract, and they needed to fill her room. I was there. I moved down fast. So fast that I didn't even quit my bartending/bar managing job in San Francisco. For the entire four months of living in Santa Monica, I commuted Friday-Monday back up to SF in my

94

old 1986 Toyota Van for three or four bartending shifts a week. Since I lived in LA, I was technically homeless in SF, so I would sleep in my van in Bolinas after working a shift. I would drive out of the Mission District in SF proper, over the golden gate bridge, and over Mt. Tamalpais to Bolinas, the surf town I didn't yet live in (remember this is now before I did that). I worked those shifts, made around $1000 in a long weekend, and drove back down to LA. Once I got back to my Santa Monica house, I slept, surfed, and chilled with my friends/roommates for the remaining couple of days left in the week. I did this for six months. For those that don't know, LA is almost exactly 400 miles from SF. So, roundtrip, plus driving to Bolinas 30 miles and back to the bar in SF every day at least three times a week, is almost exactly 1000 miles a week of driving. Just for work. Sometimes I'm a ridiculous person. Yes, I'm a Taurus.

Santa Monica has no surf. I mean, there might be the occasional swell from an unusual direction that gives fluke waves, but pretty much the closest surf is Venice Beach, which is now a gross tech capital, tourist town and ugly beach break. No thanks. Instead of south toward Venice, looking north is Topanga Point or further up to Malibu. Malibu is an iconic surf town with the historic First Point wave at Surfrider Beach. Unfortunately, now, it is the lamest surf spot ever due to the crowd. Everyone that lives there are entitled, and no one will continue the traditional surf etiquette and rules in the water that everywhere else in the world adheres to. Everyone drops in on everyone. Ten or twenty people all paddling for the same wave. It's really lame and unfortunate because it's a great righthand logging point break. I won't surf it.

If I go up into Malibu for waves I'm going north. Northern Malibu has fun, lesser known, under the radar, farther to get to, less crowded waves. I know there are a bunch of spots along the way near Point Dume and Zuma, but I never had a strong connection with those. I always went to the north end of Malibu. Malibu has something like twenty-one miles of Pacific Coast Highway between the Palisades and Ventura, and these spots are all the way at the Ventura end. I love Zero's. Zero's, in Nicholas Canyon, is a sick lefthand point break that I have surfed in solid conditions. It breaks over a rock reef with some boulders that make the point area very shallow, but the wave breaks left into deeper water. I've surfed it a handful of times with my buddy Anthony, who showed me the spot years ago, but it needs a south swell to work.

Next, heading north is Leo Carrillo. This spot is a ton of fun on a longboard. Leo Carrillo is a super chill right-hand longboard point break. This spot usually doesn't have a lot in terms of size, but the wave can be quite long. I sit pretty much on top of a huge boulder that sticks out of the ocean where the developing waves break off, and I catch the right peeling waves from there, riding into the shallower shore. I've had plenty of fun days out there logging!

Farther to the north is Staircase Beach. As in the name, it has many stairs to get down from the cliffs onto the beach. I have had a blast surfing there a couple times, but once I got pretty spooked. I was out on a bigger, messier day and had a hard time struggling on my longboard to get back in. It has sat on my shit list since, although before then I had fun sessions.

Lastly, County Line. County Line is awesome. It's on the border of Malibu and Ventura with nothing around except Neptune's Net, a sort of biker destination and casual seafood restaurant that I love. County Line is great because of its wave diversity. It has a righthand point break farther to the north and more beach break waves to the south with a few different peaks, so depending on how crowded the point is, you have options. While living in LA, I picked up my 9' 2" Gordon & Smith pig-style longboard, shaped in 1957, from a retro shaper in Ventura. It's the board that I almost knocked myself out with in Bolinas. I was so excited to surf it on the way home, I stopped at County Line for a session with my same surf buddy Anthony from Venice Beach.

I had to ride it leash-less, as it had no leash plug to mount a leash to, which was fine. I was used to riding longboards without a leash on a lot of different waves, so I figured it would be no issue, even though I had never ridden this board before. I paddled out with it. Anthony caught the first long left as we are both goofy and hunting for lefthanders. Immediately after Anthony's ride, I caught the next left and rode it surprisingly far. I was about to hop off the back of the wave but decided to mess around and buzz by Anthony on purpose as he was paddling back. I barely missed him. I rode super close to him for fun and ended up losing my balance and falling off the board. Since I had no leash, the board continued to ghost-ride the wave without me on it. In front of the wave was a sea wall, next to the beach made up of massive boulders.

"Please, please, no, don't hit the wall, don't, please!!!" I prayed.

SMASH!!!!! Right into it. I swam over to it, grabbed it, and looked at the damage. The entire nose of the board had exploded.

"Nooooooooooo!!!" I yelled.

I got out of the water as quickly as I could to stop the board from taking on water. My session was over on the first wave I'd ever surfed on it. I damaged a piece of surfing history. I was bummed out.

A few days later I called my brother Jesse. He worked as a furniture designer and builder. He was great with metalworking and woodworking. I had an idea.

"Hey Jesse, can you build me a triangular nose block for my surfboard that I just destroyed?" I asked.

"Yea, I can try, bring the board to my shop and we'll size it up." He said.

I brought the 32lbs heavy board to his shop, and in about an hour I watched him create out of thin air, a perfectly three-dimensional, triangular nose block that would fit onto a cut and sanded down area on where the old nose used to be. A perfect fit. Thanks again Jesse, you're awesome! We glued it overnight with clamps. The next day I sanded the glue down and glassed it with polyester resin. The new nose block even had the same rocker angle (bottom of the board's shape around the nose) as the rest of the front of the board's bottom. I couldn't believe how good it turned out. I had a board again! Without this successful surfboard surgery, I wouldn't have been able to give myself two black eyes a year later in Bolinas!

After four months of living with Steve and Jon in Santa Monica, we moved together to a rad mountain house high in a canyon of Highland Park, the most eastern neighborhood in LA before Pasadena.

After being so close to the ocean in Santa Monica I got spoiled and was frustrated with my two-hour commute each way from the east side to go surf. To avoid the traffic, I started leaving my house at midnight to get to the beach in a half-hour. I parked my van on the side of the PCH Highway, somewhere near County Line or Leo Carrillo, and passed out until sunrise when I surfed. I had to alter my life so drastically just to surf. I would then only have to deal with one traffic commute back home instead of both ways. I did this at least once a week, but it was still getting on my nerves. Never allow hurdles to be put in the way of your passion!

I called up Anthony in Venice Beach one day. I asked him if I could crash at his house for a few nights and have a mini three-night surf trip.

"Of course!! Let's do this!!" He said stoked.

We figured out when we both had four days off from work and planned it. The day came, and I drove out to Venice Beach across all of LA. Anthony and his girlfriend lived right off Abbot Kinney Boulevard, the main drag in Venice. We gave each other big hugs and loaded his boards into my van. We hit the road for the northern Malibu spots that I mentioned earlier, to spot check. We missed the glassy window, and the winds picked up more and more, completely ruining the surf. We checked about ten spots and almost called it quits. For some reason, Anthony, who was one of the most knowledgeable surfers in the area, decided we should check El Segundo. El Segundo is a less desirable heavy beach break that normally I wouldn't have any interest in surfing back then, but it was the only chance of surfing that day. We had nothing else to do as we planned to surf all day, so we drove for hours, through all of Malibu, hitting all the LA traffic. Two or three hours later we made it there and watched a surfable yet sloppy and choppy wave. We contemplated it.

"What the hell, let's go. It's the best we're gonna get today." Anthony convinced me.

We paddled out, Me on my 8'2" single fin Fineline and Anthony on a smaller 6' single fin egg. We caught a few waves. We were starting to dial in this lefthander that the beach break kept offering us, although it wasn't very good, long, or clean. The wave was maybe shoulder to head high but heavy and powerful. It was no Malibu First Point peeler. It was a hard-pitching, aggressive beach break. I paddled for a left I saw developing, popped up, and tried surfing down the line again like the last few I had. Only this time, the wave was larger, and the lip started throwing a bit earlier while I was still on it. It threw me forward off my board and into the water in front of the closing-out wave. When I hit the water, I wasn't too concerned since it seemed like a normal fall or wipeout, until the pain came out of nowhere.

The funny thing about hurting myself while surfing is that I never saw it coming. Whenever I kicked some coral reef, smashed into a boulder underwater, collided with my board, or got slammed into a shallow sand bar below, it always came as a surprise. This was a different feeling of pain than in the normal land world, outside of the water. On land, on a skateboard or falling down the stairs in my house or hitting my thumb with a hammer instead of the nail, I always saw it coming or subconsciously sensed some potential danger. In these situations, my body prepared a defense mode that sensed potential pain.

"Ok, tense up, this could suck for a minute." Your quick subconscious will say, preparing you for impact.

When I'm surfing and being tossed around underwater in the rodeo by strong wave energy, which is actually normal, I am not on high-alert mode. If anything, my body resorts to ragdoll-Zen mode, trying to conserve oxygen underwater, and I'm not struggling or the slightest bit tense. I try to enter a meditative calm state with my eyes closed. Then, when pain is introduced to the body, it's a complete surprise and shock. I always felt confused as to the degree of pain I was actually in. For the first five seconds I needed to decide, was this a broken leg or body impalement pain? Or was this a stubbed-my-toe kind of throbbing pain for a few seconds until it passed?

This day at El Segundo my body screamed "PAIN!!!!" from my leg. Without seeing, I knew I fell into the closing-out wave. When a wave throws its lip over to create the barrel, if I am not on my surfboard and my board is in that area, the wave can take the board with it around the barrel. I had just landed in the water in the area where the lip of the wave was going to smack the flat water. Only my board was a piece of debris coming at me like a weapon. It had the force of the barrel's strong energy and hit my leg like a karate chop, with the rail of the board right on the outer side of my left lower leg, a few inches above my outer ankle. This is where all your ligaments are on the surface of your leg, not protected by any muscle or anything. I immediately went into fight or flight mode, as it was an excruciating pain I was trying to process. Just like what happened when I got black eyes and possibly a concussion in Bolinas, my body told me to get out of the water as fast as possible in case I passed out.

I paddled frantically with lightning bolt pain shooting down my left leg. I paddled all the way until my fin hit the sand, and without thinking, I tried to stand up, but as soon as I put pressure on that leg, I collapsed with more incredible pain. I took my leash off my ankle and ditched my surfboard to hop until I fell onto the dry sand. I laid there rolling around because the pain was too intense to sit still. Anthony saw me and paddled in to see what was up. He grabbed my board that was floating in the shallow water.

"You alright dude?" He yelled over.

"Nope! I can't walk!" I screamed.

I really wanted to get to the van to sit down and take my wetsuit off to check my leg. Anthony became my crutch, and I wrapped my arm around him, leaning a lot of my weight on his shoulder and hopped to the car. He came back for my board after. I took my suit off. It was so painful to get my leg out of the snug tight wetsuit. There was a big ol' lump, but it didn't look like I broke my leg. I have broken many bones before, and it wasn't swelling up the same. I didn't know if that was good or bad, but considering the level of pain, I figured it couldn't be good either way.

Anthony drove us back to his house since my van was manual transmission, and I only had one working leg. We got back to his house, and I hobbled up the stairs to his front deck that overlooked his landscaping and the sidewalk. I plopped down on a patio chair. I looked up an urgent care nearby and managed to drive myself with one leg, shifting with the bad leg. It was only about ten blocks away. I hopped on my good leg from the van down the street to the urgent care front door. I'm an insane person, I know. After they took an x-ray, the result was I had a bone bruise – first one of my life. I assumed that it was less bad than a fracture, but the doctor told me that it can be more painful and take twice as long to heal. That was not good news. Especially since I used my legs to make money bartending. I stupidly took zero days off from work afterward, too. I wrapped the hell out of my leg with bandages, put on my biggest, tightest work boots, and limped around the bar for the next month until it slowly healed. Again, this is me being the Taurus that I am.

Glorious Baja

Baja, Mexico is one of the wildest places I have ever been to. I am obsessed with it, as anyone can literally do anything they want there. I mean it. There are no rules. There really are no people outside of a few small villages. There is no infrastructure and no care at all. And it's right in California's backyard. Only a few-hour drive away.

Anthony called me up one day when I was back in action after my bone bruise finally healed. It took about two months for that painfully long healing process to be over, but I was finally back. This part of my life is from when I lived in Los Angeles, before I moved back to Bolinas, then Maui.

"Hey dude, you want to go to Baja with me?" He asked.

"Duh! When!" I responded without a second thought in my brain.

"Well, whenever you can I don't have a car right now!" He responded.

The van was going to Baja! I took off about two weeks from the bars and was ready to go. I worked a weekend in San Francisco bartending, then drove down to Anthony's in Venice. I packed my van first with my boards and duffel bag. I picked him up in the afternoon. We spent a bit of time loading my van with six boards – three of his, and three of mine – cooking gear, camping gear, wetsuits, and photo equipment. I had a futon setup in my van that would fold out for a double-size bed, but we decided he would bring his camping gear and sleep in a tent outside for more space. We were all packed up, with five boards ratcheted to my loose, halfway broken roof rack and Anthony's shorty-twin-fin fish inside, and away we went. South.

We decided that we would sleep a night at his grandmother's house in northern San Diego County, then wake up around 4:00 a.m. to hit the border crossing when there was no traffic. It took us about two hours to drive from Venice to the Oceanside, San Diego hills, where we pulled into his grandmother's house in the late afternoon. He showed me in, took me on a tour of the house, and introduced me to his super cute little Italian grandmother. She had a huge turquoise stone necklace on and showed us her weed plants in her backyard.

We went out for dinner in town, went back to the house and passed out early to wake up at 3:30 a.m. to beat the border traffic. I don't exactly remember waking up for the drive, but my first memory of that early morning is crossing the border. This was my first time ever crossing a border by car, and I didn't know what to expect. I imagined there would be customs or border patrol or Mexican military checkpoints. There was nothing. I just continued driving on a highway and then I was driving in Mexico. It was so easy. It was hard to imagine there being traffic there, but apparently, it gets gnarly – hours of bumper-to-bumper traffic many lanes wide – so we totally made the right move by going that early.

Before I knew it, we were in Tijuana, the city that everyone in the USA my whole life said was "so sketchy and dangerous," but it seemed like any other city really. We jammed on the highway, passed Tijuana, passed Rosarito, another little city, and some more towns hugging the coast until we came to Ensenada. During the drive, the sun came up after we were driving in Mexico for a while, and I can picture driving on the edge of the huge cliffs overlooking the water at dawn, feeling an extra sense of awe.

"This is why I do this." I thought, proudly.

We pulled into Ensenada around 7 a.m. and decided it was a good place to get some breakfast and camping provisions. We walked into a grocery store and shopped around for a while, contemplating what types of food we wanted to prepare for days of camping on isolated beaches. We decided on eggs, quesadillas, chips and salsa, and beer (back when I still drank). Anthony found these Mexican cocktails in cans, like margaritas and palomas. We picked up a few six-packs of those too, with some ice for the cooler.

Anthony is a seasoned veteran surfing LA, San Diego, and Baja. His dad had been taking him down to Baja surfing since he was a kid living in San Diego. After going grocery shopping and eating at a little breakfast restaurant next to the grocery store, we got back in my van to continue driving south. Anthony was digging in the back and pulled out two Mexican cocktails and put one in my driver's cup holder.

"Cheers!!" He yelled with his canned cocktail in his hand.

He cracked his open and was looking for me to clank his can with mine.

I looked at him with lowered brows and confusion.

"I'm driving, what are you doing? I can't drink!" I said.

"Of course you can Dave, welcome to Mexico." He responded with a smirk. Apparently, after you get past Ensenada, there is not very much for forever in Baja, and it's super normal for everyone to have a beer in the car when you get to this point. It was true, there was no one on the road at all. We were in the middle of the desert.

"Alright, what the hell." I said.

I cracked my can open. After we drove for a couple of hours south of Ensenada, we made our turn off the highway west onto a little dirt road. We took this road all the way from the inland highway straight to the small cliff edge at the ocean. This dirt road was nothing more than a dirt track. I drove up dirt ramps, down dirt gullies, around eroded cliffsides that looked super sketchy as if they could fall into the ocean at any second, then drove north after T-boning the ocean. The movie *Mad Max* could have been filmed in Baja. There was so much dirt-desert and nothing else. It felt like I had time traveled to the post-apocalypse, where there were no people, only desert. We finally found where we were looking for, a little pack of a few houses and houseboats parked on land, on the cliffs, overlooking the Pacific. It was its own tiny village. We made it to Cuatro Casas.

Cuatro Casas in Spanish means four houses, which there were, and a few houseboats. That was it. It was the name of the surf break, cliffside hostel, and campground. It had a big in-ground graffitied pool for skateboarding that we could see the waves from. It was absolutely zero-frills, but if you planned to surf the amazing righthand point break out front, camp, make a fire, and score some coffee and breakfast in the morning, this was the place. Our first stop.

Anthony and I took turns carving the bowl with the skateboard I had in my van. We rode on my big soft-wheeled board meant for pool skating, trying to pump harder and getting higher on the pool's cement walls. We both pumped high enough that we grinded the concrete pool coping (top edge of the ramp) a few times each, back-side while carving. The skateboard's deck was an old stylish retro coffin shape mixed with a fish tail. It was my brother Jesse's and his friend's collaborative deck company called "Manooga" out of New Jersey. Manooga is an urban dictionary term. The meaning of the word is the action of when a man's balls get sweaty and stick to his leg. I shit you not. This is the name of their company.

There's one American man who owns Cuatro Casas. He's a salty, surly, grizzly, sailor-type of dude with an unknown age, forties, or fifties, with a plethora of legends of why he's there, both legal and not. I forget his name, nor should I say it for legend's sake, but I have spoken with him a handful of times from paying him the five bucks to camp on his cliffs, buying his firewood for my campfire on his cliffs, or begging him for coffee in the mornings. He's an avid boogie boarder and rode dawn patrol early-morning sessions shred-ding his boogie board. He's missing a finger, too, or half of one. Just adds to the mystery of his legend status.

We pulled up to the cliff edge and checked the surf. It was per-fect for longboard rides. Pretty thick shoulder-high sets rolling in on the reef. The cliffs we were standing on were probably one-hundred feet tall. I'm horrible at judging heights. Another way to gauge the cliff height, I'd say, is if I jumped off and hit the rocky shore below, I'd be dead for sure. No question. It was that high. Even though the waves looked super fun, we decided to drive further down the road to a few more spots first. I hadn't lived on Maui yet, but this was my buddy Chris's favorite saying and surf spot strategy.

"You don't leave waves for waves." Chris on Hawai'i, always said.

I have since started following this train of thought myself, but not back then. We took off and headed for shipwrecks.

The next surf spot we were headed to is called Shipwrecks be-cause there was a skeleton of a ship jetting out of the ocean, and the waves broke off the ship. I was so excited to see a shipwreck surf spot. We took the dirt roads south of Cuatro Casas right next to the cliffs and ocean. We stayed parallel with the ocean for a while, going through a myriad of different dirt road obstacles. From huge steep hills, down into washed-out, dried-up basins, to more eroding dirt cliffsides. The van was a champ, but also my 1986 Toyota Van was about thirty-one years old and only rear-wheel drive, so I was trying to baby her a bit.

After twenty-minutes, we were close to Shipwrecks. We were in a big open dirt field heading toward the ocean that was hidden behind a small berm of land. We were just on the outside of a fence, where inside was the tiny community of houses at Shipwrecks. We were so close but wanted a peek at the ocean before entering the Shipwrecks community, so we left the dirt road and tried driving thirty seconds to the ocean. Before I knew it, I hit a mud patch, tried coasting through it, but came to a stop.

I tried giving the van some gas and every time I hit the gas pedal, my rear wheels would spin and sink deeper into the mud. I tried this a few times with Anthony pushing, but I ended up sinking farther and farther and blowing mud all over Anthony from the wheels spraying. I got out of the van and looked at our current situation. We were screwed. The rear bumper was on the ground, that's how much we sank. My wheels had disappeared.

We opened the van's sliding door and popped open the cooler. Took out two beers. Cracked them open and started thinking. We got into our wetsuits and started digging with our hands. We were trying to uncover the rear wheels of the van. The mud was so thick that when we would dig with our hands, what we dug out would stay and not sink back. One of us was on each rear wheel on our stomachs, digging as if we were paddling on our surfboards. It was a hilarious sight, I'm sure.

"Didn't think this would be the way my first paddle would go down here." I joked with Anthony.

Never should have left waves for waves. We could have been scoring at Cuatros Casas right now. After a while, we uncovered both rear wheels from the mud. I had some wedge-shaped firewood in the van under my bed that we used to jam under the wheels and hammered into place with my skateboard, smashing the wood with the metal trucks of the skateboard. With Anthony pushing the van and me driving, we tried rocking the van little by little to get some natural momentum going until the van teetered. I gassed it and popped out of the mud patch. We were free! We took a few photos of the muddiest we'd ever been in our lives and hopped back in the van to Shipwrecks. I avoided the muddy quicksand pit of death, got us back to the dirt road, and took the turn into the tiny community around Shipwrecks.

VIII-Stuck in a mud pit near Shipwrecks. Baja, Mexico. 35MM

There was a hand full of homes or rental properties right there on the beach that all looked sort of vacant. The house farthest to the south was occupied, it looked like someone lived there, but the rest were empty and seemed abandoned. We parked and looked at the waves for a while. It was super clean, knee to waist-high, righthand peelers. The waves were peeling to the south of the shipwreck. There were lots of sea birds perched on the rusty metal frame of the ship, with lots of white bird crap that had dripped down the individual beams. The ship was nothing more than a rusted metal skeleton of what was once a ship.

We were already in our muddy wetsuits, we changed into them for the dirtiest part of digging out the van's wheels on our bellies. We just grabbed our boards off the roof and paddled out. Anthony and I took turns one after the other for a few rides. We were the only surfers out. We caught all righthanders the way the waves were peeling after breaking off the ship's hull.

After a little while, we started to smell something that was totally rank. It was making us want to hurl out there, but we couldn't figure out what it was. We caught a few more waves, and I eventually noticed something bobbing in the water that was kind of large near us and the ship. I paddled over to it. Floating there was a dead, bloated, rotting, festering, seal carcass that had one, very large, approximately two-foot wide, single, clean chomp bite mark taken out of its midsection. I yelled over to Anthony. He came to check it, too. It just seemed too spooky and stinky for us to stick around, so we paddled in and got out of there. Who knows how long that seal was floating there, bitten. It could have been only minutes before we paddled out, and even if it was long, the seal was chumming up the water we were in, and we were the only ones moving and causing a ruckus… A shark could have smelled the dead seal but seen and heard us surfing in our black wetsuits. It was too risky. We bailed. We got out and walked back over to my van with our boards, took our suits off, and dried off.

This was the first stop that Anthony decided to whip out his camping kitchen and cook some lunch for us. He was a solid cook and bartender back at his house in Venice Beach, but I was interested in seeing his skills on the small camping burner. He whipped up some egg and cheese quesadillas with this garlic salt that he was obsessed with, and they were phenomenal. He brought a Coleman brand fold-up camping picnic table that he cooked on, and we ate on, too. It was handy considering the amount of space it took up folded up (barely much at all) in my van.

After we finished our lunch and were packing up to spot check elsewhere, we were startled by gunshots.

"What the hell was that???" I screamed at Anthony.

"I don't know. But look!!" Anthony yelled and pointed. A man came bolting out of the only house that looked like someone was living in it with a gun blazing and did not hesitate.

"POW POW POW!!!" His gun went off one shot after another, repeatedly pulling the trigger...

He was shooting at another man who was somewhat in the water, and this man had a gun and shot back! It was a legitimate Mexican shoot-out!!! Our lunch setup was approximately 50 meters away from this shoot-out. We threw the entire picnic table, unfolded with our stuff on top, in the van, slammed the hatchback trunk as fast as we could, started the van, and floored it out of there. As we looked out the side of the van when we were speeding away, it looked like one man had pulled in the crab traps of the other man and got caught. Then he shot back once he was being shot at. We did not stick around for the outcome. There really were no rules in Baja. It was the wild, wild, west, with cowboys and all.

We took off out of there in a frenzy and headed south back on the main dirt road without even thinking which way we were going. We regained composure again after a while.

"DID THAT REALLY HAPPEN!!!???" I asked Anthony about 1000 times.

"Yea dude, what the hell that was nuts." He responded and sipped his beer.

We decided to check the next spot to the south to have more of a surf after the potentially cursed Shipwrecks. We were still hungry for waves. We drove another twenty minutes to the next spot south, called Punta Camalú.

The dirt roads or tracks always had crazy obstacles I would have to negotiate through, especially since the van was a rear two-wheel-drive rig. I got close to this abrupt downhill section that became flat and had a very steep uphill section after. I was not sure the van was going to be able to conquer it. Anthony and I jumped out of the van while it was in park to take a closer look on foot. It almost looked like it was a wash from a flash flood or something, but there was no real way around it. We both decided that I would have to haul some serious ass on the downhill to be able to get enough momentum for the uphill. Anthony got out of the van and filmed the attempt.

I reversed and gassed it hard. I came up on the downhill, bottomed out, compressing my stomach into my thighs from the speed hitting the flat, and hit the incline. I felt myself running out of speed and I tried giving some gas to the dying momentum. All this did was fishtail the van until I ran out of speed completely and started going backwards down the hill. I tried a second time, failing also…until the third and final attempt. I booked it as hard as I could with as much speed as the van could get, starting much farther away. I was trying to make the van fly, and it did leave the ground at the beginning flat to the downhill section. I gassed it on the bottom and uphill sections. I just barely crested the crux on top of the incline section and continued onto the flat. I had done it. Success! Anthony jumped back in the van, and we took off.

We pulled down this windy dirt road turn after driving for a long time next to these little farms. This place had an open restaurant in a building that looked like it was either half demolished or only half finished. Either way, once we parked on top of the cliff, we were stoked to see more waves. When I got out of the van and opened the hatchback trunk, I realized that my rusty muffler had been broken and dragging on the ground for some time. I ripped it off the rusty exhaust pipe it was still barely connected to with my bare hands. I walked it over to this wooden stump overlooking the ocean and placed it on top, as if it were an art piece. There's no recycling or trash pick-up in a place with no town whatsoever, and there was tons of rubbish around the restaurant, so the muffler fit in well.

We chilled out a while, walked down the steep dirt road to a boat ramp and the water that was meant for launching little fishing boats, and watched the waves. They were beautiful small righthand peelers but were even smaller than Shipwrecks, which means as we were heading south the swell was getting smaller—and Cuatro Casas was the largest— earlier in the day. It was getting closer to sunset, and we decided we were just going to shoot some photos, make dinner, and cliffside chill. We'd surf more the next day. Anthony set up his tent next to my van, we watched the sunset with dinner (more of Anthony's world-famous garlic salt quesadillas) and had beers. We met a couple camping next to us who were taking six months to travel all around Mexico and Central America via Volkswagen Van. We shared beers and tequila around a fire with them, and eventually passed out.

IX-Swell lines from the cliffs. Punta Camalu, Baja, Mexico. 35MM

We awoke the next morning and packed our camp in the van after coffee and another egg quesadilla breakfast. There was even smaller surf that morning than the night before, so we had no reason to stay. We said goodbye to our new camp friends and took off south.

Anthony had a handmade map of surf breaks that his dad and dad's surf buddies made by hand from back in the 1980s, and we were using it as a general guide. Obviously, the spots we were stopping at were not founded by his dad, they were spots that have been surfed for many years, but it was still amazing to follow his dad's surf map. It was like a treasure map!

We ended up driving for hours farther down the barren, open, paved road. The farther south we drove, the less cars there were on the road around us. It was literally just us. Baja is an empty desert.

We had to make a pee stop. Anthony and I went our separate ways by a few meters and pissed on some dirt, rock, and little cacti. He's a landscaper and saw some cacti he wanted for his house in LA. We went back to the van and emptied a twelve-pack of beer into the cooler, and using the empty cardboard box, Anthony went cactus foraging.

"If you kick a cactus over with your foot, you can grab the root and not get stabbed trying to pick it up." He taught me.

He had a few softball-sized cacti that he put in the empty twelve-pack and put the cardboard box underneath my futon in the van. We hopped back in and took off. Anthony, as the directions co-captain, said to turn off the paved road. We drove for a little while and entered a small community that seemed to be surrounding a tiny airplane runway. It was fenced off, but the road I was on was weird and janky, and after a minute we realized we were driving on the tarmac by complete accident.

"Shit!! Is this runway still operating?? Do you see any planes trying to land??? Let's get outta here!!" We screamed.

We suspected it was abandoned. We later found out that the few houses around were occupied with some expats from the USA. We finally found the beach. This beach had some sand but transitioned to river rocks before the water, meaning it was probably a river rock reef, which was why we were there. This wave was an Anthony pick, and I did not even get the name of this spot. We parked the van under the only tree around and got out to check the surf.

It was good, not great, but good, and big enough – maybe waist to chest high. We suited up and had a go at it. I took my log and Anthony took a mid-length. There were rights and lefts, which meant, of course, Anthony and I were hunting for the lefts. We surfed for a while, then got out for some lunch. We only bought provisions to make the same meal over and over, so we continued to eat garlic-salted quesadillas.

X-Van camp near abandoned air strip. Baja, Mexico. 35MM

We decided to stay there all day and set up camp. My van was parked in a bad spot for a campfire, so I moved it out of the way. When I started driving, I told Anthony to start filming. After I was moving and in second gear, I opened my door and with my foot on the open door, jumped out onto my windshield from the driver's seat. I then bear-crawled up the windshield and on top of the roof, onto the stack of tied down surfboards. I jumped on top of the stack of three boards that were ratchet strapped upside down and surfed my moving van. Some would say I surfed the ghost whip (driverless car). I wasn't going incredibly fast, but I was in second gear, rolling down the dirt road. I got down on my hands and knees on the roof and flung myself from a pull-up position back into my van and slowed it down and turned around. Success! Baja was made for everything. And Anthony didn't film it after all…uggggh.

That night, we cooked more of the same meal again and had some beers around a firepit about fifty feet off the water. We had a bunch of laughs with a husband and wife that lived in one of the local houses up the dirt street. They were retired USA expats. The guy surfed, and his wife collected and painted the river rocks off the beach every day. Her front yard was littered with hundreds of painted river rocks, hippie-style. They were neat, quirky people for sure, and we stumbled into their peaceful secret slice of life. The next day, we woke up on the beach again and packed up. We were headed for the Seven Sisters. Before we took off, the old man's wife gave us each one of her painted river rocks. Mine had a mandala-style flower on it. She was an awesome hippie lady!

The Seven Sisters are a series of seven righthand point breaks that are not too far north from the border of the Baja Del Sur province. We had planned to make it down this far to check the surf. We were about twelve hours south of the US border. After driving hours farther that morning, we finally arrived at our first sister. Anthony was the navigator, with his dad's thirty-year-old, hand-drawn map, and I was just the driver, taking directions. We were hoping that these southern spots were picking up some different swell because we had already been noting the swell was getting smaller and smaller the further south we headed.

As we pulled into this cove off the dirt road, we could see the ocean was pretty much flat. Maybe if we had a stand-up paddle board we could catch these tiny peelers in the shallow water, but it was just a tease, showing us the long peeling waves that could exist on a micro-scale. We were bummed, but we had a feeling this was going to be the case. We posted up for a while and made lunch. There were a handful of other cars there – Americans, Mexicans, and Europeans. We went for a swim and walked around the rocks. Anthony saw some big black urchins on the rocks and took a couple to eat. Apparently, you can crack an urchin open and eat the innards raw (which is Uni at sushi restaurants), but only if it's female. He cracked one open and slurped the insides out. I chose to let mine live free back in the water and tried a tiny bit of Anthony's.

We ate lunch and decided to check one more sister before heading back where there was more swell. We drove to the last dirt road from the beach and took it up. I mean, literally up. We went over a huge mountain and thought my van wasn't going to make it. I started sliding backwards at times and had my tires spin out a bunch. We finally ran into another guy in a Toyota Tacoma 4x4 who said we made it through the worst part. He was a surfer from Alaska and drove his truck all the way to Baja from there. So cool!

We got down the other side of the mountain onto flat ground again, and the dirt road started turning into sand – soft sand – as we came up close to the beach. We drove by a truck passing us in the other direction. I gave a wave and continued driving. I started getting worried that the van was going to sink in the sand. I looked around and the sand was softer on the sides of the tire tracks I was in from a previous vehicle. After another minute, my van's rear tires sunk into the sand, and we were stuck. Again. We could see the ocean from there and could see that it was flat. No waves. Great. I tried to gas it a few times, which only made it worse, sinking the tires deeper into the white sand, all the way to my bumper. Again. We got out and walked up the road a bit to see if anyone existed nearby, and there was not a soul or vehicle in sight. We figured we just saw that truck pass us a minute ago so there must be someone else coming soon. We tried digging the tires out, but the sand remained soft as deep as we dug. We didn't have any more firewood in the van either, which is what we used to put under the tires the last time we got stuck in the mud by Shipwrecks.

We split up and walked around scavenging for debris of any kind that we could put under the tires for traction. I stumbled upon two sheets of plywood that were probably four feet long by two feet wide. With nothing else around on a pristine beach, it was as if the plywood strips were dropped down from the universe, just for us. Perfect! We were so excited we each took one and dug it in under a rear tire immediately to try to get out of this situation. I started the van and gave it some gas. The van's rear tires shot the plywood strips out like a catapult, launching them! We tried again and again and again. With enough sand dug out under the tires, the plywood strips finally worked and got us moving again. We were getting good at this.

We were stoked to have the van rolling again, but we knew there were no waves here, and we were less excited about that. We parked at the base of this huge rocky, desert, cactus hill and walked to the water. After our close inspection and disappointment of flat conditions, we walked back to the van and saw that my left rear tire was completely flat to the bone with a visible nail in the tire.

"Shit!!!" I said.

"Did you bring a spare tire like I told you to?" Said Anthony.

 "Nope." I replied sheepishly. "I forgot."

I completely spaced out on buying a spare tire. It was my first time in Baja, but I knew it was a rule coming here that I needed to bring at least one spare. I saw Jeeps with two spare wheels strapped to their roof on the way down. Baja was no joke. There was also NO help there. It was late in the afternoon, we were on a deserted beach without waves, with a flat tire, and probably fifty miles away from cell service.

"Well, we've got water, beers, food, and camping supplies... Let's just camp here." Anthony thought out loud.

I agreed with him that it was really our only option, and maybe we could flag someone down driving by that night or the next morning for help. We set up our camping picnic table, popped beers, and prepared dinner. We also walked around and shot a bunch of photos. That night, we stared up at the stars in complete awe. There was so much nothing around us that the night sky was full of intense white dots everywhere, Milky Way and all.

The next morning, we awoke still in the same situation that maybe we forgot we were in for a few hours while asleep. Reality set back in. We figured anytime now a car would drive by. Our plan was to wait. We hiked around the mountain and went to the beach. We ate and drank more beer. No one came. All day. Not one car. Not a single one. Not a soul.

It became night again, and we started getting worried as we only had one more gallon of water in the van and we were in the desert.

"In the morning, no matter what, we're driving away if no one comes. We gotta go," I said.

Anthony was on the same wavelength. Another night passed of us looking at the stars and burning random desert debris in a makeshift firepit we made. The next morning came, and we cooked up some eggs with tortillas and had coffee. Still, no one had driven passed us.

XI-We just wanted waves! Broken down at a Seven Sisters surf break. Baja, Mexico. 35MM

XII-Broken down for three days. Baja Mexico. 35MM

We decided to pack up the van with all our gear and hit the road on a flat-as-a-pancake tire. Our tire was so flat we were riding the rim one hundred percent of the time. At first, we were on soft sand so that wouldn't hurt the rim or the flat tire too bad. We backtracked the way we came. We had to go over the big, sketchy desert mountain, which we surprisingly made it over, driving at a snail's pace. Then we had to pass the original Seven Sister where we stopped and ate urchin two days earlier. Surprisingly, we made that too.

After driving on a dirt road for a few hours, without a direction or destination, Anthony got a single bar of service on one of our phones to load a map. We found the closest town on the map that was still twenty-five miles away. Maybe this wasn't the closest town in reality, but it was the closest town that existed on the map. We went for it.

We drove those twenty-five miles on dirt roads going about ten miles per hour. It felt like forever. It took about four hours of driving on that rim to get to this little, dusty town. They had a one-pump gas station, one convenient store, and one dingy restaurant. Think, tumbleweeds and as remote of a desert as it gets. The gas station/convenience store had no repair shop garage or anything, so we asked the convenience store clerk in our crappy Spanish if there was anyone in town who could fix a tire. Between Anthony's and my Spanish, we collectively could speak about as well as an eight-year-old. We weren't helping our cause very much, but the point got across.

The next thing we knew, the convenience store woman was pointing at a building across the street to a few houses down the road and said a man's name. We drove to where she pointed, and the man came out.

"I can fix, no problem, no money necessary." He said in broken English.

We were astounded. In the USA, if someone knew we needed a tire repair, they would have exploited our situation and charged an arm and a leg. This dude just didn't care. After he patched our existing tire's hole, I gave him five bucks. We went back to the convenience store for a snack before hitting the road with a sweet, repaired tire! I drove well over twenty-five miles on that flat tire, and it didn't destroy the rim. I couldn't believe it!

We popped out of the convenience store right in front of a tall man in a very expensive looking black suit, visually loud snake-skin cowboy boots, and an enormous, black bucket-style cowboy hat. He got out of a brand new, black Escalade with all dark tinted windows.

I was never more afraid in my life. I was toe-to-toe with a Mexican Cartel member, and we locked eyes. His eyes were crystal blue and sharp, I can still picture them on his desert tanned, distinguished face. His presence there screamed "red flag, this is odd and out of the ordinary!" We were in an extremely poor, dust bowl-like village, and he and his Escalade stood out like a sore thumb. Once I realized what I was looking at, I threw my eye's gaze to the floor and tried to become as small as humanly possible. That was not easy— I'm fully covered in tattoos, and I know I have somewhat of a loud look— even in the United States. I ran back to the van and managed to get out of there and on the road with Anthony without issue. If we made one stupid mistake, we could have been buried out in that desert.

At this point, we had driven about as far south as we planned, and there was no swell at all. We figured if we headed back up toward Cuatro Casas, we would pick up some swell again and actually surf on this surf trip. As we left the little village, we saw an amazing righthand point break set up that was also flat. It showed us its potential again with a tiny long right peeler. Teasing us. We got back to the paved highway and headed north for hours. The only stops we made were desert pull-offs for pee stops. We ate in the car and managed to get back to Cuatro Casas for a sunset surf session and finally scored some good size waves. NEVER LEAVE WAVES FOR WAVES! ESPECIALLY GOOD WAVES! Although, we had a hell of a trip because we did leave those waves. We camped on the cliff at Cuatro Casas that night with some Anthony-cooked dinner and beers. We paid the owner of Cuatro Casas, the surly, salty sailor, five bucks to take a shitty old rusted-out wheelbarrow full of firewood to burn at our camp ten feet from the cliff's edge. I brought the wheelbarrow back to the backside of his hotel and skateboarding bowl. He had a serious compound set up. We made a sweet campfire, stared at the stars, and planned to surf early in the morning before we drove back up to California. We were accompanied by the two huge Doberman Pinchers that the surly sailor owned. They popped into our camp out of thin air, using the darkness to sneak around. They scared the crap out of us but all they wanted was some head pats.

Il-Cuatro Casas. Baja Mexico. Digital.

We woke up the next morning early and torched some water for coffee. We planned for a surf, but it was cold, and our wetsuits were still wet from yesterday's sunset session. Sometimes obtaining the motivation for surfing when I'm groggy, tired, stiff, cold and sore is very difficult. It's totally mind over matter! Honestly, I've never once been upset that I paddled out in my entire life, EVER. Beforehand, I always debate it. Is it worth it? To put on my (sometimes still cold and wet) wetsuit or pay for parking or whatever the excuse. **IT IS ALWAYS WORTH IT**. Even if I don't catch waves, which is rare, I am in the Mother Ocean or under the sun, having a time.

People wish they could be there instead of their boring or hectic lives in an office job or whatever. But I am there. The moment I get on my board in the water and start paddling, I'm stoked. Then I start catching waves and I'm no longer tired or groggy. I freak out with excitement. I am free.

(Secret) Rhode Island

Rhode Island, The Ocean State, has the best surf in the continental USA. That's one hell of a statement. Every break in the world has its day when the universe or surf Gods shine their spotlight down and give it all-time phenomenal conditions. Places like Hawai'i and California are so famous for surfing because of how consistently decent or great their breaks are. But the east coast has its gems too, more under the radar, as opposed to the super famous breaks, due to its seasonality and cold winters. After surfing California, Hawai'i, and other phenomenal surf destinations for over a decade, I have a good idea of what epic surf is, and Rhode Island is freaking unbelievable. Rhode Island is the smallest state in the USA but has over 400 miles of coastline, and every inch of the state is thirty minutes or closer to the coast. Pretty wild stuff.

Its problem is that it sits on the Atlantic Ocean. Swell is super inconsistent in terms of the entire year, but there is one season that makes the whole east coast of the USA light up. Hurricane season. Hurricane season window in the Atlantic Ocean exists from June through October, but realistically more swells occur from the end of August or the first week of September through October. This is always the peak of the season. Last year in 2021, we had a record number of hurricanes and tropical storms in the Atlantic during those months. The great part is the storms don't need to hit the coast, or Rhode Island specifically, in order to give it swell. As long as a storm exists in the Atlantic, remotely near the continent, it will kick off energy to all the coasts. Outer Banks, North Carolina; Jersey beach breaks; Montauk, NY, and Rhode Island to name a few. They will all light up like fireworks with amazing warm water (mid-70s Fahrenheit) waves!

If you look at a map, you'll notice that Southern Rhode Island has four fingers that jet out as peninsulas facing south. The sides of the peninsulas run vertically, facing east and west. The first is still connected to mainland western Rhode Island but has a smaller peninsula sticking out called Point Judith. This is the first finger, the next three are the islands, and then the peninsula that connects with Massachusetts to the northeast. With swell coming from the south, the coastlines of these peninsulas are amazingly ideal for producing long beautiful waves. Also, a ton of the shallow waters surrounding Rhode Island have some sort of reef on the ocean floor. Rocks, boulders, kelp beds, and even a type of coral exist there. All these reefs provide breathtakingly consistent point breaks all around Rhode Island.

The way hurricane storm systems work in the Atlantic Ocean, not that I'm a meteorologist (all surfers kind of pick up a meteorological knack after a while), is by starting on land over western Africa between the dry and lush part of the continent. This area is notorious for producing thunderstorms. These thunderstorms then get pushed west out to sea by Africa's prevailing east winds. The warm, moist air in the Atlantic Ocean near the equator beefs these storms up into tropical storms and hurricanes, like putting fuel on a fire. Those prevailing east winds push the storms all the way over through the Atlantic, growing the entire time, until they get close to the east coast of the USA. Over the USA, we have prevailing west winds, called the jet stream, from west to east. The competing winds from our jet stream moving east and Africa's wind moving west often push these storms north until the jet stream winds eventually win and the storms are pushed back into the Atlantic again. The storm gets pushed much farther north, and the jet stream throws the storm system toward Europe at a higher latitude. Sometimes, the jet stream does not overpower the African wind, and the storm will move over the land on the east coast and eventually peter out, as it has no more ocean moisture feeding it. During these storms, there is almost always swell energy being pushed north along the eastern coast of the USA, and Rhode Island is sitting patiently, waiting to accept it with open arms!

◇>>>>>>>◇>>>>◇>>>>><◇>

I attempted to move back to Los Angeles from Maui, which I
didn't really want to do. I was at the Kahului International Airport on
Maui, after being dropped off by my buddy Chris in his big Ford diesel dually pick-up truck, in order to get my ten-foot coffin-shaped
surf-travel bag to the airport. After he dropped me off at the sidewalk, I unloaded, hugged Chris, thanking him, and headed in to
check my bags. At the counter, they told me Hawaiian Airlines
couldn't accept a bag over fifty pounds. The bag weighed ninety-
nine and a half pounds because it had to be under a hundred pounds
from Oakland to Maui when I moved there. For that trip, they took
the bag no problem for $200. Now on the same airline, they were
refusing to take the same exact bag. Same size, same weight. I asked
what options I had. They told me to try walking it over to their cargo
area and pay cargo to ship it back for me.

I walked in the direction they told me to go, which turned out to
be about a half-mile away. I had to drag my ten-foot board bag that
weighed ninety-nine and a half pounds the whole way with wheels
that didn't spin. I also had a fifty-pound rucksack on my back, long
pants, a light jacket, and boots since I was flying into LA at night in
the winter when the temperatures were colder. By the time I got to
the cargo office, I was completely drenched in sweat, Hawai'i was
hot! The Hawaiian woman behind the cargo office counter looked at
me like I was crazy.

"The check-in counter told me to come over here to get my
board bag back to LA." I said with sweat dripping off my nose.

"Do you have a commercial account with us?" The Hawaiian lady responded.

"Nope." I said, sensing some bad news.

"We can only ship items for account holders." She responded.

"So why did your company's people tell me to come all the way
over here then?" I asked, still trying to be polite, but it was starting to
fade.

They saw my frustration and decided to help me.

"We can't take your bag, but if you want, we can offer you plastic wrap and cardboard to create two separate bags to check if you
want to split up your boards and things?" She said, trying to help.

I was surprised that they were willing to help me like this.

"This situation is crazy, but you ladies rule!" I said. "Let's do it."

We took my four boards out of my coffin bag and split them up, two and two, with some clothes and soft things as protection in each. After zipping my board bag back up at forty-nine pounds, we put cardboard and clothes all around my other two boards. Then, we wrapped industrial plastic wrap around it a hundred times, making a cocoon, and it was secure!

"You want a ride back to the terminal check-in area? I can drive you." The now amazing Hawaiian woman said.

"No way, are you serious!? Yes please!?" I said gratefully.

She pulled around her personal monster truck, no kidding. It was a very lifted truck that I could barely get in, but she helped me load my now two board "bags" into her truck bed and drove me the half-mile back. She helped me unload my bags out of her truck, and she gave me a big hug.

"Good luck!" The nicest Hawaiian woman in the world said, waving as I walked back into the airport to start the process over again.

I couldn't believe it! Karma was on my side that day. Until I walked back into the airport. After they accepted my newly separated bags under their new weight limit restriction, I had to take them to an area to be checked by a TSA agent. I'm not kidding, this guy actually took a knife and cut open the cocoon we just spent so much energy making. After my lack of drugs and illegal substances inside, only surfboards and clothes, the bag passed his inspection.

"Have a nice day." Said the TSA agent and he walked away.

I felt violated. I had a huge mess on the ground and had to try to put it back together after he destroyed it. I put everything back into a pile and put the cardboard over it and tried re-wrapping the pile with the cut plastic wrap. It didn't really work, but the plastic did sort of stick to itself. I kind of just plopped the mess on the conveyor belt.

"Screw it. I don't even care if I see this again." I said to myself. I was broken. It's *messed up* how *messed up* that whole system is (that sure makes a lot of sense, Dave). I mean, to me, that's wrong. They can send me through the sniffer to see if I have any drugs or bombs and have x-ray machines for my carry-ons but need to open manually or destroy my bag that's going to be checked? That makes no sense! The whole system is idiotic, including all the personnel working there. Mouth-breathers. Ok I'm done, I'm Zen again. Tangent over.

I also had to check Rodeo, in her kennel, but I did this first before my board bag debacle. This is the reason why I get to airports four hours in advance. I'm always traveling somewhere ridiculous and half the time the ticketing check-in attendants just put their hands in the air when I walk up with my strange requests. I would have missed my flight if I didn't go super early!

I ended up making it to LA that night and met my brother Jesse who picked me up with his tiny Toyota pick-up. I got Rodeo first and let her out of the kennel. I always put the kennel on my skateboard, like Hawaii, and had Rodeo on a leash out of it. It's much easier to push a kennel on wheels. I put my bags in Jesse's truck and had to keep running back for more bags to the baggage claim special bag area. Everything I checked was special. My makeshift board bag was a total disaster. It was a pile of garbage on the floor with my clothes and blanket scattered around next to my boards and the plastic wrap, but my boards were amazingly still intact without any damage! I took a handful of clothes and one board at a time to Jesse's truck at the curb until I got it all, including the ten-foot board bag. We had to ratchet strap it all down as it was overflowing the bed of his little, old truck. He turned his hazards off, and we took off. I was officially done with that. I was over it. Welcome back to the mainland.

I hung out for a few days in LA when my Dad asked me if I wanted some seasonal work in the summer at the beach in New Jersey, helping them run their bed and breakfast. He had asked me before, and I denied it as I was busy living my Californian or Hawaiian life, but this time, they caught me in transit. It was only seasonal work, so I accepted. I was now east coast bound for the summer months.

My buddy Anthony, who I went on the Baja trip with, moved to New York City with his girlfriend, so I reached out to him since I would be close by.

"I surf the Jersey beaches all the time. Let's hang out! But Rhode Island is what's up!" He responded over text.

"What's in Rhode Island?" I asked, super curious.

"The best surf in America." He responded and added "Don't tell anyone."

I kept it to myself for about three years until I wrote a book about it. Sorry buddy.

I took some savings that I didn't spend on Maui and bought myself a 2005 Honda Element with 180,000 miles for $3700 outside of LA. I wished it was a van, but it did the job. My last Californian van from the 80's died in the beginning of a trip from L.A. to Alaska. It got stuck in second gear and parts to fix it didn't exist any longer. I sold it to Rick in San Francisco, for $200. He sold it to another buddy for a back Tattoo. Barter style.

I loaded my stack of surfboards on my Element's roof rack, took out the back seats, and built a bed platform in the back. I was ready to drive cross country. As I was leaving, a girl named Bethany I met in LA, asked if she could tag along, split gas, and drive across the country with me.

She was from Jersey, had family there she wanted to see, and would fly back to LA after. I was into the idea because driving across the country alone sucks. I've done it countless times, and it's always a bummer. She worked at a cafe in LA and was let go from her job because of the pandemic shutdowns, so she was free.

We made a quick plan and hit the road.

Our first stop was a campground I always wanted to go to in New Mexico called the Cosmic Campground. The Cosmic Campground is protected by a Dark Sky Sanctuary, which means there are laws set in place restricting commercial light pollution at night. That means it's an area with great star gazing, and the locals want to protect it. There are sixty of these dark sky sanctuaries in the USA, and something like 195 all over the world.

We drove for a few hours north off the I-10 freeway to the middle of nowhere in the western-central region of New Mexico. All dark sky sanctuaries are in the middle of nowhere. They inherently must exist far from a city, even a small city, for great night sky viewing. It's something like fifty miles or more in all directions from a significant city's light source. I had never been to one before and was hoping to see the Milky Way Galaxy, like I did when I lived on Maui, near the Haleakala Volcano.

After hours of driving on country highways, we made it. It was a beautiful area without cell phone reception (all the best places are). We passed high-elevation forests, outcroppings, huge boulders, and ended up on dirt roads in a high desert. We drove up to the campground gates, and it was closed due to the pandemic. What a bummer. But I looked around and realized that we were in Gila National Forest. National Forests are free to camp in, so we decided to camp off one of the dirt roads adjacent to the campground. Fifty meters outside of the fence. Perfect! Score! A pandemic won't keep me from campin'!

We set up camp and made a fire before it got dark. We ate some cans of vegetarian chili, and I had a few protein bars. I played guitar while Bethany, Rodeo, and I just looked up. We were a little disappointed because the stars weren't coming out very strong this night. It was somewhat cloudy, and we could see the stars but not intensely or any remnants of the Milky Way that would deem this place extraordinarily special. We had fun, anyway, laughing around the fire and playing music and cooking. Bethany didn't drink or partake in any drug use either, like me. At this point, it had been around a year and a half or two years since I drank or did any drugs, which is relevant to bring up for what we saw next.

As we were still hanging around the fire at about 21:00— 9 p.m.— we heard something in the sky near us. We looked up above us.

"What the hell is that? It's not a normal plane, we're not in a jet path, and we haven't seen or heard any other low-flying planes? What the hell is that? It's coming straight toward us!?" We said, trying to reason.

The next thing I knew, I was looking at a plane or craft of some sort directly above us in the sky. It was about as high up as a commercial passenger plane that flies over a highway right before it touches down on the runway in the airport. Like in the movie *Wayne's World* where they would hang out on top of their car, "The Mirth-Mobile," just outside the airport limits and let the planes buzz by them overhead. It was that close! We couldn't really make out its shape, which was odd, considering how close it was to us and how slow it was moving. It seemed triangular, because it had three lights blinking white, one on each corner. The center was transparent, and I felt like I was looking through it to the stars in the sky above.

We were losing it!!! We kicked over our soda water cans and ran into my Honda Element and shut the door. We didn't know what this thing was, and we weren't screaming "aliens!!!" but we knew it was abnormal. It kept on its trajectory after it passed over us and continued in the night sky until it was out of sight. It had a noise, too, like a rocket engine combusting the whole time. We stayed in my Element's camper bed another fifteen minutes until we noticed something from a completely different quadrant in the sky. About ninety degrees from the flight path of the first UFO, we saw a second unidentifiable flying object coming toward us from the horizon. Or it could have been the same one as there was only one in the sky at a time.

This one was seemingly similar in shape but much further away. Without our eyes blinking, we watched it through the side-back window in my Honda Element moving in our general direction. We witnessed how I can only describe as the craft shooting out a pair of orange flames or flares of some sort that projected forward out of the craft. They were a very bright orange/red color and were kind of like two parallel fireballs with tails. They would linger for a second, then fade away into black and be gone, with only the craft left. It did this over and over and over and over every ten seconds until it flew by us to the side, disappearing into the sky again. We were totally, completely beside ourselves. I love conspiracy theories and shows about aliens and the like, but I found myself in that moment, just like my shark sighting in San Francisco. I was trying my damnedest to figure out what it was we were looking at, trying to classify it into something easily explainable. But we couldn't. We just had wide open jaws and amazement. Maybe military? Who knows. It was a wild experience. We saw a third and last craft another seventeen minutes later. We were timing them, but this one didn't have the orange flare things. We stayed up a while after that waiting for more, but whatever it was vanished and left us back to our Cosmic Campground stargazing.

The next morning, I perked up the campfire and made us some cowboy coffee. We packed our camp and took off to the beach in New Jersey. The Cosmic Campground. What are the chances that we saw a UFO at THE COSMIC CAMPGROUND!!! Are you Kidding me!!?? Stoked!!!!!

III-Cosmic Campground, New Mexico. 35MM

We continued to drive across the entire locked down country for the next three days illegally. Every new state we entered on the highway had big, digital construction signs saying: "Not Welcome." Or "Go Home." We stopped for gas at one gas station in a crappy part of Oklahoma City where the gas price was $0.99 per gallon. I filled up my sixteen-gallon Honda Element tank for $16 and continued on our way.

We made it to Jersey without any problems, and I started working at my family's bed and breakfast doing general maintenance when the hotel was closed during the early pandemic in March/April 2020. I immediately started surfing the Jersey beach breaks. Except my 4/3 wetsuit (4mm thick at the core and 3mm thick at the limbs)

was only meant for California winter water temperatures that only get to the low 50s, and in late March the water temperature in Jersey was in the mid-40s. This was the coldest water I had ever surfed in, and this wetsuit also had holes in it like my first wetsuit. I was used to San Francisco winter water temperatures in the low 50s, but this was more frigid and painfully cold. Also, with the holes in my suit I had little defense against it.

That year, I went through five months of working the B&B and surfing every swell that came through. In the early season, there were a few larger 5' to 10' swells, but as the summer progressed, the swells got smaller and smaller. I paddled out into a few 6' or 7' foot swells, and it was intense. I wasn't a good shortboarder yet and would have my smallest mid-length boards out on a 6.5' swell hitting the jetty beach breaks. They were fast and aggressive. I caught some over-head rides but mostly was out of my element.

I did get better at surfing beach breaks since that is all New Jersey really has. Sometimes phenomenal ones too, but generally not super long rides that a point break would offer. I improved my surfing in faster waves. Often a point break, even if it's large and much overhead, can be a slower wave. Beach breaks are much punchier, so popping up for a steep drop-in and getting in front of the breaking section can be a big challenge.

August came and the Atlantic Ocean became the Atlantic Lake. Flat as a pancake. For about three solid weeks my boards sat on their rack and never touched the water. That was until the first hurricane of the hurricane season blew past us like a banshee from hell. That day there were double to triple-overhead (2-3x the size of a person or more) lightning fast, grinding barrels, with an angry lip that was throwing so incredibly fast it was hard to believe. It was amazing and terrifying. I, still to this day, after surfing for over a decade and in over ten countries, have never seen a wave like it. The biggest tubes I have ever seen, all with an offshore wind. A couple of hours later, the surf had calmed slightly but was still macking (firing, pumping). I grabbed my 7' Andreini single fin, mini-gun board, threw the wetsuit on and ran to the beach. I stood there in knee deep water staring at the massive, aggressive surf waiting for a lull or an area that seemed like I could sneak a paddle out. After standing for forty-five-minutes, I never found one. That was the only time in my life I turned around and walked home. It was too big for me at the time, and I didn't have the confidence to paddle out alone. The next morning, I was off to Rhode Island for the first time to try my hand at their point breaks that were getting hit with this same hurricane swell.

I woke up early the next morning and hit the road with a bunch of boards and camping equipment in my Element. I drove 227 miles from Ocean Grove, New Jersey to Point Judith, Rhode Island in under four hours. I had done six months of my own research on different breaks there and was planning to hit them all on the westside of Rhode Island.

I did not realize until I arrived there why the Point Judith area was so amazing for surfing. Point Judith is a very small peninsula that is the southernmost point of Rhode Island's mainland, not counting Block Island, sticking out into the Atlantic farther than any other point. It is on the west side of Rhode Island that's connected to Connecticut. I call it mainland because if you go farther east, Rhode Island becomes a series of islands, where Newport is located, accessed by a series of bridges.

Point Judith is only about a half-mile wide from east-facing coast to west-facing coast and much less at the southern tip of the peninsula. FOR SURFERS, this means that if the wind is blowing any direction, there will still be waves to surf on at least one side of the peninsula! If it's an east wind, the west side will have great offshore wind conditions, and vice versa with west wind and east shores. If the wind is coming out of the north, closest to the peninsula point on the south will be offshore, and if the wind is coming from the south, it's a crosswind on the east and west coasts, which is not ideal but still surfable.

In most surf areas in the world, there's one coast and three directions of wind are bad or not ideal. This place is a surf haven. Since it's only half a mile from one side to the other, checking everywhere is easy! I could not believe it when I realized this. It's like Maui when I used to live there. If the wind was blowing shitty onshore at one beach, we surfed the other side of the island, and that same trade wind would be offshore because the coast faced the opposite direction. Only to get from one side of Maui to the other was forty-five minutes to a few hours, depending on which coasts. In Point Judith,

130

it was five minutes. This was amazing. AMAZING! A surfer's playground!

I wasn't a Rhode Island local, but from what I've seen, Point Judith has about five different general breaks. The most popular is The Lighthouse. The lighthouse is a spot that's technically on the south tip of the peninsula. With the hurricane swells hitting it, coming up from the south, the swell energy produces long, peeling, righthand waves that are incredible. It's more of a shortboard spot but not exclusively. This spot is awesome to camp out for a while on top of the cliffs and watch the surf, almost comparable to the Santa Cruz, California vibe.

The whole beach is rocks, but the rocks are what make the waves epic. To the north of the lighthouse is Pilgrims. This was honestly one of the most fun waves I have ever surfed in my life. It's on the east side of the peninsula, farther north away from the peninsula's point. I have surfed 3' overhead to double-overhead grinding yet beautifully peeling point break surf there with offshore winds. Some of the best days of my life. I caught one towering right peeler that was easily the length of a football field. The largest, cleanest, longest righthander I ever caught in ten years, from a hurricane swell blowing by. All the spots on the eastside of the peninsula are righthand point breaks when a hurricane swell comes from the south. North of Pilgrims are more waves too, just like Pilgrims, but with more peaks and potentially less people.

There are two breaks on the west side of the peninsula point and lighthouse. One, I'm not sure of its name. It's probably called "The Lighthouse Left," or that's what I call it. It was really close to the lighthouse but on the western tip of the peninsula, meaning it was a lefthand point break. Opposite the righthanders on the east side. Also, out of the handful of hurricane swells I have surfed there, this lefthander tended to be a bigger and more intimidating wave than the lighthouse righthander. I surfed it once on my 7' Andreini mini-gun-looking single fin mid-length board. A local and I started chatting. He found out it was my first time surfing that spot on that big of a day with that board.

"Damn dude, you're crazy," He said and paddled off.

I guess implying it was an intimidating wave to show up with a shorter board and catch a bunch of crazy long lefts? I surfed the lefts so far that I started ending my ride early on purpose to save shoulder burn on the forever-long paddle back to the lineup. In order to access this spot, I parked on the dead-end street (it dead ends into the lighthouse), and I walked about thirty meters through what looked like a cornfield, only it wasn't corn, it was like a grain of some kind or a huge weed that looked like tall corn stalks. Once I got through the mud path through the "cornfield," I made it to the lighthouse lefthander at the rock beach.

XIII-Pilgrams break with waning hurricane swell. RI. 35MM

XIV-Mud path to surf, Point Judith, RI. 35MM

The last spot at Point Judith is called the K's, or K38/39. This spot is completely different from the other four. It is surrounded by a jetty almost entirely to produce a safe passageway for boats to enter and exit. Obviously, the boats need a place to enter, so there is one opening in the sea wall. At this south-facing opening in the sea wall, the swell sneaks in only one direction, which organizes the waves an unbelievable amount. Also, with the rock reef and kelp around, it really felt like Santa Cruz, California again! It provided the longest, friendliest lefthand point break for longboarders I have ever seen. It has a shorter righthander off it as well, but the left was the main attraction. This is the wave for developing your logging skills. Cross-walking, hanging-ten, or just dialing your single fin into a perfect wave. This wave got crowded with all the longboarders, but it was so worth it.

Matunuck. Ma-tune-ick. This might be one of the best lefthand point breaks on the east coast. Or the west coast, too, for that matter. Surfline (the surf report app) calls Matunuck the west coast of the east coast. Matunuck is a tiny town in Rhode Island west of Point Judith, only by a couple of miles, but driving takes longer as it's separated by a whole bunch of waterways and marinas. The only way to get from one town to the other is by the highway going out of the way.

Matunuck has a much different vibe than Point Judith. Point Judith is a tourist destination in the summer for its beaches and seafood, so it has a bunch of restaurants and hotels nearby in a spread-out neighborhood setting. Matunuck is less of a tourist destination besides its surf. It's a surly, salty, rusty, little forgotten town with small, modest houses and a trailer park, one bar, one restaurant, and one surf shop. All the houses are a made of dark wood that are usually wet from the consistent fog. The locals are more apparent here too, proud of their epic wave. It is an unbelievable wave. The first time I surfed it, I was paddling out on my 8'2" single fin Fineline into a 7.5' hurricane swell. I know my longboard length and big hurricane swell don't exactly match, but remember, it's a perfect point break, so there's a waveless channel to paddle out through. It was big, but when I paddled out, I paddled around the surf completely, not having to paddle through one wave (point breaks are the best for this). It was as if I was looking at San Onofre in San Diego if it was legitimately massive. I surfed San O before when the conditions were about head high, or maybe a bit more, and thick, but this was next level.

Next time, I'm taking a shorter board for sure, but back then I was less of a shortboarder. I remember paddling into a doozy bomb of a set wave, and the cobblestone/boulder reef forced the wave to lift off, creating this tall embankment, like a flat, banked ramp at a skatepark. From there, the wave continued to jack up getting steeper and steeper, until it finally walled up vertically. I had open real estate to ride the wave left forever as it escalator'd down in front of me, where the wave was still developing. I paddled, popped up and dropped in on a strong left angle as it walled up. I remember flying so unbelievably fast that the front of my board was popping up off

133

the water over and over again. The nose of my board slapping the water sounded like "wap-wap-wap-wap-wap-wap." It was a bull ride just to stay on the board. I planted my feet and rode it out until I carved back up the open face and went at it again and again until the wave finally mellowed out far into the shoulder, at the channel.

Matunuck doesn't have a very big beach. The break is located right behind the one bar/restaurant's outdoor patio that's stilted up in the back with pier legs. When the tide was high, it consumed the entire sand beach, and the ocean slammed under the bar's patio. This made it difficult to get in and out of the surf around those times. Also, it was a far paddle out – at least on a bigger day – a football field, maybe two. There were also a few other peaks to the east that I have not surfed yet but plan to on my next trip. One spot is called Deep Hole and it was right next to the proper Matunuck's point break. Every time I want to go check out Deep Hole, I see the Matunuck point looking incredible, and I can't seem to walk past it.

I felt it was necessary to support the surf shop, the food truck/coffee shop (in the surf shop parking lot), or the bar to give back to the little town that gets infiltrated with an influx of surfers whenever there was a significant swell. Thank you, Matunuck, and thank you, Rhode Island.

"I never leave Rhode Island." with an anchor chained to the words, is one of my favorite bumper stickers in the world.

The perfect way to end a day of surfing a hurricane swell at a point break from sunrise to sunset was by kicking up my feet around a fire at a campground in the forest. The largest campground in the USA was only about a fifteen-minute drive from this surf mecca. It was a bit pricey; campsites were around $35 a night, but so worth it to have somewhere to go after the surf day. Camping in quiet nature and getting great sleep. I was still on the hunt for a free camp spot somewhere nearby, but this campground worked great. Having a fire was so worth it.

I plan to continue to adventure around and hunt for surf during hurricane season farther into Rhode Island and eastern Massachusetts. There was much more there I hadn't discovered or surfed yet! I heard there was a good left point break up there at the border, so I went on one of my trips, and sure-as-shit, it was firing. This beach was beautiful, and I had not seen one like it on the east coast. It was a big cove where I parked my car right on the sand in front of the water line. This style of cove resembled California with its houses on top of the eroded cliffs at the beach. I walked the beach to the east, and I walked into Massachusetts. Right across the imaginary state line border. There were big boulders sticking out of the ocean providing a fast, barreling lefthand point break, just waiting for me. I'll go back with my shortboarding skills. In between Point Judith and the border of Massachusetts are a bunch of islands with south-facing shores and potentially great surf. I will hunt for more surf the next hurricane season I'm nearby!

PuRA VidA BAbyyyy Santa Tere

I was adrift. I was stuck out at sea. It was my birthday, May 10th, 2021. Santa Teresa, Costa Rica had a 5.5' @ 18 seconds swell hitting as my birthday present, and my best friends Rick and Brett were with me for it. The day prior, we surfed Santa Teresa's main beach, and it was around 3.5' @ 16s. It was a blast. Super clean, super fun, some good size, and at no point were any of us overwhelmed by it. My birthday was a little different.

The day before everyone in town was out surfing, and it was packed at sunset. On my birthday, there was close to no one out, maybe five guys sprinkled scarcely down the entire beach. They were the only ones who were willing to take the punishment. The three of us took the dirt road in my car down the beach from the main road in Santa Teresa. We passed the Selina Hotel and the skateboard bowl ramp on the left. We pulled up and parked under the trees at the beach. We got out and had a look with coffees in our hands.

"Oh my god!" We all said at once.

XV-May 10, 2021. Birthday Surfline live cam screenshot. Santa Teresa, Costa Rica.

I already saw it from the Surfline live cam on my phone, but the cam was very far away from the surf and on top of a hill. It was not exactly accurate. The high camera angle of the live cam gave us serious *cliff eyes*. It looked unreal. There were swell lines forever into the ocean's distance. A view I had never seen in real life before. A view that I, as a surfer, had always dreamed of seeing, but up until this point, had never seen as current conditions. There is a coffee shop in Mill Valley, California, between Bolinas and San Francisco, on the north side of the Golden Gate Bridge, that I stopped at many days while commuting to the city from Bolinas. On one of their walls near the bathroom, they had a huge, entire wall-sized print of a photo of swell lines like that. I stared at it every single time I was in that coffee shop. Now I was going to live it in Santa Teresa, Costa Rica. With the *cliff eyes* we had, we were so excited to get down there and paddle out, having no idea just how big it really was…

My friends and I used to ride our Harley-Davidson choppers down the Pacific Coast Highway south of San Francisco to a secret place we named "Thunder Cliff." We illegally renegade camped on some private open land we could sneak our bikes in through a few construction barriers that blocked cars from entering. We would hang out, have fires, and camp on the cliff edge listening to the thunderous sounds of Northern California's exposed coastlines' heavy waves smashing the cliffs all night. We watched the waves, never understanding how they were making such a loud sound with such a small wave from hundreds of feet up on the cliff. The reality was that the waves weren't small at all, it was our *cliff eyes* lying to us, as they, always from above, made it looks smaller than the conditions really were.

I had taken some screenshots of the Surfline live cam that morning on my birthday at the house in Santa Teresa before we left. Beautifully satisfying swell lines, forever into the ocean. Because of the angle of the cam from the top of the hill overlooking Santa Teresa's beach, I couldn't quite perceive the true size of the surf. We also wondered why no one was out!

After standing on the beach for a while with heaps of doubt, we all decided to give it a go. The three of us were also at completely different surf levels. I had been surfing the longest out of us, around ten years consistently. Most of my surfing years were spent on logs or mini-Mals (mid-lengths, small longboards, funboards, eggs, things in the 7'- 9' realm), in California, and in smaller to average-size surf. Rick had been surfing for almost as long. Or maybe he had an unsuccessful crack at surfing prior to when I started, but he really started longboarding with me in San Francisco. He had not surfed as consistently as I, with gaps of years in between without surfing. Then there was Brett, who had been surfing for much less time, three-five years, but he picked it up in New Zealand and Australia, then on Maui and the North Shore of O'ahu. Brett had basically only surfed epic waves his whole surfing life and was much more comfortable surfing shortboards in bigger conditions than Rick or me.

We all paddled out. I was on my 6' fish with glassed in fins (not the best board for these large beach break conditions I know, but I got better at shortboarding later). Brett was on his Al Merrick high-performance shortboard under 6', and Rick, poor Rick, was on a rented 9'0" log. I had my doubts, but I was with my best buds, and we were going to try to catch some of these huge, terrifying waves together on my birthday!

Brett got out first. He had the best board and skills for duck diving. I made it out a few minutes later, on the fish. And Rick, Rick never made it out. He got punished time after time on the inside, until he gave up trying to get out on the log and just caught some inside reforming waves and white wash (broken waves). Brett and I were together, out back, and went for a few waves as we were being dragged by the current north of the parking area and finally found our courage. I caught a few towering well overhead waves, but for

138

the most part, they were more on the brink of close-out sections. I would have a steep drop-in, look down the line, and see the lip crashing down hard from above. I would try to dive through the wave or ride out the transition, ending straighter, facing the beach. Hopping off my board to dive under water to try to avoid the strong white water crashing down on me.

After a few of these that were not that much of a good time, I paddled in, leaving Brett out there, and walked the beach looking for a better wave section somewhere else. I saw Rick sitting on a palm tree that decided to grow sideways a few feet off the ground before growing up again. He looked a little defeated. I walked over.

"How was it buddy?" I asked.

"I got destroyed!! I couldn't get out with this thing! I tried catching a few reforms on the inside, but it's just too big out there for me. So, I'm chillin' here." He responded, pretty content.

Rick is such a good soul. Some surfers would be pissed off they couldn't catch waves, but Rick was just truly happy to be there.

I watched Brett from the beach being choosy with waves and found a few that offered rides a little better than the ones I caught. His skills and patience were noticeable.

After talking with Rick, I went hunting down the beach for a better peak. One with some actual left breaking real estate. About a football field south I saw the waves breaking a little more consistently and smaller for a few sets. It looked much more manageable. Maybe this was the spot. How stupid I was. It was all the same beach break. There was nothing protecting that area from direct swell that was any different from where Brett still was. For some reason, I saw these smaller sets and thought I had found something. I paddled straight to it, no problem. Then it all changed. As soon as I paddled out to the (not any) smaller waves, it went flat. I waited a while, then came the onslaught.

The tide was coming up while we were out, and this probably added to the swell's intensity. Or, perhaps, the swell energy peaked while we were out, but the first of many sets came through on a completely different energy level than anything we had seen earlier that day. Legitimate mountains or buildings of water propelled through the ocean toward me.

At this point, I was not a seasoned shortboarder. I was still downsizing to a fish. I had my Hypto Krypto 5'10" but wasn't super comfortable on it or on bigger waves. Meaning, I was still a beginner shortboarder, even though I had many years of experience surfing longboards. It's a whole different world. My first instinct was to panic and paddle deeper to beat the crest of the wave from breaking and destroying me on the inside instead of duck-diving. I paddled for my life, kicking my feet, paddling as hard as I possibly could. I managed to get over the waves in that set by the skin of my teeth.

I immediately noticed the amount of height I had traveled, from the trough of the wave to the peak and to flat water on the backside of the wave again. It was significant. I felt like I was flying, weightless, in outer space.

"Damn that was crazy! Okay…" I said to myself. "Maybe that was a fluke set." I hoped.

I was now much deeper out. I waited. A minute later, a bigger set of four waves blew through. Even from the new deeper position I had just paddled to, I needed to paddle for my life again. I had to paddle even deeper to try to beat the lips of the waves from breaking. I was worried that the strength and size of these waves were too much for how buoyant my fish-style board was. It wouldn't duck-dive well, and I was afraid of being pinned under that strength for who knows how long. This is a rookie fear. I made it once again, barely, by the skin of my ass, over the peak as it jacked up like an angry freight train coming toward me and I was on the tracks. I waited again. Too afraid to move, confused to paddle in or out or anywhere. Here came a third set... I could tell that the waves were building in strength with every set. I paddled out as hard as I possibly could with all my might again. There were three, four, or five waves per set, and every one of them seemed to intensify significantly. I was so upset, angry, scared, and terrified. I was in awe of the beauty and the strength of nature while I was in it, completely vulnerable. I started yelling. I paddled as hard as my body would let me, my back, my arms, my shoulders, my neck, my hands, my ass, my legs, and my feet, were all on fire from fatigue.

"Are you freaking kidding me, what the helllllllllllllllllll!!!!!!!!" I screamed alone in the ocean with these powerhouses.

These sets were absolutely not the same energy we were surfing earlier when I was next to Brett. Those waves were large, but these were on a different scale of massive – a completely different intensity. After how far I paddled to avoid being annihilated from these sets, I was so far from shore it was scary. All the features on land were too small. I was adrift. For one of the first times in my life surfing, I didn't know what to do. I cursed myself for actively putting myself in this situation. I could have avoided this entirely if I wasn't a dumbass, thick-headed, idiot trying to prove my toughness. There was almost no one else out for a reason.

"Ok, I have to get myself out of here... Now, remember you love this." I told myself.

Another set came. And another. I was still paddling deeper with every wave. After a few hours, I drifted to a new part of the beach closer to where I left Brett, but I was so deep there was no one around me, I couldn't even see another surfer in the water in any direction I looked. I started to coach myself.

"Ok. This is what we're going to do. After the last wave in the next set, whether it's number three, four, or five, because every set is different, we're going to paddle as fast as we can and chase the backside of that last set wave to shore. If we get caught on the inside, try to catch a wave, surf it, and ride the white water all the way in. If we get caught under, just chill." My inner coach told me.

As I write this now, after seeing the *Dune* remake movie, this quote comes to mind: "Don't give into fear, as fear is the mind-killer." But that's what it was. I had to put fear on a shelf in my brain, knowing it was there but leaving it alone to actively attack the situation at hand.

My time had come. The last wave of a set blew by. It was the largest wave I had ever been in the water with in my life. I paddled in hard and fast. I was sucking wind like I was running a marathon, but I wouldn't stop. I never stopped. No matter how hard my arms felt like they were going to detach from my sockets and leave me stranded in the ocean without my top limbs, I kept going hard and breathing even harder.

I figured I had a few minutes before the next set. The higher the wave period (in the surf report) and stronger the swell, the more consistently organized waves become. On this large day, the ocean was pretty calm until those three to five set waves blasted through, then it became flat again. Usually, there would be a few, maybe even ten, minutes in between sets. This was my escape window for navigating through the building-sized aggressive waves around me. I paddled and paddled and paddled. I was so far out. It took me a long time to get to the normal break area again, where the lineup was when I was with Brett earlier catching the large but smaller waves before the behemoths started.

Once I paddled inside, a wave came. I was in a good spot to catch it as it was forming and jacking up. This was a smaller inside wave but still overhead. I caught it and rode it left, pumping and making big carves on my twin fin fish. The wave closed out after a surprisingly fun ride, and I rode it straight in on the energy of the white water as long as I could, like a beginner. I fell to my belly back on the board and paddled more, still in the whitewash energy. I got to the shallow water and ran out. Holy shit. I was still alive. I made it out. Happy friggin' birthday, Dave. Surfing gave me life on my birthday. The best gift I could ever receive. New life appreciation. More modesty. Hell yea. I'm an idiot.

I met back up with Brett and Rick on the beach. Brett had been out of the water for a while, and they were looking for me wondering where the hell I went. I told them the story. We left for some birthday café lunch.

Legends & Happiness

I have always dreamed of living off the grid. I want to throw my phone away. At times, I have. We live in a complicated technologically social world that doesn't have to be complicated or technological. There's a real beautiful world all around us. I go through bouts of living this way and prefer its simplicity. It's important to do things for ourselves not for other people's satisfaction. In the climbing documentary *The Alpinist* about Marc-André Leclerc, most of the time refused to let anyone watch or document his climbing. Even his dangerous solo climbs. He climbed alone. Only for himself. He didn't even have a cell phone. Sponsors had to seek him out. They bought him a cell phone, and he refused to let them know when he was climbing, leaving their phone behind. This is legendary in the modern world. He could care less about being famous. Same goes with Yvon Chouinard. He gave away his multi-billion-dollar company, Patagonia, to forever help fund global warming research studies, protect natural lands, and fund movements toward bettering the earth, making him no longer a billionaire. A true dirtbag in the highest regard. This has never happened in history. How much more of a boycott to the negative aspects of society can either one of these men give? Their focus, Mother Nature. I respect these men.

I have tried to minimize buying crap I don't need. Some of the best times in my life have been when I didn't have much. Some of the most creative times in my life were also when I had little...

I love that my life is still unwritten. It gives me excitement thinking of the unknown. Every step of life shouldn't be planned. I attempt to wake up and live in the moment as often as possible. I try distancing myself from the average American consumer bubble and have never been happier. At times I stopped paying for a monthly cell phone plan and love existing in the world untethered. I ask real people for real directions. It's like I'm a kid in a candy store when I exist in the world this way. I'm temporarily free from the all-knowing and all-seeing phone. It's awesome. It's an incredible feeling to think about something and actually ponder it. Without pulling out the all-knowing phone from my pocket, instantly gratifying how impatient I have become for useless knowledge. It's beautiful being incapable of asking the internet about every single stupid thing that goes through the mind. It's like being back in the 1990s. We dress this retro way, why not live it? We need a revolution against everything fake, all the distractions. For me, it's a waste of time and life. I'd prefer to take a trip or draw a map or paint a picture or grow a plant or play a song or learn an instrument or write a poem or mail a letter or have a conversation or play in the dirt or patch my jeans. Humbleness. Be real. Exist. GO OUTSIDE. BE SIMPLE. These are ways I have found happiness.

Pura Vida Local Style

I became a temporary local in Tamarindo, Costa Rica. My dad, in his early retirement, decided to buy a small condo down in the Playa Langosta (Lobster Beach) area. He did this with the idea that he would be down there maybe a couple months a year, but he rented it out for some of the busy season, and other times, left it empty for me to use. Literally, I have no money. I've always saved money for extensive periods of time for lengthy trips or moves, and then spent it all. This became an incredible opportunity to be able to exist in Central America without accommodation costs.

I decided to go down to Costa Rica the first time the condo was available to me. Back in October 2020, it was one of the only places in the world that was open to travel to during the pandemic. I wasn't about to sit on my ass for two years. Mexico was also open, and I went there as well, but I was looking to go farther than Mexico, so I set my sights on Costa Rica.

I went down without any real expectation. I didn't really research the surf or different towns I wanted to surf. I just went. I figured I could use my Dad's place as a home base and branch out from there. That first flight there, there was barely anyone on the plane besides me.

We were deep in the pandemic. I was almost the only one in the airport, and one of about six on board my flight. I had to spend the night in Houston, TX to catch the only flight I could to Liberia, Costa Rica the following morning as most of the flights to Costa Rica were cut. This was a spooky flight. I can't remember exactly how much I spent on the flight, but I think it was under $100 each way, maybe less, which is an insanely cheap price compared to normal times.

I made it to Liberia, a small city in the northwest region of the country in a province called Guanacaste. I took a shuttle to Tamarindo, a beach, vacation, tourist, traveler, surfer, expat town. I made it to my Dad's place and experienced the town empty. There was no one in town, on the streets, or on the beach. Three quarters of the businesses in town were closed or boarded up. I had never been there before, but this felt a bit spooky, like the flight. Anywhere I went, like restaurants, surf shops, etc. everyone greeted me with surprise.

"Wow you're American!!?? You're the first American traveler I've seen in eight months!! Please tell your people to come back!!" The Costa Ricans said to me every interaction I had in town. They were reliant on money from tourism that came to a screeching halt, and their economy was crushed.

I experienced Costa Rica from a more local's perspective versus a traveler. We had a small Chinese SUV, and I cruised Costa Rica for the winters of 2020-2021 and 2021-2022 spending about ten months there in total. Every day, I walked or drove to the local surf between Playa Grande (Big Beach) to the north, Playa Tamarindo just down the road, Playa Langosta across the street walking, or Playa Avellana (Hazelnut Beach) a fifteen-minute drive away.

I rarely went to Playa Grande, as it's very exposed to wind, has bad conditions often, and is the farthest drive out of anywhere local from Tamarindo – about thirty minutes. I needed to pass a bunch of beaches with good surf first to get there. It was pointless. That being said, once I watched a sunset session there from the sand when I arrived too late to paddle out. I witnessed double-overhead surf, with offshore winds, producing perfect large, hollow barrels. AKA the best possible conditions for that spot. Barrels so hollow that surfers were standing straight up tall, even with arms in the air above their heads, in disbelief of how much space there was inside each tube. It was like a painting of a surf scene that I swore could not be real. But it was. I was staring at it. Aside from that, whenever I checked Playa Grande, it was wind-blown, crappy, or crowded once people existed there again after the peak of the pandemic. Not my favorite. I know others love it.

A better spot that I did love (technically on Playa Grande's most southern shore) is a break called Casitas, meaning "little houses" in Spanish. This spot I had to take a thirty-second boat ride over from the Tamarindo beach, crossing the possibly crocodile infested river, upstream from the Tamarindo river mouth wave. The boat was about three bucks round trip, and it saved my leg from being bitten off. This really happened to a surfer in the early summer of 2022…

An American surf tourist from Arizona was surfing the Tamarindo river mouth with a bunch of other surfers and a ten to fifteen-foot long adult Saltwater Crocodile was feeding in the ocean, out of its usual upriver home. It bit the surfer's leg and pulled him under attempting to barrel roll and drown him. He fought for his life, got away, and managed to get out of the ocean. He was rushed to the hospital, which in Costa Rica is far away, where doctors had to amputate what was left of his leg and stop the bleeding in order to save his life. This was wild news when I found out. I have surfed there minimum, a hundred times. I even thought I saw a croc in the water near me one day. I paddled into shore and got out of the water because of it. I saw some funny looking green, thick, spiky, reptile skin in a square shape above the water just floating around. It didn't look like a plant. Also, it's all sand bottom there, there is no reef or kelp or seaweed around. It looked like it was attached to something below, but I couldn't tell what. I felt a primal fear and bolted, paddling for my life. The surf there was close to shore, and it didn't take me long to get out. I think about this as a real possible threat from time to time out there.

On one hand, it was like the shark conversion.

"You're more likely to get struck by lightning, than getting attacked by a shark." They always say.

But if there's sharks *AND* crocs, now the percentage has gone up! Also, I disagree with this general statement because, I'd say, it was pretty-damn probable that I would get struck by lightning if I chose to stand on top of a 14,000-foot mountain in Colorado in the summer during a storm with a metal rod in my hands in the air. Wouldn't you? Wasn't this more like the same probability now? We're not surfing in a public pool that was safe from these creatures. Except maybe a croc in Florida, but I'm not going out of my way to surf public pools in Florida anyhow. Instead, we were throwing ourselves into croc or shark infested waters in wetsuits, as if to impersonate a seal on Halloween, jiggling and wiggling around out there, clearly trying to be bait.

If I surf in San Francisco's red triangle hotspot of Great White Sharks every day, isn't that the same as being on the mountain top during a thunderstorm with the metal rod above my head? Either way, I still do it. I try to leave fear to the side and do the thing I love (but maybe with heightened senses...).

After the boat took me to the northern shore of the Tamarindo river, technically the southern shore of Playa Grande, saving myself from crocs, I walked along the sandy riverbank until I reached the ocean. Casitas was here in front of a few small houses on the beach at the ocean. Casitas has a rockpile reef mixed with sand bottom for a better, more consistent wave than the beach breaks around. This was better for less aggressive, more friendly surfing, or if there was a big swell, and it was big everywhere, for more rideable waves with better transitions that weren't quite as fast to close out.

As I progress in shortboarding, I keep an eye out for breaks that are more aggressive and faster for the shortboard. But sometimes, it was fun to be on a more friendly wave when it was big, to be somewhere not quite as intimidating. Casitas also had a super nice lefthander and a fraction of the people compared to Tamarindo. I think many tourists lacked the knowledge to take the boat over. I could also pretty much see the break from the tip of the Tamarindo beach to check if the boat ride was worth it or not.

I have only seen the Tamarindo river mouth wave work great about twice in two years. Of course, the first time I ever surfed it, it was phenomenal, and I thought it was always like that. Turns out, it was never like that. It had head-high, long, peeling, glassy lefts. I surfed it on a log, and it was amazing. Since then, it's a version of bad, even with good winds. The joke I had with my German friends in town was how we called that wave the "Tamarindo Close Out." Or "The Shit Hole." It was the worst and shortest wave around. It tended to jack up and close out the whole beach almost at once. Sometimes, on better days, it would run left, but it was so fast that only a very skilled shortboarder or tiny grom could keep up, still for only a couple of seconds. Once in a long while, there might be something rideable longer than that, but it was rare. It was also super crowded, as it's the main break in town and known as the "official beginner surf beach of Costa Rica." I don't know who came up with that, but it was hilarious because it was the worst wave around.

I was surfing the Tamarindo close out river mouth wave one afternoon, when the offshore winds held after morning, and I had most of the break to myself. There was only one other surfer around, and he was far from me. I kept catching this surprisingly fun lefthander, considering I was surfing the Tamarindo Shit Hole wave. It was just a very convenient break. This guy with shorter blondish hair came from out of nowhere and paddled over right next to me and paddled for the wave that I had just caught a few times. It was awkward. With surf etiquette, I'm not saying that was wrong, but I don't think I would paddle straight up to the only other guy after watching his ride and try to have a go at it. I would have found my own peak elsewhere. This was a little off-putting.

"Get out of here guy!" I thought to myself. We then continued to rotate, catching the peak that I initially found. We didn't talk or anything, and eventually, the wave got worse, and I left. For some dumb reason, I went back to that same wave the following day instead of a better break, and the same thing. The same blond-haired guy was out there again. Only this time, he was out there before me.

"Hey dude, have you ever been to Casitas?" He asked, yelling over to me.

"No, where's that?" I responded to the guy who I thought I didn't like.

"It's right over there on the other side of the Tamarindo river mouth." He said while pointing to the beach on the other side of the river.

"Do you want to go over there?" He asked, and continued, "I think it's better than here, this place sucks right now."

"How do we get there?" I asked.

"By a quick small boat ride over the river to the Playa Grande side, right over there." He said, with his slight European-sounding accent, while pointing.

"I didn't bring any money with me, how much does the boat cost?" I asked.

"It's cheap like $1.50 each way. It's cool, I'll pay for us. My name is Felipe... I remember you from yesterday." He said being super friendly.

I was blown away! My competition in the water yesterday was trying to be my friend today! Just goes to show how much of a dense idiot I was.

"Felipe, I'm Dave! Nice to meet you, dude! Sure, yea this place sucks shit right now. Let's go check it out." I said after changing my opinion about him in a split second.

We got out of the water and walked the beach to the area upriver, where the boats waited for people wanting to cross and the water was deeper. We flagged one down and the local Tico (Tico means local Costa Rican man, Ticas are ladies) boat driver took our boards from us, and we hopped in the small tour boat. These boats gave crocodile tours upriver and fit around ten or fifteen people per boat.

Felipe introduced me to Casitas, one of my favorite waves around. It was chill, friendly, and had a nice left. He told me he was Argentinian. I was stoked, as I had never met anyone from Argentina before. We surfed there together for a few hours, and I returned the favor by paying his boat fare a couple of days later, back to Casitas again. We traded phone numbers and surfed together a bunch. My first local surf bud! He worked at a local, fun Spanish restaurant, and I came to visit him a few nights a week to eat at the bar and chat with him while he made cocktails. It was fun to have a new local buddy in town!

I love Playa Avellana. If there was swell in the water, I would be at Avellana by 6 a.m. This beach is about fifteen minutes south of Tamarindo. Avellana is a long beach with something like eight different breaks on it, if not more, all relatively close together. I haven't surfed every peak because I always stick to the uncrowded ones. I usually surf right out front of Lola's Beach Lounge or La Purruja Restaurant. La Purruja is also the name of a break that's over shallow reef out front of the restaurant. I usually surfed between La Purruja and the beach entrance from the parking area next to Lola's. This was an unbelievable lefthand point break over a semi-shallow rock reef. My favorite surfing in Avellana. Most people didn't surf it because they were afraid of the shallow rock reef. Not far from there are boulders sticking out of the water making it more daunting.

Like always, whenever I do my research and try to avoid the masses and surf areas without anyone, as soon as I start catching wave after wave, surfers come out of the woodwork like roaches, flocking toward me. It is a pet peeve of mine. I don't surf like that. I

150

always looked for my own peak or my own ride where there was no one else around, if possible, not staring at other peoples' rides, bum-rushing them so I could have it for myself."

"I want exactly what that guy's doing!" I guess they all say?

Surfing is art, but that's not art. That's a version of theft in an area of many peaks especially. Anyway, this lefthander was long, with semi-fast, walling up transitions that were SO fun. It was usually around chest to head high on the good winter days, but it can be much bigger. In Costa Rica, the large swell season is from May to November, and the smaller swell season is from December to April. It's common for big 5'+ swells at high intervals to blow through in those summer months, while in winter months, it's possible for larger swells, but it's usually smaller.

To the north at Avellana, is an A-frame point break from a rock pile that offers a left and a right. This is normally crowded, and I don't surf it that often, even though it offered great rides when it was on. There's a longboard wave after that down the beach, followed by a bunch of lightning-fast shallow shortboard peaks. These shortboard peaks I only paddled out to once, and I've never surfed the longboard wave. It has always been too crowded.

The most quality wave is the Avellana river mouth. This wave is amazing. The break to the north of that is called Little Hawai'i, But I think the Avellana River Mouth should just be called "Hawai'i." I saw it breaking a few times, and only surfed it once, but the locals say it's under the radar and one of the best waves around. Not far south is Playa Negra, the most known wave in the area. When conditions got big and Playa Negra was firing, the single point drop-in on the amazing, barreling point break was fought for by every local and skilled surf traveler all at once. It's hectic, macho, and not chill. I won't surf it with that crowd. The Avellana River Mouth was more hidden. It couldn't be spot-checked easily from a car or a short walk, as it was a long full twenty-minute beach walk each way.

The day I surfed the Avallana River Mouth, I was with my neighbor/buddy Matt, giving him surf lessons, and took him out there on a day that was bigger, 4.5' @ 18 seconds. That day, we started by checking my favorite left reef point, straight in front of the car park, but it wasn't working well. The rest of the beach was packed with surfers, so we walked farther down. We paddled out in the fast shortboard beach break surf and got tired of it quick. From the water, I noticed the river mouth waves farther down the beach. It

151

was incredible looking, but at the same time, I thought it was intimidating, larger waves. Either way, it was the only answer to a better, empty surf session. We walked all the way north to the river mouth wave with our boards under our arms on the deserted, empty, tropical beach. We watched it break at high tide. (I've been told to go at a lower or mid tide.) The swell was so strong that it had no problem punching through at high tide and looked seriously epic. I couldn't believe my eyes! Why was no one surfing this!? It was Hawai'i out there!

We paddled out and there ended up being one boogie boarder out there we couldn't see from land. We hung near but inside the boogie boarder who was a local Costa Rican, giving him the respectful priority position to catch a few waves first.

"Hola." I said with a smile and a wave, and he smiled back.

The sets that came in were no joke. They were powerful and thick, a bit overhead, and because of the rock pile under us and the offshore wind, the lip would hold and hold and hold, until it hit that rock pile and threw super hard. My seasoned surfer brain calculated the drop-in point quickly. I needed to paddle in and pop up just before this point, but Matt, who was still in a heavy learning stage, had never been in this type of surf before and was getting steam rolled over and over. It was hilarious, but technically, I took him out on a wave that was well above his paygrade. Sorry dude. That's how we learn right? He never complained once either. That badass from Oklahoma put his head down and stayed determined. It was awesome to watch. Most beginners would be terrified.

"Hell yea Matt!" I tried to prop him out with support while he was getting a whiff of the rodeo.

I caught a handful of righthanders. They offered a much longer ride than the alternative lefthanders. I was on my Hypto Krypto shortboard, and this was THE first day I successfully caught legit waves on it. I remember noticing the strong differences between my thicker polyester fish that I was used to riding. The Hypto Krypto is an epoxy board. Those are the two main different materials used to make surfboards. Polyester boards have been around since the 1950s. It's a stronger, heavier, stiffer glass that's traditional and generally used for longboards, mid-lengths, fish, twin fins, and alternative shapes. Epoxy resin has been used to glass surfboards since the late 1990s and is much lighter in weight, thinner, and more flexible. These attributes give the polyester boards more drive, so they can glide on their own easier, also allowing them to drop-in earlier on a wave and keep momentum, while epoxy boards have more pop from their light weight to constantly pump for speed.

This situation was my first encounter understanding the differences in board materials, and it was very noticeable. At first, I would pop-up and attempt to carve the board like my fish, just glide and cruise the board without much effort, but it would noticeably slow down and I would lose all my speed. I had to compensate by pumping the board – bending my knees, twisting my body, and hopping over and over while making little turns up and down with the board to grab the water with the thruster fin set up (three fins). The first few rides I took weren't great, but after a few more, I got better at it.

I was farther north and caught a few lefthanders. It gave me the ability to understand the board from my preferred frontside, facing the wave, which was terrifying at the end of the ride as the wave sucked the water back from the rock pile in about one foot of water right in front of me. The water was clear enough to see the danger below from standing on my board. I bailed out the back of the wave into deeper water. The last wave I caught was a right again. I pumped, beating the fast-throwing lip right behind me on an overhead wave, but I decided to get greedy and ride it all the way in as far as I could. I thought it was all sand bottom over here, and I was wrong. It's all rock reef, and once again the wave closed out with me in a lower position on the wave, not able to jump over the back, and I jumped off into the closing barrel. Through the cycle of the barrel, my board karate chopped my leg, gave me excruciating pain, and I hit the rocks below cutting my leg. I quickly got out, as it was close to shore. I limped on the sand and saw I was bleeding down my leg. I looked at my board and the impact to my leg had caused a pressure bubble next to the rail. Bummer. But at least it didn't crack the epoxy. Matt got out a second later after his session of annihilation. We laughed about the crazy awesome wave. He knew he was in over his head but had fun with it anyway.

We walked back to the car, and as I was toweling off, Matt put both our boards back in the hatchback trunk for me, as he was borrowing one of my boards and wanted to help. I didn't check, I just closed the trunk, we drove fifteen minutes home, bouncing on the dirt road littered with potholes, like Swiss cheese, and pulled into the condo parking lot. I took my boards out and saw that Matt stacked the boards one on top of each other with fins touching boards, and my Hypto Krypto had three new slashes in the epoxy from the board I loaned him!

"Dammit, Matt!" I said and laughed.

"Don't stack boards like that, look!!" With the look he had on his face I could tell he was so embarrassed. He didn't know what to say.

He was so apologetic. I scored that Hypto Krypto for like $240 in California, when they usually ran $500 used, so I wasn't upset at all. I just laughed, brought it in the back, and repaired it with some more epoxy resin.

Down the coast further south is Play Negra, as I mentioned. This was the most famous wave around. It handled big swells and was a beautiful, barreling righthand point break. All the locals had it dialed in and knew exactly where the barrel section was. This was why it was super difficult to catch waves there on good days. The lineup was always packed. Even if I paddled out and caught a few, the general vibe at breaks like that isn't fun. It's too stressful. If I only get one wave an hour, and it's finally my turn, and I catch it, I don't enjoy that pressure. Half of the time I'll wipe out for some stupid reason associated to nerves that I'm finally on a wave, and then the locals will want to give me even less waves after. Not my vibe. Surfing isn't supposed to be a competition... It's supposed to be honest fun!

I was talking to a friend who I met at the gym, and he told me that just past Playa Negra is the best lefthand point break anywhere around, and not many people know of it.

"Oh reeeeeeaallyyyyyyyy? Please tell me more." I said, devilishly intrigued, like Mr. Burns from the Simpsons.

"It's called Cajones, and it's a series of points, depending on how big the swell is, but that's where I always go to boogie board, and it's epic. It can get really big. If it's small at Avellana, it's bigger there, always." This Frenchman told me.

"Shit man, let's go!" I responded.

This is when I feel a little guilty for writing about secret spots, but honestly, is anyone even going to read this? Does anyone even read anymore? I think most of America is too distracted by bullshit in these modern times to pick up a book. I'm assuming maybe my brother's future kids will read this if they care in thirty years. If that. It's still a secret then. Boom. I broke zero surfer codes of ethics.

My French gym friend took me to this secret spot about a week later when we had a good 18-second period in the report. The SW swell was 2' @ 18 seconds, and I thought the day would be chill. Those conditions seemed great fun but not massive by any means...

We pulled up after a crazy route of getting there that I would never remember, and I looked out at the beach. It was anything but chill. I couldn't believe my eyes. I had underestimated the spot and the 18-second interval.

"Are you kidding me??" I said in disbelief.

I was a bit nervous to paddle out. It was proper big. I brought my 6'0" fish because I thought it was a smaller day, even with the strong period.

"I wish I had my shortboard. Shit." I said.

"I told you." My gym friend responded in his French accent. "It's always bigger here."

We waxed up our boards and paddled out.

"Don't paddle over there, it's all rocks and there's strong current. Paddle over here even though you think you should paddle over there. Then once you get beyond those rocks, paddle toward the break." The Frenchman instructed.

I was very thankful for the tip, and he was right. I followed his boogie board and advice. We got out and some seriously large Hawaiian style sets came steam-rolling in. I was genuinely scared and paddled deeper to try to avoid getting smoked by one of the waves until I got my bearings. There were only three other people out – two guys and a girl. All shortboarders. Based on these conditions, there should have been fifty people out. I couldn't believe the lineup was so empty. I could see Playa Negra down the beach, and I could see a hundred little surfer heads sticking up out of the water there. We were about to score.

I waited for a while and eventually tried getting into one. I messed up and judged the wave wrong. I was stuck on the inside for a set, getting slammed and pinned on the rocks below. I was shook. I contemplated getting out. I tried calming myself down. I decided to curb my fear and paddle back out, mostly to not get made fun of later by the Frenchman. He came over to me.

"No, let's go. It's time. You must sit inside, over here." He instructed.

"Screw it, let's do it." I said, abandoning all fear.

I paddled in and caught the next set wave. I dropped in and popped up on the thick, fast, beast of a wave. I flew down the line, on this beautiful overhead transition.

"Owwwwwww!!" I screamed from adrenaline!

I was so excited and stoked! I paddled back and caught another screamer. This was surfing. Not getting out when I was afraid but being patient and finding the spot that worked for the board I was on. Also, doing research and networking to find a great spot that was not the most popular to get my own waves. I caught wave after wave. I was on fire. I got comfortable with duck diving the thicker fish through the bigger waves that broke on me. We stayed out for hours and we went in after the tide had changed so much; the conditions weren't as good as they were when we initially paddled out. I was so proud of myself that I didn't let my initial fear ruin one of the best surf sessions I had in Costa Rica. I thanked my buddy loads for taking me to his less known spot.

My most local beach I would surf often was right across the street from my house. Playa Langosta. Every single morning of every single day that I spent in the Langosta house, I woke up at or before sunrise, made coffee, and walked across the street out to the surf. I walked a dirt trail that had monkeys hanging from the trees. I check the spot directly in front of my place first. It's littered with rocks, most sticking up out of the water unless it was high tide, really the only time to surf it.

Then, I would walk farther down the beach, looking for puka shells and sipping my coffee. I took some puka shells home with me but made sure to pick up more trash than shells, so my shell-taking was karmically balanced. I made necklaces, bracelets, and anklets for my friends from the puka shells.

After a five-minute beach walk, I reached the Langosta river mouth wave. This was a crazy wave that I surfed many times, some successfully and some not so successfully. This wave was by far the shiftiest, sneakiest, most confusing, fickle wave I've ever surfed. It has a few different rock piles before a river mouth sandbar. Also, there is a separate shallow reef bed next to it, possibly forcing energy to the river mouth from the side. Either way, this wave would play games with my head daily. It appeared like it was going to break for ages, but it never did. In fact, it would mellow out (meaning the ocean floor gets deeper again after a wave began to form, mellowing

156

it out) before hitting a rock pile farther on the inside and pitching its lip, surprisingly hard some days. I have watched some waves break on an outer, deeper rockpile, then reform and break again on the inside. But every wave was different. Some don't break outside but break on the inside. Some do an S-curve, still breaking over the inside rockpile but looking like they should break farther to one side first, then not doing so. It's trippy. A pain in the ass, indecisive wave. It seemed like a longboard spot, until that lip threw on the inside and it became a fast, steep, left, sometimes barreling, making it best for shortboards. Every damn day it was doing something different, and it was hard to dial. I went to see what personality the wave had every morning.

Langosta has one more break that was a little local secret. South of the river mouth, there is a wave down the beach called "The Ocho." I'm not sure exactly why it was "The Eight" or what is "Eight" about it. I've also heard it called "Cape Town." This is a different type of wave than all the others. It's a one-of-a-kind wave in all the greater Tamarindo area. It's a low tide wave. Everyone knew in Tamarindo you had to surf mid to high tide. The tide swings, from low to high or vice versa, in this general region of northern Costa Rica are significant. It could be about two and a half meters different from low to high tide! That's about eight feet! Eight feet higher or lower surface water from high tide to low tide. In areas where the water drained back, the beach would have half of a football field length of newly exposed sand beach or reef. Cape Town was a nice secret if I was trying to surf near a low tide. This spot floods out at higher tides with more swell and only works when most water drains out. Also, it was walkable from my house! I had to cross the Langosta estuary river that fed freshwater out to the ocean at the river mouth wave. There weren't any crocs in that river... right? Well, at low tide it was only about two feet deep, and I could see the sand and rock bottom, but the crocs were out there... Then from there, I would walk about ten minutes down the beach. It took about fifteen minutes to get there from my door. I could mostly see what was happening down there from the river mouth, too, so checking it was easy if I squinted hard enough.

The same trip Brett and Rick came down for my thirty-fourth birthday, before we all went to Santa Teresa together for my actual birthday, we first hung around the Tamarindo area and surfed for a week. One day it was low tide, and we were hungry for a morning

157

surf session. We checked The Ocho/Cape Town wave. It seemed small but fun, and it was the only game in town for a low tide surf, so we grabbed our boards from my house and walked down there.

We paddled out, which again some of these beach breaks were less than a ten-second paddle, and this one was no different. I knew where the break was – near a rock on the beach that became exposed at a low tide. I always thought this spot was a beach break, but it turns out there was a very specific little rock pile or one big boulder that the waves broke off consistently. I learned this when I was surfing it on a negative tide (sometimes the tides get out of whack and become more extreme, due to a full moon, and this low tide was way lower than usual), and I could see the rock underwater. Some dude even stood on it.

Brett, Rick, and I all paddled out at the visible rock on the beach, and there was no one else out. We had an offshore wind, 83-degree Fahrenheit water (28.5 Celsius), a few feet of playful swell, and this beach break/rock point break ALL TO OURSELVES!

The wave wasn't huge that day, but it was big enough to shortboard, which Brett and I were. We had three hours of wave after wave after wave.

"This is like Hawai'i, only there's no one here!!!" Brett yelled at one point. He couldn't believe it.

"If this was Hawai'i, there would be fifty dudes out, and maybe in this same time, I'd have caught only four or five waves. We've all caught like thirty waves!!!" He said energetically.

It was then that Brett saw a new beauty of Costa Rica. We surfed until we were exhausted and starving.

Portugalllllllllll

I had never been to Europe. Not once. I traveled inside the United States for years on motorcycles, skateboard trips, and on surf trips. After surfing for over a decade, I finally needed to start branching out for better surf around the world. Once I had my eyes outside the USA, I chose west, over the Pacific, or Central America continuously. My warped perspective of Europe seemed like a destination for backpackers looking to stay in hostels and go to pubs in different European cities. That sounded boring to me. All those cities are landlocked without surf!

After working the hotel season in 2021, I decided it was time to get to Portugal. I found a dirt-cheap, round-trip ticket for about $350. I guess because the world was still afraid and not traveling? I also rented a car for a month for only $250. I was set. I was leaving September 28th, which was perfect for cheaper prices for accommodations as it was after the summer tourist season. Autumn was when the Atlantic Ocean, especially over there, was pumping with waves too.

I finished working at my family's hotel during the busy season at the beach in Jersey and was keen for an adventure. On my flight over the Atlantic Ocean (my first time), I watched a documentary on this wild dude from Brazil who bodysurfs big waves. His name is Kalani, and the documentary was about how he would bodysurf Nazaré, the surf spot with the tallest recorded big waves ever surfed in the world. Pro surfers were interviewed saying how bizarre this guy was because he just swam out from the sand with average fins on his feet, nothing special, swimming under the massive 40'- 90' waves to swim out to the lineup with no gear or team. Solo. This dude blew me away. He also made the big wave surfers look like total wimps. They get a jet ski ride from the local marina to the safe part of the lineup, deep behind the big crashing waves, and get jet-ski-towed into surf them. Kalani swam out himself, negotiating the terrifying waves breaking in front of him, and paddled for his own waves as they broke on him, like skyscrapers falling in an earthquake. He would duck dive swim 50'- 100' down under every wave. This guy is a complete badass and freak of nature. This was the coolest thing to motivate me for a new place that I knew nothing about.

Finally landed after the overnight flight, and the airline staff corralled the passengers to a passport control building that was vacant without personnel. We waited for about an hour until the few hundred people just decided to leave the building and walk elsewhere. As a stampede, we found the correct building to enter and finally got through. Between my lack of sleep, jet lag, and being in a different country, I felt like it was magic that I made it through at all.

I decided not to bring a board with me to Portugal because the flights charge an astronomical amount, $200-400 each way, and I figured I could just buy another board out there for that price. Then, I wouldn't have the hassle of carrying it and potentially damaging it in transport. Also, I prefer not to support the overpriced airlines. I caught an overnight flight with just my rucksack on my back. I boarded around 9 p.m. and with the five-hour time change and five-hour flight, I landed at 7 a.m. in Lisbon, Portugal.

I used the airport's free WIFI and called my rental car company to come pick me up with a shuttle, because, of course, the sweet deal I got was from the company far from the airport. I got picked up and was in my new tiny Euro ride headed toward the beach an hour later, and since my overnight flight landed so early, I still had the entire day. My first stop was a tiny village outside of Péniche, near Ferrel, called Casais Brancos, where my local accommodation was.

I drove through all the crazy, curvy streets of Lisbon and got lost. I ended up at a dead end, facing a sketchy project building with lots of seemingly homeless around, and folks that looked at me like I didn't belong. I quickly U-turned and got out of there, but I did notice some amazing graffiti art on the buildings on the way out. I got back on track and out of the city. I decided at the last minute to drive to Ericeira first, as it was on the way to Péniche. This took less than an hour to drive straight west to the coast. Ericeira is a very old fishing village built up on the cliffs overlooking the Atlantic. This area has become a hub for surfing and is a pro surf tour destination due to its phenomenal surf breaks all around.

Ericeira is a perfect example of an old-world Portuguese town that was one of the coolest places I have ever been, especially as an American. The USA is not an old country. Honestly, I have never even seen anything older than 100-200 years in the USA. When I was standing in front of a building in the town of Ericeira or the Nazaré lighthouse that was 600 years old, my mind didn't know what to make of it. I was kind of in awe that it was still standing, slowly crumpling, and it was much more beautiful than something built yesterday. Six-hundred years old means that about eight generations of people have died since it was built. That was surreal.

I arrived in Ericeira and parked in the parking lot north of the downtown streets at the cliff. I got out of the car. It was cold, damp, and foggy. I couldn't see the ocean from the cliff. The fog was too dense. I walked over to the edge and looked down. From here, I could barely see. The surf was big and unorganized from strong consistent 35mph onshore (poor) winds. I had to put on a heavier shirt and walked around the old cobblestone streets of downtown Ericeira.

After I walked around for a while looking in the old buildings' storefront windows, I got back in the car and headed north again toward Péniche. I drove near the coast for maybe thirty minutes until I reached another town called Santa Cruz. I had surfed Santa Cruz, CA in the USA tons, so just because it was a recognizable name, I figured I would pull off the main road and see what this Santa Cruz had to offer. I parked and jumped out onto a big beach. There was no surf happening here at all. This was the opposite of the Santa Cruz I was thinking of – the surf mecca in California – but I walked around for a few minutes on the sand anyway. I noticed next to me, on the same area of the beach, what I thought was a pair of boobs face up to the sky! I double took and, sure enough, a woman was tanning topless. I recalled the stereotype Americans knew of Europeans – that they do this – but my jaw was lying somewhere in the sand in amazement. I regained my composure and took off. I didn't want to stare too long!

"Did I just see a unicorn, or is this normal here?" I wondered.

I kept driving north from Santa Cruz to a small village town outside of Péniche where my first accommodation was located. I booked it because it was unbelievably cheap, cute and in the outskirts of the vicinity I wanted to check the surf in. While still working at the beach hotel in New Jersey, I watched a lot of the live-surf cams on different surf report websites around Portugal a month in advance to try to plan some waves I might want to surf or regions of Portugal I might want to surf in. My favorite wave I saw on a surf cam was a beach called Praia Baleal. In Portugal, they speak Portuguese (I know, "duhhhhh"), which is a crazy difficult language to see and hear but has some vague similarities to Spanish. In Spanish, beach is called "playa," and in Portuguese, it's "praia." I remember sitting in the office of my Jersey beach hotel watching the surf cam for Praia Baleal.

"Holy shit!!" I yelled.

The surf in Praia Baleal looked amazing!

It looked like long, easy, slow, glassy longboarding waves, point-break style coming in with some height. I figured this would be the best place to start surfing in a new country where I know nothing. I checked myself into the $31 per night studio apartment for two nights and drove another ten minutes to check Baleal.

The main street of Baleal was small with stores and little restaurants on either side. I took it to the beach. It's a simple, cute little town with mostly surf schools, restaurants, accommodations, and skateboarding ramps. The town clearly catered to surf tourism the closer I got to the beach. I have a funny distaste for staying in places like these. I'm not sure why, but I think I try my hardest to live as a local when I travel – under the radar – than live as an obvious tourist. There's nothing wrong with being a tourist, I just want a more local experience in new places. I crave more culture, cheaper meals, and accommodations. The same reason why I don't like to visit somewhere for only a few days or a week. I prefer to stay in places I want to be for a longer time to get a deeper sense of the culture I am interested in learning. Proof as my accommodation was in a more affordable village, inland from the beach area, surrounded by local Portuguese people.

The town's center was a circle with a few local cafés, pubs, and a mini grocery store that felt much more local-style Portuguese. I got out of my tiny Euro rental car in the parking lot at the beach and ran over to the edge of the cliff. I was so excited that I was finally there and about to catch some waves! I looked over the cliff edge. The conditions were shit! Like super shit! There was not another surfer around anywhere! Even on land... Bad news!

"Uggggghh…" I sighed.

I pulled up the surf report map and saw where some other popular spots were nearby and drove to check them too. I looked out for surfboard rental places, too. I planned on buying a board but didn't yet. I was board-less! I needed to change this quick! I went to check out Péniche. Péniche was only a few-minute drive from Baleal, only it seemed to be the hub of the area. Much larger than Baleal, Péniche is more of a tiny city, comparably. There are large grocery stores, a few gyms, lots of houses and buildings all near each other and built up a few stories tall. Péniche has its own touristy upscale restaurant strip over a canal, but it's not my vibe. Although I did later find an all-you-can-eat sushi restaurant in there for cheap, which was way more my style!

I drove west through Péniche's peninsula to the point that stuck out farthest into the ocean. More horrible conditions. Péniche is unique because it has a peninsula kind of like Point Judith in Rhode Island. Only here it was not the peninsula itself that usually had good waves but the adjacent beaches with their rock reefs. This type of unique coastline is what offered super fun waves, but definitely not today.

To the south of Peiniche is Supertubos. Supertubos, a famous, super shallow, extremely hollow, barreling beach break that can reach double to triple overhead. It's known for its fast-as-lightning, grinding barrels in very shallow water. It's gnarly. It was one of the fastest beach-breaks I had ever seen. Within a ten-minute drive, there were all these different spots, some beach breaks, and some rock reefs. But everywhere I went that first day had no surf whatsoever. After checking all these spots, I threw in the towel and decided to find a gym and exercise.

After I showered and left the gym, I looked for a café for lunch. I eat a lot because I exercise a lot, and I decided to look for a café to hold me over until I bought some groceries for dinner.

I walked into this local café with a Delta Espresso sign out front, implying that it's not a hip cool-kid expensive café but rather an average, typical café. I asked what kind of food they had. The café was different from any American café already because of the people in it. There was a fútbol game on the TV and a handful of old men and some wives were drinking beers watching it. American cafés don't really mix coffee and alcohol so much. Either it would be a bar, a brunch/restaurant with alcohol, or a coffee bar. It's not usually all three. Especially with the sports bar component and modesty.

"Hi miss, what do you have to eat here?" I asked the older Portuguese woman.

"Egg sandwich, tuna sandwich, pastry." She responded with very broken English.

"Can I have an egg sandwich, a tuna sandwich, a double espresso, and a bottle of water please?" I asked politely.

"Four Euro." She said.

"Are you sure?" I asked, confused by how cheap it sounded.

"Yes, four Euro" She repeated.

I felt like this was too cheap, so I tried leaving some extra dollars for a tip on the counter.

"No no no, too much, you take." She said in a way like she didn't want to owe me any favors later.

There was no tip jar, nothing. She truly didn't want my money. The currencies between countries are always changing, but at the time, €1 was equal to $1.15. My lunch was $4.60. I sat down at a square wood table next to the wall of windows. She made my espresso and walked it over to me. After I sipped it and watched the fútbol fans on the other side of the room for a few minutes, she brought my sandwiches. I was surprised to see two sandwiches be placed in front of me, because I didn't pay enough for two sandwiches! They were also served on fresh rolls baked that morning at the local bakery down the street. They were simple yet delicious, with the best cheese I have ever had chopped thick from a large brick.

If I ordered this at an American café in San Francisco or LA or NYC where I have lived, each sandwich would be $10-$15 plus a $5 double espresso and a $2 bottle of water. Add that together plus tax and a 20% tip you're looking at $35 to $40. It was almost one-tenth the price!!" I was amazed. I thought I had found the cheapest place in all of Portugal!

After the café, I drove back to the mini grocery store and picked up some eggs, bread, bananas, canned tuna, and a few other little things for some simple dinner and breakfast. The same thing happened at the grocery store, too! I paid less than €20 for a whole big bag of groceries for many meals! I went back to the little village and my little studio. I ate some more eggs and tuna (practically the same as my last meal) and researched more surf breaks in Portugal. I was

164

also looking for my next town to stay in after my two nights here were over.

I book one accommodation for the first few days of landing somewhere new and then figure it out spontaneously. Maybe this is hectic for some, but I prefer it. I like to search around different spots to surf based on swells that I don't know about too far in the future! About an hour south was the bigger surf hub town of Ericeira (Eidyseida Portuguese pronunciation, Eddy-sera English pronunciation). I figured I'd check that town out next, so I booked an older lady's back house for four nights. It felt good to at least have my next place secured, only forty-eight hours in advance. I went to bed and hoped to surf Péniche the next day.

I awoke with excitement. I thought for sure it would be my first day catching waves in Portugal. I made coffee, eggs, and toast. I ate and quickly jumped in the car with a banana and a road coffee. I drove back through Baleal and back to the cliffs. I peered over the edge of the cliff to examine the surf conditions. They were still atrocious! It was a mish-mosh of unorganized windy soupy shit out there.

"Ugggggghh…" I sighed again with heaps of disappointment.

I went walking on the nearby cliffs for a while, until I decided to get the hell out of there. I figured, since the surf sucked, I would drive north to Nazaré.

In the surf world, there are "big" waves, and then there are "big waves." That might sound stupid, but any surfer can say at their local break, "Man, the waves were big today! I surfed some big waves!" Then there are "big waves," meaning waves that are over 40' and often times too big to paddle into. In the 40'-100' wave category, surfers usually need jet skis to pull them fast enough to keep up with the over 40' wave's intense energy.

There is a certain type of surfer who surfs these large waves, a "big waves surfer," who has different gear entirely from a classic surfer. It is its own sport altogether. These guys have unique boards called guns that are very long and pointy that no other surfer would use in average-size waves. Many have foot bindings, kind of like a snowboard, to keep your feet attached to the board while flying down the face of the huge waves moving way faster than a surfer on a smaller wave. The risk is much higher when surfing big waves, because if the surfer doesn't make it successfully, they will be pinned under 50'-100' feet of water and foam. It's also much more likely to get injured along the way. Many big wave spots around the world have taken the lives of unlucky surfers trying to surf them.

I have witnessed Mavericks breaking at 50'- 60', in northern California just south of Half Moon Bay, but I was particularly excited to check out Nazaré, even when it was flat! Nazaré has so much hype around it being the biggest wave ever surfed. It felt special being there. I have watched it break on film so many times, I couldn't believe it when I was standing in front of Nazaré's iconic lighthouse right at the point. It was all pretty glamorous for my surfer brain.

I continued driving north from the Baleal area, where my accommodation was in Nazaré. The environment was changing the farther I went. It reminded me of northern California. It got colder, foggy, and tons of pine trees appeared out of nowhere. I eventually needed to stop for gas and found a gas station in the middle of nowhere around a bunch of empty land. It looked like people would drive back on dirt roads to camp (of course I went and checked it out afterward to note a free camping spot) around more pines in the forest. The attendant put the gas in my Euro car for me and the price was 1.56 Euros per liter, and I needed twenty-eight liters. €50 total for three-quarters of a tank of gas in a tiny car! Gas was pricey here!

I kept driving north with tunes blasting, sipping coffee. Simon & Garfunkel, you are great anywhere! I used to listen to the same three songs on Maui the first time I lived there with my brother Jesse when we were barely adults. Every morning for a month while showering at sunrise and putting the scabies cream on our entire bodies (don't get it, it sucks), I would blast "Sound of Silence," "Cecelia," and "El Condor Pasa" in the bathroom. Then we would go hiking, avocado picking, and cliff jumping into the lagoons in the jungle, or hitchhike to go bodysurfing in the waves before I ever surfed. Here they are again, Simon & Garfunkel, blowing my mind in Portugal.

I arrived in Nazaré after about an hour of driving through more and more dense fog. I soon realized that there were two parts of Nazaré: Nazaré low and Nazaré high. Nazaré low, in my opinion, was a small city. It has tight streets and was built into a mountain's cliffside. The buildings were quite tall. This had an urban feel for sure. I was in the south part of Nazaré (low) where there was a massive sandy beach, and the water was flat – no waves at all. I was confused. I was in Nazaré, where the hell was the big wave spot?

With a bit of café internet research, I found what I was looking for. I had to leave that area and go around to the top of the cliff/mountain to Nazaré part number two (high). There was a tram that transports people up and down the steep sloping mountain between both parts of Nazaré. How bizzare! A town that a huge cliff dividing it in half. I was on my way to the beach and saw a little café. I stopped in for an espresso, just to pop in somewhere and check it out. Nazaré number two (high) must be the older section of town because it was reminiscent of Ericeira in the old-world way. It was fun to see everyone living in such an old place. There was a large older woman missing many teeth behind the counter of the little café who started making fun of me in Portuguese the moment I stepped in. It was great. She kept pointing at my tattoos and laughing hysterically. She gave me an espresso in a dixie cup. I attempted to banter with her, but we had zero common words, so I thanked her and left. I drove straight to the lighthouse. I needed to be there to see where the largest waves in the world took place. Even if it wasn't happening now, I wanted to take it in and experience the place where it occurs.

I had to park a few blocks away and walk the streets over to the entrance. I started noticing the crowds of people walking toward Nazaré realizing that this was a world attraction. I was not prepared for its level of interest. There was a massive truss entrance with banners all over it, saying it was one of the world wonders. It was almost like a theme park. I was immediately turned off, but it was only at the entrance, mostly to corral people when the wave was on, when tons of people came to view it. Nazaré wasn't currently breaking, so it wasn't nearly as hectic.

I walked through the massive outlandish entrance and down the cliff road to the lighthouse. There it was. The red lighthouse perched on the edge of the cliff facing Mother Atlantic. I walked up to it and read its sign. It read, "1577." I touched the old crumbling brick walls as I entered.

"Today, I am standing in a building built in 1577." I said to myself.

My mind was malfunctioning. Lack of comprehension existed in my little brain. I paid €1 to enter the museum that was revamped after being abandoned and dedicated to teaching people about Nazaré. I was stoked. I'm not really a tourist like this usually, but in my head this was cool. Afterwards, I sat on the cliffs overlooking Nazaré Norte Beach's surf, looking just beyond the big wave spot to the north. This break is still no joke. It's an exposed, heavy beach break. It was well overhead that day with only a couple surfers out. I saw the waves crashing from above – directly overhead – an angle I usually can't see waves from. When they broke and crashed, they would create these beautiful organic designs that formed a mural of patterns that satisfied my eyes until they would melt away and disappear back into the sea. I walked back up the cliff to my car. I researched a gym in Nazaré and worked out for a few hours, still waiting for good surf conditions. I drove back down to Baleal and slept the last night in my first accommodation.

I awoke and planned for a drive south back to Ericeira where I would be spending the next few nights. I took the coastal road south. This was maybe an hour and a half drive, but I made a few stops. Why not if the surf sucked?! I pulled off at this one café near Santa Cruz, inland, not at the beach, right off the main road. It was called the Atlantic Café. I parked, walked in, and said hi to another older woman behind the counter. She was very nice and spoke almost zero English. I ordered the same thing as the last café in Péniche: an egg sandwich, a tuna sandwich, a double espresso, and a bottle of water. I expected the price to be much higher than the first café, as that must have been a fluke.

"Five Euros," she said.

"No wayyyy!" I thought.

It was only fifty cents more expensive.

"Maybe this is just what things cost here?" I pondered.

I tried to leave a few dollars for the woman as a tip.

"No, no, no," she said, refusing, and handed it back.

This was the second time a café woman refused to take my tip. I didn't see how trying to leave more money was bad etiquette, but maybe it was? We tried talking, as she was very friendly. I understood she was asking where I was from because clearly, I wasn't from there.

"USA," I said.

She looked surprised. I thanked her for the delicious sandwiches with the best bread and cheese I'd ever had and took off back down the road toward Ericeira.

The road was small. It was a local road, not a highway of any kind. One lane in each direction. I headed farther south, eventually driving through Ribamar De Cima, the small town just north of Ericeira. Portuguese pronounce "Ribamar" as if they are clearing their throat. It's wild to hear. Americans don't make that noise with English, and the Portuguese roll their eyes when I attempted to say it.

Ribamar was where my accommodation for the night was – a little back house of a main house where an older Portugese woman lived. It was still early, and I was not ready to check in yet. I continued south to Ericeira. I parked in the same big open parking lot at the cliffs that was at the edge of the beautiful old fishing village district, where I parked the first time. The fishing village streets are Ericeira's main downtown. I walked around the snaking uneven cobblestone streets enamored by the historic beauty mixed with modern culture. There were surf shops, cafés, macrame shops, gift shops, bakeries, bars, restaurants, everything under the sun, embedded in the hundreds of years old buildings.

The town's central hub was a square open park area, where one café with outdoor seating jetted out into the middle of the street, and across the way was an open area with benches where people would congregate. There was another café adjacent to that, and a few streets opened to the square, spilling out tourists from hotels, hostels, surf rental companies, etc. It was an all-around great people-watching spot. I think Europeans enjoy people-watching more than Americans. Seems like everyone loved to see, be seen, and just hang out. After having another beautifully inexpensive café meal, I walked more uneven cobblestone streets back to my tiny Euro car and drove back to Ribamar to my accommodation. I met the woman who owned the property. She was in her fifties. She took me around back to the guest house. There were amazing views from the patio and my front door of the Atlantic Ocean and views of a cove with a surf break called São Lourenço, which was a pumping righthand point break. This cute place set me back only €54 a night. I couldn't believe it.

After I brought my rucksack and grocery bags in and cooked myself a meal, I went hunting for a used board on the internet. Renting a board in Portugal was expensive. Some shops charged €40-50 per day, plus a wetsuit! I clearly wasn't doing that! I found a guy selling a cool-looking board for €350 with a fin. It was a 5'10", 21" wide egg (a board shaped like an oval) that was shaped by a local infamous shaper in Ericeira. It had three fin boxes for a single fin or a thruster set-up (three fins), with one single fin included. I figured this might be the all-around board for a place like this, if I could only have one board. Since it was a 5'10", I could shred bigger waves, as it was a shorter board, especially if I put two more thruster fins on it. I could also surf small waves on it as it was 35 liters (measures the volume of the board, and a 35-liter shortboard is a lot of volume) with a rounded nose and 21" —wide for a shortboard. I could still have an easy time getting into smaller waves, longboard style, too. AKA a wave catching machine!

I went for it. I bought the board in a grocery store parking lot in Ribamar De Cima from another fellow American who was headed back to New York. The board was in almost perfect condition, with one tiny repair done to the side of the nose but that was it. I figured that's about $400 USD for a practically new board with a fin. That's a good deal. The next day I went to the local surf shop and bought a cheap pair of Futures fins (brand of fins) for the two smaller side fins next to the large center one that was included with the board. I already had a leash with me, so I was ready to paddle out for €370. Score. That definitely beat a new board price of €800 plus fins.

I decided to paddle out almost across the street from the surf shop, Boardriders, at a beach called Praia do Matadouro. I could see amazing lefthanders running all the way from the road, and there were a few surf schools giving lessons on the inside sections, so it didn't seem too sketchy for a first paddle out in a new country. I walked down the steps to the reef beach with massive sections of slab stone jetting out from different angles of the sand. This slab is what a lot of famous Portuguese surf breaks are known for. This type of reef is what makes these waves unique. They're consistent and powerfully epic. But the slab is unforgiving. Unlike coral, cobblestone river rock, or other types of reefs, slab is solid. No water can pass through it; therefore, all of the wave energy has to move over it. This makes the wave energy more powerful, and after surfing different types of waves all over the world, this energy is very noticeable.

I paddled out. I was getting acquainted with my new, short eggstyle board. Paddling, duck diving, sitting. Just seeing how the board reacted to my movements and balance. I was in the lineup and a wave came that looked like a pretty good, head-high size, and I went for it. I paddled toward the massive cliffs in front of me and got picked up by the wave. I popped up and the board felt stable under me as I went left to my frontside, down the face of the wave. Before I knew what I had gotten myself into, I was in a situation known as, "sure death." The wave had sucked some water back from its trough and exposed some rock reef right in front of me. I was going to hit it. I was hauling-ass down the line, and I was going to smash straight into this gnarly-looking, jagged, diamond-shaped rock that just poked its head out of the ocean. I was toast. I clenched my body, clinched my face, braced for impact, and… Somehow, in an instant, I was now flying in the air, as if I was floating. I hadn't jumped, I was confused at first, but I realized that this slab energy was so strong it literally flung me off the wave itself. Somehow, miraculously, or because the tide was high and maybe the backward moving backwash wave (yes, this is a thing) hit me at that exact moment and was super strong. I have no idea, really. Some kind of miracle wave threw me into the air over the exposed rock (and my doom) entirely, and I landed in the water on the other side, unharmed. I was stunned. I was preparing for sudden death or at least sudden pain at the very least. Then, I was surprised by getting launched in flight and having the experience over without any pain introduced to my body that I was expecting. It was a weird feeling. I dodged a bullet.

"Holy shit." I said to myself.

That was my first wave ever in Portugal. I took a deep breath and paddled back out.

"Well… now let's surf… just not there again." I said to myself.

I stayed out surfing for the better part of that morning, having tons of fun on my new, easy to ride, shorty egg.

Portugal is a simple place. Everything there is easier and has a refined beauty. The people, the lifestyle, the fashion, the food, the culture. The longer I live, I feel like my life is heading toward the remote bohemian beach lifestyle. I make sacrifices of having less in order to live in a peaceful, isolated, beautiful place. I got that feeling in Portugal around the coastal surf town areas. The accommodations were not fancy but perfect and cozy. A lot of meals were just bread and cheese, but it was the best-tasting bread and cheese I'd ever had in my life for very little money. The women were gorgeous and stylish in a modest and simple way. Everyone was kind, chill, and patient. I vibed so well with this culture outside of the beaches and surf spots. I started falling in love with it.

The next day, I tried driving down a few hours south to a town called Odeceixe (can't even begin to say correctly in Portuguese) but had some complications. I needed gas as I was leaving Ericeira and was about to get on the highway. I found a petrol station that was self-serve. This was the first time I'd be pumping my own fuel in

Portugal. The first time fueling up was heading towards Nazaré, but there was an attendant who pumped it for me.

I pulled in and waited in line. This gas station was set up to where I pumped first, and all the cars waited in line after to pay at a drive-thru window. I remembered the car rental employee told me to make sure to put *gasoline* in my Euro car not diesel. I got out and there were three pump handles, only one with marked words on it in Portuguese. I took out my translation app and translated what it said on the pump handle.

"Gasolina Simplés," the gas-pump handle read. This translates in English to "plain gasoline." Plain gasoline is exactly what I wanted. In the USA, I would say, "regular," but "plain" seemed to mean the same thing to me. I pulled out the black-handled pump and tried to put it in my tank's fill hole. It didn't quite fit, like the car's fill hole was too small for the pump nozzle. I saw above the hole a green sticker that read "Gasoline Only."

"That's exactly what I'm trying to put in here." I said.

I pushed hard and got the pump nozzle to squeeze into the fill hole. I only had about one-eighth of a tank when I pulled up, so I filled over three-quarters of the tank until full. I put the pump back, sat in line, and paid the attendant. I left and got on the highway toward Odeceixe. I drove for about five minutes, until I began to cruise up a steep hill on the highway and my Euro car started bucking violently. It started softly, then it became harder and harder. A flashing red engine light popped up on the dashboard. My speed was getting less and less, so I quickly pulled onto the shoulder and came to a stop right at an exit on the highway. I kept trying to start the car again and again until the car's engine stopped kicking over.

"Shit. What the hell just happened?" I said to myself.

I called the number on the rental car's key chain and talked to a representative.

"Hey, let me guess, the black-handled gas pump... Is that diesel?" I asked sarcastically.

"Why yes, of course, that is why we put the green gasoline sticker above the gas tank fill hole, so you match the green handle with it. Wasn't it hard for you to fit the diesel pump handle in the gasoline hole? They are different sizes." They informed me.

"Why didn't you explain matching the colors to me when I picked up the car?" I asked them, as this must happen to others, hence the reason for the green sticker in the first place.

"Duhhhhhh." I thought.

My mind wanted to shatter with frustration. I felt, at that moment, like I just bought a one-way ticket to being forced to buy this car. I now owned a broken car in Portugal.

"I guess I'm moving here," I thought.

"Look, I translated 'gasolina simplés' to English and it means 'plain gasoline.'" I told them.

Plain gasoline doesn't mean diesel to anyone (does it?).

"Anyway, can you guys help me? What are my options right now on the side of this road? I paid the full insurance, so I have full coverage." I asked with doubt.

"Full coverage does not cover negligence. Your options are you don't have a car anymore, and we tow away this one that you put the wrong fuel in. Or you pay us €450 to deliver you another replacement car that you also need to pay the €180 of full coverage on." The representative informed me.

In total, it looked like €630 for breaking their car. So much for full coverage. What a scam. I think full coverage is a total scam. They will find ways to force us to pay if they want. Isn't every accident in the world caused by momentary negligence? In that case, a rental car company's full coverage has NEVER covered anyone? It's just an extra fee? It sounds like a scam to me. I'm looking into using car rental insurance that supposedly comes free with certain credit cards, currently in my wallet right now. So I can stop paying these extra money-grabbing fees.

With conversion rates, €630 was about $725 at the time. Plus, the full tank of diesel gas, another hundred bucks wasted. I was all in around $825 for this stupid mistake.

"Yes, I guess I have no choice. I need the replacement car, so please send it ASAP as I am literally waiting here outside on the side of the highway." I said to the car rental man.

After I hung-up, I panicked that the car was dirty inside — another way for them to charge me more. I quickly packed up everything I had back in my bags and pulled any trash, dirt, sand, or food out and packed into one bag I'd take with me.

I made the car look pretty good on the inside. After practically living in it for days, I had my things packed up and ready to move over into the new ride. I walked past the exit ramp and peed in these tall bushes against a fence separating the highway. About forty-five minutes later, the tow truck showed up. In two minutes, he had swapped the tiny new Euro car off the flatbed truck and put the one I broke on. I signed one piece of paper, he tossed me the keys and laughed at me a little bit, then took off.

"Not bad!" I said.

In an hour and fifteen minutes, I had a new car.

"Even though I spent a ton of money on a stupid mistake that should have been free because I already paid for full coverage..." I thought about it more, totally annoyed.

Once again, I was mobile. I tossed my board and bag into the car and took off south again. After a few hours, I made it down to Odeceixe where I tried checking into my new accommodation – a tiny home in someone's backyard. I called, knocked, and there was no answer. After a little while, I started to think I was at the wrong address, knocking on the wrong door. I thought the neighbors on the street were going to become suspicious of me. Finally, I got through on the phone with the host. She was out, so she was going to send her 94-year-old mother to check me in. This tiny old woman opened the front door and told me to follow her into the house. She showed me around to the backyard where the tiny house was. She spoke great broken English. She was quick on her feet and agile walking up the tiny house's wood stairs, showing me the bedroom. I couldn't believe this woman was in the best health I'd ever seen a person of that age. It was adorable. Night was coming, and I figured I would just get dinner, pass out early, and have a long surf day the following day.

I couldn't get to the beach soon enough. I'd heard that the southern Algarve region of Portugal was where it was at! Supposedly, it was a warmer, drier climate with some great surf. I did some research and talked to a couple of locals. I decided I would drive to Praia da Arrifana. Arrifana is a crescent-shaped cove that's lined by tall cliffs protecting the waves from shitty northwest winds. It was mostly a beach break, but with a few boulder areas that offered a point break as well.

I arrived after a half-hour of driving. I took a curvy street to the cliff tops, passing a few Euro-style cafés with a ton of Euro-style people everywhere, mostly hanging around their campervans. I parked my tiny Euro car. I walked over to the cliff edge and checked the surf far below. There were some great lines down there, but the break was unbelievably packed. There were so many surfers and beginners out that the ocean looked like surfer soup. It was so packed that it made my memory of Malibu seem empty.

I noticed that there was a nice lefthander breaking into the cliffs and no one was riding it. It was easy to see from the hundred-foot-high cliff. I found my spot! It was probably sketchy with rocks or shallow reef, but I figured it was a great place to start. I changed into my wetsuit without a towel outside next to my car. I got completely naked and squirreled into the elastic wetsuit until I quickly pulled it up over my crotch before anyone walked over and saw. I needed a changing towel. Then, I waxed my board and started the insanely long walk down the very steep hill that felt like forever to the beach.

XVI-Surfer soup. Eyes on my empty left. Crowded Arrifana, Portugal. 35MM

I walked down the super windy, steep, mountain road barefoot with my 5'10" egg under my arm. I passed a bunch of Euro camper vans parked on the side of the street and walked farther and farther down. Europeans have a funny take on the surfing lifestyle. It was seemingly more important for them to visually identify with the surf lifestyle than necessarily be good at surfing. Most Americans are not as visually loud. Of course, in any surf town in California, surfers look like surfers, but Europeans look like they spend lots of money on their clothes, vans, boards, travel bags, sunglasses, hairstyles, and everything they can to identify with surf culture. I'm used to people that just surf, so it was a funny experience and made me smile as I passed by.

I finally reached the beach and walked to the right toward the cliff that I parked my car above. I saw the lefthander breaking and paddled out to it. I was all alone. There were hundreds of people in the water about half of a football field away and beyond, but no one was close to my spot. I waited. After a few minutes, my wave offering a lefthander came, and I caught it. It was about shoulder to head-high, semi-fast, and walled up nicely. I caught it and rode the shoulder of the wave for a while, pumping up and down facing the wave on my frontside. I finally saw a rock sticking up out of the water right in front of me as the wave sucked the water back, and I jumped backward off the wave into deeper water avoiding it.

"That's why there's no one over here..." I thought.

I had no problem after knowing where the rock was. I still had quite a bit of real estate between the peak of the wave and the rock, so I paddled back for another and another and another. After about a dozen rides, I started drawing attention from the closest pack of surfers who paddled over to ruin my solo session. Sure enough, a handful of them started catching the wave I found, and I caught less and less until it was too much, and I got out. It was a killer session regardless, and I scored harder than anyone else in the huge crowd! I walked back up the steep hill the same way I walked down, only it was much harder on the walk up after the surf session. I managed to get away with getting naked for the second time, taking my wetsuit off next to my car. I really needed to get a towel for changing...

The next morning, I awoke in my backyard-tiny house and did not have another accommodation booked for that night yet. I was thinking of what to do as I liked the Arrifana vibe. Ericeira was super cool, but sometimes too much, and besides the Arrifana surf town, the area I was in was more calm, empty, and more Portuguese, which was awesome! Also, the warmer, desert surroundings and climate were super nice compared to up north, so I kinda' wanted to stay.

I got up out of the second-story bed in the tiny house, overlooking the cute, little backyard, and packed up my things back into my rucksack. I walked down the circular staircase to the kitchen and tried making myself some eggs and coffee while trying to decide what to do for the day and where to spend the night. There were no pans in the kitchen anywhere, so I took six eggs out of the carton, cracked them open into a bowl, and put the bowl in the microwave while my coffee water boiled.

After doing some research, I wanted to check out another beach south called Praia do Amado. From the map, surf apps, and forums, Amado looked like it had great surf. It was also protected from the strong winds from the north with big outcropping cliffs and tapering coastlines, like Arrifana. I choked down my gross microwaved bowl of plastic-tasting eggs that I had to scrape out with a fork, put my bag in the car, and took off south for Amado beach.

As I left Odeceixe and got on the main road, I saw a Eucalyptus grove and smelled it in the air. I have this ongoing mental checklist in my head whenever I see Eucalyptus trees in the wild, like back in Bolinas, because they are so foreign to me as I grew up in a suburb of New Jersey where nothing like that existed. It was so exotic to me. I notice that Eucalyptus trees only grow in places that I find to be extremely beautiful, special places in the world, too. I have kept a tally in my head whenever I saw them at the coast in northern California, in Hawai'i or Australia. I was passing a grove of them where I was in southern Portugal. Still holding true to my belief that they only grow in beautiful places that I find special. They are evidence that I am on the right path, in or around something epic.

I drove for almost an hour and decided to pull off and check a spot just before the cliff outcropping that protects Amado beach, meaning here would be completely exposed to wind and swell. It was an easy turn-off, so I took it just to check. The beach was called Carrapateira. This place was incredibly exposed, had very large waves and was extremely wind-blown to shit. There was one sole kite surfer out, flying around. The ocean was angry and hectic. Carrapateira was beautiful if I could ignore the constant oppressive wind. I had parked on top of the cliffs to the south of the beach, and there was nothing around besides a few other travelers in vehicles and an open desert. I parked and walked north to see the beach better from above. There was a wood walkway that led all the way down the beach around the open desert dunes, but I had no reason to walk all the way down as the surf looked *no bueno* from where I was standing. I ran into the desert behind a bush, took a pee, then took off south to Amado, just a few minutes away.

I drove on some crummy road to a dirt parking lot with a bunch of Euro vans and people chilling. I saw camper vans day camping with wetsuits hanging off their rearview mirrors, drying in the sun. I figured I had arrived. I parked and walked by a few little van camps, one with a European girl changing out of her wetsuit without a care in the world that she was topless for the world to see. I love Portugal.

I kept walking while trying to be polite and not to stare with my American eyes and made it to the cliff edge to check the surf. Holy... Shit... It was good. It was reallyyyyyy good. The beach had a few different working breaks. I was staring at one right out in front of me on the cliff below. A rad lefthand point break off its rock reef. I looked down and a guy was sitting on the rocks holding his head and had watered-down blood all over him. There were a few people attending to him and holding his board. There wasn't much sand exposed on the beach, as the tide was reaching high, almost making it up the beach to the big rocks the bloody man was sitting on. It was a little daunting to see that at a new spot, before a surf, with some stronger waves. I figured there were so many beginners here, he probably just had a beginner mistake, causing the injury. I went back to my Euro car to put my wetsuit on. I got in my car and closed the door, pushing the driver seat all the way back as far as it went to give me room to get naked because I still had no changing towel! I claustrophobically got it on, waxed my board, and took off for that lefthander in mind.

I surfed for a while, catching a bunch of high tide lefts that were breaking closer and closer to the beach. It was unnervingly shallow, so I eventually got out. I caught ten big drops that were overhead by a couple of feet. It was fun, but it took some serious duck-diving as the swell was nothing to laugh at. The view from the surfer's perspective was amazing. Desert cliffs turn to sandy beach with nothing around AT ALL. Peaceful!

I got out and dried off with some clean T-shirts from my bag acting as towels and quickly flew out of my wetsuit and into my short Wrangler cut-offs. I put my warm thermal long-sleeve shirt on and walked around the cliffs after slamming a protein shake. It was such a treat to be somewhere that was not developed or commercialized. Too many places of beauty in the world are being destroyed; another reason to leave the American bubble that I know...

I drove back north later in the day with no plan for where to spend the night. I did have, in the back of my mind, a contingency plan to car camp in the compact Euro hatchback. I wanted to camp at least one night to save accommodation costs, and I thought maybe tonight's the night.

I felt like I knew Odeceixe well after walking the streets and getting dinner there the night before. I went back, searching for dinner again. I looked around the small but compact little village that had a tiny downtown. I found an ALL-YOU-CAN-EAT-SUSHI restaurant and, of course, I had to try. I ate the amount of food for three men for €14.99. I had difficulty breathing afterwards because my stomach was so full that it wasn't allowing my lungs to expand very far... But it was so worth it!

After dark, I decided to try to sleep in my car along the river at the base of town, maybe a couple of blocks from the busier streets with stores and restaurants on them. Those busier winding streets all spat out down the hill to this quiet street next to a park with a river, and distant view of the ocean. I pulled up and parked near a few other camper vans that were clearly doing the same thing. I got out and situated the seats for maximum sleeping room, which in the tiny Euro car, was not enough. I pushed the front seats forward, folded the back seats down, took out some clothes from my rucksack and laid them around me. I made a little nest out of them trying to create a buffer from the hard plastic on the back of the seats that was now my mattress. I brushed my teeth, spit in the grass on the side of the road, and hopped in the back, closing and locking the doors after me. It wasn't too bad, a bit uncomfortable, but with a free price tag, it was doable. I peed in an empty water bottle, screwed the cap on tight, and tossed it on the floor. A true dirtbag.

I eventually passed out after putting in my earplugs. There were some people walking the river path talking that I wanted to drown out, so after putting in my foam earplugs, I was much better. I dozed off for a while in an uncomfortable C-shaped position.

POLICE SIREN NOISE!! POLICE FLASHING LIGHTS right behind my car in the street. I was startled awake suddenly with adrenaline and fear. My heart was racing, my mind was planning what I would say or wondering what they would say, still in a half-asleep state. I stayed low in the car. I was lying much below the windows, and I didn't sit up to give myself away. I thought I would let them come over to the car to see me. I looked at my phone and it was 12:30 a.m. I tried to extinguish the cell phone light the best I could. They started talking through their megaphone from the police car, but in Portuguese, so I understood nothing they said. I stayed laying there, silent, and motionless. I looked around and noticed that because of the nighttime temperature drop, my windows were completely fogged up. This was a dead giveaway that someone was inside breathing hot air. Still, I didn't give myself up. I just laid there. I figured I would make them come over and knock on my window. I decided I would play dead, because heavy sleeping with earplugs in was not a crime if I recalled correctly. I couldn't get in more trouble for being a heavy sleeper, right? I didn't move.

I couldn't believe it, but after another minute of panic and holding my breath, they drove off! Success! I won the standoff! I started doubting if they were even there for me, but I figured so. I had read and talked to other travelers about how the police are cracking down on people sleeping in their cars instead of paying for accommodations. Especially in the warmer southern climate of the country where more tourists visited.

"Well, if they're gone, I might as well stay here and go back to sleep." I thought.

I tried to find a better position while angled diagonally in the hatchback with my knees bent to fit. I dozed off after my heart calmed.

MORE SIRENS GOING OFF! POLICE LIGHTS BEHIND MY CAR AGAIN! I WAS STARTLED AWAKE! I checked my phone, trying to smother the phone's light in my car's interior. 2:15 a.m.

"Shit," I whispered. "They got me for sure this time. Maybe the first time was a warning, and this time I go to jail…That must have been what they said on the megaphone before…" I thought with bad, nervous butterflies in my gut.

I still didn't move. I stayed laying still, motionless, with the same plan as before. If they came over to the car and knocked, I would get up, but if they didn't, I wasn't moving. I heard the policemen talking to each other in Portuguese, but again, I could not understand any of it. After an even longer time with high anxiety, trying to barely breathe, they took off. I started wondering if they were only there to deter me and were just messing with the campers. Either way, I went back to sleep. I awoke one or two more times that night from flashing lights driving by, but they didn't stop again, and they never knocked. I have been in my camper van/truck/car in the USA, where police have knocked and forced me to move before, but it seemed like maybe in Portugal they don't do that. They still won the war because I slept like crap and wouldn't sleep there again. I am smarter than that, too, but I was lazy and was looking for a place to sleep in the car after it was already dark and didn't have a good lay of the land. Rookie mistake. Next time, more planning would be necessary to park somewhere in open nature with no one around outside of town before dark.

I was up early before the sun the next morning. I took off north again and booked an accommodation while driving for Ribamar, a village just north of Ericeira. This was a four-hour drive from the south Algarve region where I had car camped. I was driving back to get a taste of The World Surfing Reserve.

The World Surfing Reserve is a badass organization meant to preserve outstanding surf zones around the world and their surrounding areas, never be destroyed or changed. They have protected surf breaks in Portugal, Mexico, California, Australia, Chile, Peru, Costa Rica, Brazil, and more. This proves that some of the waves I was surfing were some of the best waves in the world. It was extremely cool to see energy spent to protect something that I consider beautiful and naturally amazing.

As I drove back, I noticed a man or shepherd chasing a herd of running sheep across an overpass as I drove under it. I laughed hysterically. It looked like he was not herding them but chasing after them as if running in the wrong direction. There was one black sheep in the pack. He was my favorite and the only single one I noticed. I loved how Portugal's life was so much calmer and more old-world like that. I have never seen anything like it in the USA. I drove up to the top of the Ribamar hills where the windmills were. My small rental house was at the top. I pulled in, spoke with the host, and got my keys. I took a nap to help my lack-of-sleep brain for an hour, then took off for a spot check. On the way, I got some café sandwiches and espresso. Classic.

When I arrived in Portugal, I never had an espresso in my entire life. I had plenty of Americanos, a watered-down espresso, as a European would say, but never a straight-up espresso. I have become a

181

bit of a coffee connoisseur in my more recent years. I don't drink alcohol, smoke, or take drugs anymore, so coffee is my only real vice, and I embrace it strongly. I lived in San Francisco for years and eventually built a healthy coffee shop habit. I would buy bags of coffee beans from the shops and make amazing coffee at home. My favorite being from Ethiopia and a few other African countries. It tastes wildly different, more acidic, fruitier, thinner, and more complex. I love it.

At my family's hotel, where I worked the last three summers, I roasted my own African beans DIY-style out of an old 1980s popcorn popper. I bought beans from Ethiopia, Kenya, Burundi, or even Sumatra. I would buy unroasted, green coffee beans, wholesale, from a distributor who got them from the farms that grew and dried them. I would get pounds of the coffee beans delivered to my house and roast my own. I wasn't great at it, especially with my DIY caveman setup, but it sure beat paying over $20 per bag when I would blow through that bag in a few days! I cut the cost by about seventy-five percent!

When I arrived in Portugal and tried ordering a coffee, they just stared at me with a confused look.

"Oh, you're American. Do you want an Americano?" They would ask, which was a bit degrading.

They were pretty much asking, "Oh, you want us to water this down for your weak American palate?" Being the traveler I am, I tried to be more of a local in new places, and I started drinking espresso like the locals did. I noticed that it was a completely different experience! I took tiny sips instead of big sips, and the flavor was so strong and intense. But once I got used to it, regular coffee was weak and boring. Some Portuguese people will walk into a café, order an espresso, shoot it like a tequila shot at the bar, pay, and leave ten seconds later, never sitting down. It was crazy. I always preferred to slowly enjoy my coffee whatever time of day I was drinking it, but some Portuguese treat it a little differently. I was used to having my coffee to-go, exclusively, in a reusable or disposable/recyclable/compostable cup, and there, this didn't really exist. Or they gave it to me in a dixie cup, which was disappointing and wasn't fun to drink from. I started having my coffee in the café, like the rest of the townspeople, and engaging in the conversion there more, too!

I did not surf the rest of that day, I just checked a few spots and got dinner. My brain and body were too worn out from the police the night before and being cramped in the car. I ate and rested that night getting ready for a long surf day the next morning.

I awoke feeling revitalized! I was ready for anything! I made some breakfast and coffee and took off to spot check around Ribamar and Ericeira. I was so excited to see what a giant 7.5' @ 18 seconds swell was doing to these amazing breaks.

I drove past the break called Matadouro, the first break I surfed in Portugal, where I almost hit that boulder and flew through the air. I checked it on the ocean road and could not believe the size of the waves coming in. They were towering. Massive. No one was out. It was hard to tell just how big it was with no reference of anyone surfing it, but the faces were beyond double, more like triple overhead. And relentless. Stacks of set waves coming in one behind another with their lips pinned open by the strong offshore wind.

"Gulp." I said, with doubt.

I drove north to Praia De Ribeira D'ilhas (impossible for me to say like the Portuguese) and parked in the dirt parking lot, which was crazy packed compared to other days I had been there. I wondered why so many people were here.

"Everyone is here surfing this huge swell?" I questioned why I was so wimpy if this was true.

I walked out and saw tents and heard commentators on loudspeakers. I saw WSL (World Surf League) posted everywhere.

"Ohhhhh, that makes sense. There's a pro surf contest on this crazy big swell." I understood.

People were everywhere – all over the beach and lining the cliff tops above. I walked up the cliff and went for a walk on the dirt trail. I saw these unbelievable sets coming in from the high vantage point, and the slab reef created a super long righthand point break connecting all the different sections that were thick, slower, steeper, more pitchy/ hollow, and faster on the inside. It was currently the women's pro surf league contest.

I don't really follow the WSL, so I wasn't sure who was there, but I watched for a while. Anyhow, the swell was keeping me out of the water, I guess… It was so big the competition had multiple jet skis out there for the surfer's safety, and during the time I was watching, one girl had to be helped with a jet ski and another girl got swept up onto the rocks on shore and guys from the audience on the beach ran over and saved her. She was all bloody, but ok after they helped get her out. It was a big day to say the least.

I was walking back to my car after the contest was over and struck up a conversation with a Portuguese girl who was with her son sitting on a hippie blanket watching the contest. They were cool, and we talked about everything under the sun and life itself. It was a spontaneous, deep, great conversation. I hung out for a bit, then left for a café lunch and to spot check other breaks nearby. I checked the surf at the other local World Surfing Reserve spots and was totally blown away. I checked spots like the righthander Coxos, Pedra Branca's left, Reef's right, and Cave's right. All legendary waves. I shot some photos and watched the sunset on the cliffs at Pedra Branca, my favorite cliff hangout spot, down the dirt road. I found an urchin skeleton on Pedra Branca's beach below that was beautiful! Score! That night, I hung out on my back patio staring up at the stars for a few hours. Since I was on top of the hill with no city lights close by, the stars were incredibly bright. I saw bits of the Milky Way while enjoying the quiet, calm night.

I awoke the next day and drove up to Péniche. It was a weekend, and the accommodations always got more expensive in Ericeira on the weekends, so I booked a place in Balial, near Péniche for two nights. This was far less expensive, so I saved some money. I then tried to find some smaller surf around.

I have surfed double-overhead conditions in places around the world before, but I had also surfed those breaks first when they were smaller. It was super intimidating to paddle out to a new spot that I knew nothing about when it was that large. I wouldn't know where to paddle out from, where the currents were, or where the shallow reefs or boulders were hiding. I figured with this large swell around, some of the spots near Baleal would be fun as some of the waves there were gentler. And I had already surfed it when it was smaller. Also, I thought that Supertubos, the famous barreling beach break, would be amazing just for spectating!

I drove up there from Ericeira and checked into my affordable, hip hotel/surf hostel that was €40 per night. I spoke for a while with the owner, who was a traveler himself. He was a Portuguese man, maybe a little older than me. Once he found out I was American, he told me about his travels in Brazil and USA. The hotel was empty besides one other guest who was a surfer from the Netherlands. I talked to him for a while in the communal kitchen. He told me how he was designing a surf app for the surfers up there in Netherlands who rely on crappy wind swells for waves. The swells were super inconsistent, so he wanted to connect people together to rate the surf every day to try to better forecast the wind swells that occasionally offer decent surf, which as of now was difficult to forecast properly. Wind is a fickle, always-changing aspect of weather. It's amazing what ideas some people come up with!

I had a surf in Baleal that was bigger but good fun. I found a lefthander that would T-bone me straight into a huge, exposed boulder, and I had to pull out of the wave last minute to avoid smashing it. This is clearly a constant theme in my surfing. This was a ton of fun, so of course I kept riding it over and over. Afterward, I checked Supertubos which was firing. The wave was a hollow overhead barrel, absolutely firing in just a few feet of water above the sand bottom below. I was watching dudes getting barreled and absolutely destroyed by it, depending on the surfer. It was great. Occasionally, someone would successfully fly out of the barrel.

The next day, I decided to try a different inland town, when the rates were more expensive at the beach. I heard that there was this town between Lisbon and Ericeira that was holding an event that let a bunch of bulls run free in the streets, like in Spain. I thought this would be a wild event to experience, even though I have always been on the side of animal rights.

I found an accommodation in town that looked decent enough and headed there, stopping in Ericeira first for lunch. Once I arrived, I realized that my accommodation wasn't private but a shared room in an apartment that was on the main festive street. The entire town was raging and would be partying hard all night. Also, the place was a dump, so I bailed for the sake of my peaceful sleep and found another accommodation outside that town, just a twenty-minute drive away, giving up on seeing the bulls.

I arrived there and hung out for a few hours with the hysterical and sweet married couple who owned the place and were my hosts. We talked in their backyard, and I was told I needed to go to their little downtown and try the Bacalhaus (Ba-ka-lyaw), a traditional-Portuguese whitefish dinner, and they suggested a restaurant that was famous for it. I love these types of spontaneous recommendations, so I totally went. I got there and it was a bit classy, too classy for the likes of me, and apparently, their famous dinner was not meant for only one person. They usually made servings of it large enough for the whole table. It was quite large. I told them that I exercise and surf and would have no problem eating it all, but man, was I wrong. They told me they would make me a special smaller portion than normal, and it still would have fed a family of five (the normal amount I eat).

Bacalhaus is a whitefish the Portuguese salt and submerge in olive oil for a day, then take it out, wash the salt off, and grill it over an open fire. It is served with potatoes. I took my first bite of the fish, and it was the best tasting thing I had practically ever eaten, but bite after bite, the saltiness and heavy oiliness started to get to me. It slowly made me feel nauseous. Eventually, I couldn't put another piece in my mouth. My body started rejecting it, and I would gag when I tried swallowing it. I tried to eat as much as I could because I told the server I was starving, and I didn't want to show disrespect to their local dish they were well known for. Eventually, I said I had to go, and I took the fish and potatoes with me.

I got back to the house and knocked on the front door to the hosts' quarters. The husband answered, and I gave him the box.

"Bacalhaus for you. You said you love it so much, so I brought you some." I said while giving him the plastic bag with the boxed fish.

He freaked out.

"Are you serious!!!!???? You are my favorite guest!!!" He thanked me a ton, and I left to go to bed.

The next morning, I tried cooking eggs, but it seemed no accommodation in Portugal stocked oil in their kitchens, and I kept forgetting to buy it myself, so I cut open a tuna can and used the vegetable oil and tuna juice to cook my eggs. Sometimes you just need to think outside the box and have tuna flavored eggs in the morning! The whole purpose of this adventure was to see the bulls running in the streets, and I missed it when I bailed out of that first dump apartment. I headed back to Péniche, about an hour drive.

Ericeira's surf was still too big for me and everyone else, and with the WSL at one of the main breaks in town, everything was crowded. I chose to jam back up to Péniche. I arrived and checked into this blue apartment, where every single thing was blue. The walls, tables, bed, floor… it was creepy. I was in Ferrel, a more local town next to Baleal, and was hungry for a surf. I decided to go back to Baleal beach again. It didn't have the best conditions ever, but I paddled out and caught waves around sunset. It's always worth it.

Afterward, I dried off at my car with a towel that I wisely brought from the accommodation to change and dry off with. I drove around Baleal looking for some dinner and found this place with shrimp and salmon burgers. I got one of each! Baleal is a tiny surf town that was kind of attached to Péniche, a bigger surf town, but at the same time completely separate.

There isn't much outside of the three towns, Péniche, Baleal and Ferrel, and it only takes ten minutes to drive from one to the other. It's kind of all the same world, but each town does have a separate vibe. In Baleal/Ferrel, there is mostly surf accommodations, restaurants, surf shops, and a grocery. Those two towns are down the same road from each other and are both villages compared to Péniche. There's a younger crowd in those towns, it's more affordable and has more surf and bohemian vibes than Péniche, the bigger older city. Baleal/Ferrel, or the outskirts of Péniche, near Supertubos, was better for my surf bum-ness! All offering the chiller vibes.

Over the next few days, I stayed in the blue apartment with tons of flies. I mean tons. They had a fly swatter on the counter for a reason, and man, did I use it. I felt bad, but I left the fly carcasses on the walls and floor to show the host how many there really were by the time I left. Hundreds.

I surfed Supertubos when it was small, maybe waist to shoulder high. Still at this smaller size it was lightning fast and super difficult. Supertubos has the easiest, shortest paddle-out in the world. The wave is only in three feet of water, maybe even less, so the paddle to reach that depth is around three paddles. Maybe zero paddles to get into position. It's walkable. I did manage to catch a bunch of super fun lefthanders, but they were all breaking in such shallow water and were so fast that if I wasn't in the perfect possible drop in position, I missed the wave. Being off by a split second meant I missed it. The ones I did catch were super fun even though the ride was short.

The next day, I drove up to Nazaré for a second time. I knew the lay of the land from the first time I was there and drove straight to the surf at Nazaré Norte Beach, the beach break just north of the big wave spot. I was willing to surf it because the swell up there was only 2'. I figured that was my chance to paddle out at the famous beach break. When I was here earlier in my trip, there was a 6' swell and the beach break was too big for me. Terrifying.

Nazaré Norte's beach breaks are about as exposed as it gets. I parked on the small cliff before the beach and walked down with my board on the long sand beach. I watched it for a while and decided it was in my wheelhouse. I paddled straight out and there were a handful of guys in the lineup, but the break was still empty as there were many different peaks along the beach. I was confident that, based on the report it was small, but it wasn't. A few A-frame peaks came firing through and I felt the energy of this place, even on a tiny day. The faces of the waves were overhead by a few feet. So much for 2'... I paddled a bit deeper as I was a little afraid of bigger ones dumping on me, and I tried to get used to the size. After I sat around for a few minutes out there I saw one with my name on it.

"Oh, hell yea," I said and took the left off the peak.

It walled up vertically so fast. Perfect for a shortboard. I made a big carving cutback-turn and came back up the face, pumping and riding ecstatically as it shrank in size before it petered out. My adrenaline was pumping, my heart was racing, and I had the biggest smile on my face. My first wave in Nazaré. I paddled back out, duck diving a few waves that dumped on me, and caught a few more. I was still super nervous, so after a few more rides, I got out and chilled on the beach for a while.

I don't have tons of experience in bigger, heavy surf like that, so I caught rides for my bucket list and got out before I got destroyed. I surprisingly surfed it well, but I didn't stick around long enough for something sketchy to happen. I have more experience on shortboards in bigger surf now, and at the time I was being tested, but I was successful! I put my board back in the car and walked the beach. I walked all the way south to the cliff that the lighthouse sat on in front of the big wave spot. The tide was out, and it exposed all these caves in the cliff side. I walked in and saw muscles growing all over the cave walls and ceiling. The cave must get completely filled with water when the tide was up for mussels to be growing on the ceiling. It must have been fifteen feet high. Crazy. That's a huge tidal difference, lots of water. I peed in the cave and took off. Since I'm in nature all the time, I get to pee in some pretty cool places. I walked back and couldn't help but notice the ten topless girls on the beach. There were tons! This was normal here, confirmed. I headed back to Ferrel and Baleal for some Indian food dinner.

The next day I drove back to Ericeira again. I was pinballing all over Portugal. I chose a coastal route to drive down, as opposed to the inland route. I pulled off onto dirt roads a few times to spot check to the north just outside of Santa Cruz. I saw a totally radical cliff camping spot with nothing around at all and an awesome righthand point break that wasn't receiving enough swell to surf it. I could see the little swell lines in the water, and it looked great. I took a photo of it as a little tugboat was driving by in the background. I think it's my favorite photo I took in Portugal, and there isn't even a surfable wave (it looks surfable but too small in real life)!

XVII-Tugboat right point. My favorite photo in Portugal. 35MM

I stopped at a local watering hole, the Atlantic Café in Santa Cruz off the main road and hung out with the owner who knew me by now as the tattooed American. I made it back, just inland of Ericeira, and I checked into a stone house that a husband and wife built with their own hands over a few years. It was beautiful, rugged, rustic, and real. It looked out to a river and a forest. This was inland a few miles further than I had stayed before. It was in another little compact village near Mafra, fifteen minutes from Ericeira.

After I checked into the stone house, I suited up and drove back to Ericeira to check the surf at Pedra Branca – down the dirt road to the car park and cliff overlook. Pedra Branca is the name of a lefthand point break that's one of the protected spots by The Surf Reserve and the name of the righthand point break wave to the south breaking into the bay.

I looked at that southern righthander and saw its magical wave, peeling all the way to Praia do Matadouro, the next beach to the south.

It was a wave for my backhand given that it was a righthander, but I wanted to give it a shot as it peeled forever. I walked with my board along the long wooden staircase that took me down the cliff to the slab reef and sand beach. I got to the sand and walked south a few seconds and watched someone else paddle out right between two slab pieces of rock jetting up out of the water with a deeper valley in between them. This was exactly where I found my urchin skeleton on the beach and figured they're like cockroaches – if you see one, you know there's more nearby. I got on my board and paddled trying not to touch anything or put my feet down again as I was in spiky urchin territory.

I ducked under a few waves and made it to the lineup with only four other guys out. I let them catch a few sets as I hung out in the lineup and saw one that I was positioned well for. I was up first and riding, but this older Portuguese guy on a shortboard dropped in closer to the peak and came down the line at me forcing me to pull out of the wave, giving him the wave as he was in the higher priority position. I was completely in line with all surfing etiquettes, but after the wave, the guy mean-mugged me (giving me a stink-eye) for the rest of the session. After I caught a few more, I decided to just pad-dle all the way south to Matadouro.

"Congratulations old Portuguese guy, you ruined my session. I couldn't stand your energy for a minute longer. I left for another break. You win. Make sure to do that to everyone who doesn't look Portuguese in and out of the water and see where that gets you in life as I respected you the entire time." (Can you feel my sarcasm?) "And make sure you don't travel elsewhere to surf in your life and be the visitor in someone else's local break where you must act with respect to others who don't know you." I didn't say this, but really wanted to... I mean, there were only four guys out, and he was catching eve-rything he wanted. There was no reason...

The tide was getting low, and I caught a few shallow waves at Matadouro and got out. I now had to walk back about a mile to where I parked along the cliffs at low tide. I walked on uneven slab stone and was afraid of urchins every step.

The next day, I awoke in the stone house and decided to check out a new area I had not been to yet. South of Ericeira, there were a whole bunch of breaks I wanted to check that were new to me. I was skeptical because it was technically getting closer to Lisbon, so I just assumed that meant it would be more crowded the further I went, closer to the city. I drove south and there were a few beaches, where the main road cut inland around, and I could not see them. This bummed me out but eventually the road hugged the coast again and I started spot checking. I didn't necessarily have a spot I needed to surf in mind, I just wanted to get a feel for the surf down along that area and see what it was all about. This is what I do.

After driving a while, I veered off and checked a spot that had some serious size but was unorganized. It was in front of a little strip of nicer restaurants. I continued driving on the beach road, checking the surf from the car, and the road dead ended into a massive cliff face. I turned around and headed back on the main road that took me farther south. That surf wasn't at all what I was after. I was driving only a few minutes more passing a town with cafés and seafood restaurants on this smaller beach, when a firing lefthand point break caught my eye in the background.

"Whaaaaaaaat!!!!!" I screamed!

I brought the car to a screeching halt on the road's shoulder and watched. There were a handful of surfers out and it looked to be about head high with waves breaking nicely off this outcropping cliff on the south side of the beach. The reef in front of the cliff provided sick, fast-peeling grinders (it was a bit aggressive), breaking north into the beach that was set back from the cliff. I was looking at Praia das Maçãs.

Ocean contours fascinate me. The swells here in Portugal come from the west or northwest, building energy across the entire Atlantic Ocean. When the swell energy from that direction gets to this beach in particular, the deeper water in front of the beach is too deep to produce waves. Due to this cliff that jets out into the ocean on the south side of the beach, with its rocky reef, the swell energy jacks up waves nearing the shallow rocks at the cliff point. Starting to break there, the wave energy needs to go somewhere and moves north to the deeper water breaking on the tapering shallow water surrounding the cliff towards the beach. It's magnificent. It's brilliant. The natural engineering of ocean versus land contours behind this natural phenomenon or straight up miracle is incredible.

The street was busy with cars, but it was not a highway. I was freaking out looking for parking. I needed to get rid of this car and run to the surf. It was like a strong magnet pulling me. I had to park farther away in an empty parking lot across some trolly tracks. I put my suit on, waxed my board, and ran. I got to the beach a few minutes later and sure enough, it was still breaking the same.

I stretched for a second after being cramped in the car for an hour, then I padded out. I paddled in the deeper water where the wave mellowed out and ended. This was a classic point break. Paddling around the surf in flat water and not getting in another riders' way when paddling out was the way to go.

I made it to the lineup, and there were only six guys out. Not too bad. I waited for a few sets to come through and man, did they come like a subway train. The energy was strong. The waves were hefty and thick. A little unnerving at first, but after a few minutes, I gained an understanding and started to try to time them and looked for my chance. I was in the right position for a wave, so I took my first ride and ripped down the line on my frontside. The wave's lip was a bit over my head, but I was still in front of it as it was walling up. I was seriously cooking with speed. I rode it for over twenty seconds all the way inside where I initially paddled out from, in front of the beach in the deeper water channel section. After I paddled back out, I counted the time of other surfers' rides and determined mine was at least twenty seconds. It was a long, classic point break.

"Yowwwwwwwww!" I let out a stoked howl.

My heart was racing. I immediately paddled out for more. I let the rotation of guys get theirs, but I caught a few more screamers. When the average waves came in, they broke closer to the boulders much closer to the cliff. When the set wave bombs came in, they were like water avalanches. They broke way outside in the shoulder due to it's the stronger energy, and that was where I waited. Most other guys waited farther on the inside hugging the cliff as it was more consistent there, but I was waiting patiently for the bigger bombs, and every so often, I got one. The wave would slow down, and the white water/broken part of the wave would reform into another long open section of wave on the inside. Looking from the road, I did not see these waves, and it was a different animal altogether. I was out for a few hours and the tide was noticeably changing – getting higher – and the waves weren't producing as well as they were earlier. I caught one more and called it a session. I paddled in and had to correctly time the now big pounding wave on the shore that didn't exist when I paddled out. A Portuguese father in a Euro speedo and his son watched me from the beach in anticipation of disaster, but I navigated successfully and ran out on the sand. This was the definition of impromptu, spontaneous surfing. Wave hunting and scoring!!

I drove back to the stone house on the inland road. I passed a diner-looking café on the side of the road and pulled in. I ordered two shrimp omelets with toast and inhaled both. I was starved. I got back to the stone house and had a chill quiet night's rest.

I awoke the next morning and packed my things to check-out. This accommodation required me to pay a fee per night to help fix the roads in town as a tax, which was something I had never heard of but sounded fair enough, so I paid it with a few €1 coins and took off. I said goodbye to their blind, black Labrador Retriever on the way to my car, such a cutie. I reversed my Euro car through a narrow one lane dirt road between two walls and across a creek bridge for the last time, almost clipping a telephone pole.

Yet again, I drove a different way to the coast heading to Péniche. A few minutes into an hour or longer drive, I saw a café on the neighborhood thoroughfare road and stopped for an espresso and egg and tuna sandwiches. The woman behind the counter was in her sixties. She was missing a few teeth and spoke absolutely zero English. I tried speaking very slowly or pointing at what I wanted, but it did not help. She gestured for me to wait and ran outside grabbing the shirt of this larger tattooed man who was drinking a morning beer with his friend to come in to help translate.

"Hey, what do you want? She can't speak English, but I can a little, I'm from Brazil." He said kindly.

"Thank you!! I just wanted an espresso and a couple of sandwiches if she has them!" I told the large, tan, tattooed Brazilian man.

She started making my food and coffee, and this guy just continued to talk with me the whole time I waited. He was genuinely interested in my trip, where I came from, and where I had been in Portugal. He was a super nice guy. This is something that doesn't generally happen in the USA. People are too standoffish or too busy or too afraid to have a conversation with a stranger. This guy was awesome, so friendly. He gave me directions to the break I was after and

193

wished me a happy trip as I took my food for take away. I attempted to tip her (again with the American trying to tip), and she absolutely refused it as usual. They all knew I was American before trying to tip, so my cover was already blown. I got back in the car and checked the local wave, which had some surf, but I didn't feel the need to paddle out again. I continued back up to Péniche.

I drove straight to Supertubos. I was excited to ride it on another smaller day. It always seemed to have offshore winds. I'm not sure why, but every time I checked there or surfed it, the winds were off-shore. I guess its costal positioning was perfect for the oppressive wind from the north that ruined everywhere else nearby. I arrived and sure as shit, there was an offshore wind, smaller waves, and it was perfect! Normally, I would prefer the surf to be larger, but since Supertubos was a crazy, fast, hollow, barreling beach break I wanted it to be smaller so I could try practicing my timing on it before it was overhead again. Also, when it was small, not many locals surfed it, so the lineup was quite empty. The locals were barrel hunters, and no barrels meant no fun.

I paddled out and caught ten waves. None were barrels, but I had a handful of fast lefts with a few pumps per wave. I paddled out about thirty minutes before the ideal tide and was alone for half an hour. One by one, more and more surfers joined the lineup, even though it was a smaller day. A bunch of the locals were tiny short-boarding men or little young groms (short for grommet, again, is a young wave-hungry, ripping surfer kid) who shred hard on short-boards. This was their break, and they were serious about it. I got out of the water once there were enough of them out there. I changed and ate some tuna pâté and yogurt with granola at the Supertubos bar/restaurant right in front, watching the surf.

I got in the car and drove another hour to Nazaré. I showed up later and tried to check into this cute, hip studio near the cliffs. I walked from where the map told me to park, and realized I was on the cliffs in the north part of Nazaré overlooking the southern flat Nazaré beach to the south (the beach without waves). I was on a cobblestone walking path at the cliff and Google Maps told me the €35/night accommodation was right here. I couldn't believe it. For this location alone, the price should have been hundreds (in the USA). The cobblestone walking path and the view just after it was outrageously breathtaking. Glamorously old-world. I could see so incredibly far into the ocean, and the cliff was so tall compared to the lower half of the city down below.

I called the host to check in, and she told me the keys were hidden behind a brick in the alley wall. I love this kind of shit. I went hunting for the brick in the wall that was loose, found the key behind it, and went inside to check it out.

It was a nice, clean studio with a kitchen. All I needed. I left my bag and went for a walk around the streets in northern Nazaré. I walked the cobblestone cliff path right in front of the accommodation's door and passed the train that transported people up and down the cliff connecting the two parts of town. I wanted to take it so bad, but the sun was setting, and I wanted to walk to the farther cliff near the big wave spot to watch the sunset from there. I got out there and this dreaded hippie man was set up his instruments on one side of the walking path and started playing some music through a tiny amp. He played guitar, didgeridoo, sang, had effects on his guitar, and sounded like a full band by looping his sounds together. They were peaceful sounds in an incredible place to watch a killer sunset.

The next day I awoke after a long rest and had to make some eggs in the microwave again. Damn! I really needed to buy some oil. I went out for better eggs and coffee. I noticed in Portugal that any eggs I bought from any market, convenient store or grocery had the most vibrant, bright, orange-colored yolks I had ever seen. Like a dark setting sun. And they were super cheap! I was so confused and amazed by this as an American. I think all the eggs in the USA are garbage. If I wanted eggs of this quality, I would be spending about a dollar an egg in the USA. Otherwise, for zero-quality, chemically changed, hormonal, nonnutritious eggs, they were still twice the price as Portugal's natural, healthy, beautiful eggs. Please explain this to me, someone.

After I ate, I went to check Praia Do Norte surf, the beach just to the north of Nazaré's big wave that I surfed once, days earlier. This time it was big, too big for me. While I was on the beach, I ran into the mom I'd met a few days earlier on the beach in Ericeira during the WSL women's pro comp. She was just chilling on the beach in Nazaré!

"What are you doing here!?" We both screamed at each other.

She was listening to Jimi Hendrix's "Machine Gun" on her little speaker.

"Hell yeaaaaa!" I responded to hearing my favorite Jimi song.

We talked for a while and planned to meet at sunset later that night on the cliffs where I was the night before. I recommended it, and she said had never been there before.

The bummer about traveling to Nazaré to surf is once I commit to driving there, it's kind of the only wave in town. The main huge Nazaré beach to the south of the big wave is always flat, and it's about another hour drive to Figueira Da Foz, a right point break. There probably was something to surf in between, I'm sure, but the coastline was uneventful, and it would be just as exposed as Praia Norte in Nazaré to swell and wind. If it was too big or bad conditions, that was kind of all there was. I pigeonholed myself in this predicament, so I didn't surf that day. Basically, the rest of Portugal south of Nazaré or much farther north, has so many more options of breaks that face different directions. This gives loads of options to surf in different wind and swell conditions.

Sunset came, and I met my friend from the beach at the cliff as we planned. Even though she was the Portuguese local between us, I showed her the Nazaré-big-wave-sunset-cliff-spot above the lighthouse. We hung out on a rock around a bunch of other sunset seekers and listened to the dreaded hippie man play his music again as it was his regular sunset tradition.

As we stared west into the bright, red, melting sun plummeting into the ocean with a purple explosion in the sky above, I heard the hippie man speaking in his song.

"Look behind you, a rainbow." I heard him say through his reverberated effects.

He said it so mellifluously, that the words blended into his song. I thought they were lyrics and so did all the others on the cliff watching the sunset if they were listening and could understand English. Just because, I decided to turn around and look at the sky behind me. There was a massive, vibrant, popping rainbow completely over the other side of the sky. Both sides of its arch jetting out from the land in a full-blown perfect shape. Hiding behind us in plain sight. I couldn't believe my eyes. I told my friend to look, her mouth dropped wide open, and we began snapping our necks back and forth and back and forth 180-degrees as these two beautifully intense and rare events were happening all around us!

Also, let's not forget, we were sitting on top of a rock on a sheer cliff in a place with the largest recorded waves ever surfed. Our bodies and minds were picking up the extraordinary energy of this extreme place. We were all on the same wavelength. We were one with Mother Nature. We could not fully process the site. We were trying to input the beauty into our brains, but our brains were fried and eventually gave up trying. We just stared. It was too much beauty. I have never felt THAT much beauty before. Then, the sun ducked below the ocean's horizon line, and it was over. Both spectacles disappeared in an instant. Forever. Like performance art. Never to be seen exactly the same again.

My mantra, "Fill Your Stoked Tank," is a way for me to inquire about my own or others' true happiness levels in a fun, non-prying way. I refer to my Stoked Tank being empty or full to express if I am feeling mentally healthy and happy or not. If my Stoked Tank is empty, I can be a flight risk wherever I am. At any moment, I could throw in the towel, hop on a plane, and be somewhere else doing something I love that brings back my inner child, my stoked energy, and my happiness. Or there are times like this. On a hundred-foot cliff in Nazaré, Portugal, watching a sunset-rainbow. Who even thought that was possible!? These were the moments my Stoked Tank had a serious refueling to the point of overflowing. These are the moments in which life is worth living and worth searching for. I couldn't feel more bliss than bliss. This is my religion. This is my spirituality. This is larger than me. I could see it, and I could appreciate it to its fullest. IT MADE ME WHOLE.

As we were walking back to my friend's car through town, I stopped and bought a coin wallet from a local vender woman. It was made of cork. It was €3. It felt relevant as Portugal has the largest cork forest in the world. When we started walking again, we heard this eerie music that sounded like some sort of crazy organ, Nick Cave style, that someone was playing through a window on the third story above.

We asked an outdoor restaurant waitress if she knew who was playing that music. I really wanted to know what it was since I am a musician myself and have never heard this type of spooky yet soothing melodies before.

"Oh, yea that's my cousin. He does that every night, sometimes until late. His front door is over there. Ring the bell and ask him yourself." The waitress said to us.

We were so excited to have a random adventure finding out about this unique sounding music! We walked the dimly lit, cobblestone path to the door she pointed to and rang the bell in anticipation. We waited. We waited and waited.

"Should we ring it again??" We were deciding.

We rang it again and again and again and again. He never stopped playing or answered the intercom or came down to open his door. I felt horrible if he was in the musician's zone and we were interrupting, I just really wanted to tell him he was awesome and ask what it was he was playing. He remained a mystery. My mom friend drove home, and I walked the dark cobblestone cliffside path back to my studio and passed out.

I drove back to Ericeira the following morning. After being in Portugal for almost a month, my trip was beginning to come to an end. I had less than a week left, and I hadn't surfed Ericeira as much as I wanted to. I booked a back guesthouse at the woman's property that I kept returning to in Ribamar De Cima. The place where I could see São Lourenço surf break from the front yard. I never surfed that consistent right point break while I was there, but many mornings I watched it break until I left the house.

I needed to surf Ribeira De Ilhas before I left Portugal. By this time, the WSL competition was over, and the swell was no longer the biggest thing I had ever seen. With the swell a manageable size and a relatively emptier break (it's never empty there), I paddled out. There were a few different peaks there. The wave the WSL competes on is the classic long right. It is all under slab reef, but when walking on the beach towards the ocean, if I hugged the cliffs to the right and paddled out past the beginner classes, there was another break behind there. This section offered rights and lefts depending on where I was positioned. I paddled out and surfed right in front of the cliffs, adjacent to the beach.

This spot was overcrowded and sketchy with beginner kooks (people that have no idea what they were doing) in the water everywhere. Every wave I surfed I was dropped in on by someone that wasn't even looking and had no idea I was about to slam into them. Wipeouts constantly. Or kooks hitting other kooks. I was scared of the other surfers around and tried finding peaks farther away that were emptier, but it was so crowded. I did manage to get a few righthanders and a few lefthanders in this area but no long, contest-style wave.

"Ok, I've officially surfed here at this 'famous spot.' Now I'm getting the hell out of here before my board gets a ding or worse." I told myself.

I paddled in and walked back to my car deep in the dirt lot. Situations like these in surfing honestly are a bummer. But the smart surfer usually tries to avoid spots with the crowds. I was merely trying to check a box by paddling out to the contest wave.

That night, I looked up the best seafood spots around. I found a place that a Portuguese surfer had referred me to on the main road super close to Coxos surf break in Ribamar. I walked into the seafood restaurant across the street from the ocean. I met the son of the owners, who was excited I was American and a surfer. I asked what he recommended, and I went with his suggestion, a seafood platter. All of it was fresh from the sea across the street. When he put it on the table in front of me, my eyes grew large. I had never seen anything like it. It consisted of a whole fancy cup of large shrimp with tails, oysters, mussels, clams, a seared raw tuna steak thinly sliced, sashimi style, crab pâté with ground up crab meat in an upside-down huge crab shell with dipping toast, crab legs, and a famous local Portuguese barnacle called Percebes. Gordon Ramsay himself filmed a segment of his show harvesting these barnacles with a local Portuguese forager across the street in the ocean. The owner's son showed me the video where Gordon Ramsay was in the ocean with the local but was terrified of the waves smashing him on the rocks, so he hid on the rocks while the bad ass local free dove down and cut the barnacles off the rocks underwater with his knife. It was awesome. I had to ask how to eat it because it didn't exactly look like food to me. It looked more like fantastic dragon toes.

He showed me how to hold the claw-looking part and suck the inside slippery, chewy, meat into your mouth from this sheath tube that surrounded it. It looked like the finger-sized sheath tube was made from a crazy material, like fictitious medieval, chain mail, dragon armor or something. Impenetrable by the blade of a sword, from a medieval time. All of it was dragon-esque. Either way, it was delicious. I love oysters and anything with an ocean brine or saltiness, and this had the same essence but with a different experience. This meal was also about one-third to one-fourth of the price it would be in the USA, too. I couldn't believe it. I was in seafood heaven.

I was leaving in four days! I was getting upset that my trip would be over soon, but I was going to try to sell my board before I left. Of course, I wanted to surf until the last possible minute, but I figured I would put it up for sale on the internet and see if anyone would be interested in it a few days in advance. I did all the picture taking and descriptions and posted it. I would love to have kept it, but the airlines going between the USA and Europe make it so damn difficult to check a board bag. It's $250-$500 EACH WAY, depending on the airline. That's the same price of the board or more! I can't justify bringing it back for that!

I had no clean clothes left, so it was time to do some laundry, Dave style. I didn't know of a laundromat in town, nor did I care to pay or look for one, so I did my own laundry... In the shower. This is a cheap traveler trick. I wore my dirty clothes in the shower and washed as though I was naked, then took my clothes off and wrung the soap out of them and hung them to dry. Voilà, they were clean. I brought all my dirty clothes in with me and threw soap on everything. This worked quite well, too. Especially when I used my grape-stomping method to lather up my pile of dirty clothes on the floor of the shower with soap, like I'm crushing grapes for wine on a vineyard. So cultural and classy, right? After they were all washed, I hung them to dry outside somewhere, or I'd hang a line myself. Now after one shower and an afternoon drying in the sun, I'd have clean clothes again, for free and without wasting much time or leaving the house. It was like magic. Poof.

<<<<<◇<<<◇<<<<<<◇<<◇>>>

The next day, I booked two nights in a questionable cabin that looked like it was in the hills southeast of Péniche by about thirty minutes. I rolled the dice. I love cabins. I've attempted to own one before but failed, and I really wanted a cabin experience in Portugal. At the same time, I found one that was not too far of a drive from surf, and it was dirt cheap. The first red flag was that this place was called something like "The Magic Cabin." Usually when cabins are extraordinarily cheap and look the way this one did on the internet, there was something suspect about it. Every single accommodation I

200

stayed at in Portugal was solid, until this point, so I let my imagination or lucky streak take hold that this cabin would be rad.

The mountain cabin was all wood and stilted off the ground. It had beautiful views of a village in the distance below, and it was surrounded by trees and seemed cute. The red flags were in its booking photos. It showed a hippie tie-dye, thin, beach blanket hanging on the wall like it was a tapestry, and there was a very large speaker in the corner of this one-room wood cabin. It gave off a vibe of the type of hippie who "drank the Kool-aid." I am not against this culture of folks by any means, I just have a slightly different lifestyle. I have lived in areas where we existed in the same place in the past. I booked it anyway. It was like $35 per night, which was a steal, and I figured I could enjoy nature.

On my way north out of Ericeira, I decided to surf Ribeira De Ilhas, the "famous pro contest spot" one more time. I parked at the break and once again, it was a shit show with tons of surfers everywhere. Most were insane beginner kooks. I got to the beach and looked at the crowded water with no one surfing between sets. This was seriously like a trip to the mall, and hell with the mall. I hated being in places like that. But I was there, so I paddled out. I caught one taller, steep, short left and had to weave in and out through kooks.

"Screw this. I'm done. I'm going back to Péniche." I thought to myself, frustrated.

I couldn't take it. I got into my Euro car and headed north an hour back to Péniche. This time I was after something more specific. Supertubos was a lot of fun, but it wasn't really my wave if there was any size, it was sketchy and crowded. Baleal seems like it just doesn't work great all that often because the peninsula in front of it blocks some direct swell, making it a smaller beginner spot.

I thought if I just headed farther north a bit from Baleal the west swell should hit more directly and there should be better waves. The Surfline surf report app had a few spots up there, so I left Baleal and headed toward a beach that wasn't super straightforward to get to. I left Baleal and was on a dirt road, driving through a farm for a little while with crops on both sides of the dusty dirt road. The dirt road had no road signs or anything. It was just flat country land out there. I loved it. I made a wrong turn and did a complete loop somehow on around a farm but then found the left turn I was looking for with a dusty sign reading, "Almagreira."

I took it, stayed on the dirt road, and made my way straight to the cliffs and the break. I parked and ran out to check.

"Ho-lyyyyyy shit." Slowly dribbled out of my mouth, mesmerized.

Winds were offshore and waves were firing. Shoulder-high, left-breaking, thick, beautiful, organized sets. This is what I had been waiting for the entire month I was here! There were only ten dudes out in a break that had options and was not one exact peak. I had noticed that the set waves were bigger than the rest (as per usual) and when they came the shoulder of the waves ran! Peeling far left! None of the surfers out there were positioned correctly to catch it! They were at the normal peak area, which turned into one giant close-out, skunking them all from catching the wave. I watched this happen over and over and got excited.

"That's my position." I said to myself.

I suited up and ran to the beach. There were a pack of girls close to the rocks on the beach. Of course they were topless, but my gaze was truly on the spectacular wave. I paddled out. I sat to the right— beach perspective— north of everyone far in the shoulder where on a normal wave, the surfers farthest south would pick up the peak and ride it north, farther inside (shallower) of me. I waited patiently, and sure as shit a set wave came straight at me. I love being right with surf. All the other guys were paddling deeper or farther north to see if they could pick up the shoulder, but they all got smashed from the closing wave, and I rode the open left shoulder of the thicker set wave all the way to the next beach over.

It was a longer paddle back, but I made it to the same general spot and waited again. I was still alone. The other guys went back hunting for the smaller peaks farther south again in between sets. Some surfers have goldfish brains. They don't retain information beyond the wave that broke last. Seriously, they just follow the last waves peak, constantly chasing it. It's a better and less exhausting strategy to watch the surf before paddling out to see the bigger picture of what's happening. Then, plant yourself in the best spot and be patient. It was hilarious. So again, a set wave came, and same as last time, all the guys got smashed and I caught a head-high, higher tide, thick left all the way to the next beach to the north. It was amazing. After I repeated this three more times, the other guys started noticing and paddled over to the spot to catch the ride I discovered.

Now it became more of a competition because everyone was after the set wave I had been scoring. I tried sitting inside, outside, left or right of the guys to have a better position on the wave. I caught a few more and decided that was enough, as it was becoming more of a struggle now with the crowd. So, I sat where they used to sit on the inside, caught a couple, and paddled in. ALWAYS JUKING THE MASSES.

XVIII-Favorite surf day in Portugal. Almageira, Portugal. Digital.

I had an amazing session with amazing waves. Was I crazy lucky, or was this spot always better than Baleal? It was one of my last days, so I was thinking that I might not have another chance to see. I changed out of my wetsuit and hung out on the cliffs for a few hours. I walked the cliffs all the way to Baleal Beach, maybe a thirty-minute walk. It was firing in Baleal as well, but the wave at Almagreira was much better. The left was much longer!

I started the walk back from checking Baleal, and I walked on the cliff the whole time back and found a secret spot! There was a secret lefthand point hidden in the cliffs. This break didn't have an exact road to it or a car park area nearby. I noticed a few guys parked on the farmers' open land, but it didn't look like enough cars for a known spot, so the masses kept driving past toward the known spots, like Almagreira.

I scrambled down the rock cliff to just above the ocean level, sat, and watched. There were only a couple surfers out during the hour I sat there, fixated. I didn't have my board, and just finished a three-hour session. I wasn't about to head into a very rocky shallow point break blind, but I was studying the hell out of it. Also, one guy was a total beginner on a soft top with his friend, so I think it was fine, but the location screamed, "shallow reef!" I watched and watched and was mesmerized by the waves coming in. They would build up at the cliff point and hug the rocky cliff wall until it peeled toward the beach on the inside. I watched these guys catch beautiful left after beautiful left. To this day, I never surfed that wave, and the next time I go to Portugal, I have my sights set there. It was the most quality wave around. Not overly aggressive and almost completely empty. I have no idea its name, but I will surf it one day.

After way too long, I scrambled back up the rocky cliff side to the top and walked back to my car. The cliffs were totally different between Baleal and Almagreira. Closer to Baleal and the secret cliff lefthand point break, the tops of the cliffs were full of the succulent grass that existed on California's cliffs too. Closer to Almagreira, the cliffs became more desert-like with outcropping red rock and no life or greenery anywhere. I got in my car after shooting some photos and headed back to find the cabin on the foothill of the mountain.

I drove south and inland. I left the last village town with a paved road and headed up the hill on a dirt road. It was dark, and the road was getting steeper and steeper. The Euro car was having more and more difficulty keeping the tires from spinning as I went up. I finally pulled up to the cabin on the right of the dirt road.

I tried turning right into the driveway, but the car couldn't make the turn because the grades of where the road met the driveway were so different. One was steep and one was flat but higher off the ground. The car stalled. I turned the key and started it up again, trying and trying. I was in the dark with no one around, only trees on each side of the steep dirt road blowing in the wind. I reversed, stopped, started driving forward, and gained momentum to drive farther up the hill. I did a sketchy U-turn on the steep grade and flew down the hill and bounced up the driveway with added speed.

I opened the gate and pulled in. It was *really* dark, I could hear some animals in the distance, like crickets and an owl, cutting through the steady howl of the wind. I grabbed my bag from the back of the car, turned my phone's flashlight on, and headed to find the front door of the cabin on a dirt trail. I took my first step onto the elevated deck from the trail.

"Ribbit!!" A huge fist-sized bullfrog belted from under my step, jumping into the grass below.

I nearly stepped on it!

"Jeez!!" I yelled as it scared the piss out of me.

I walked around the deck and used the key from the key box to open the front door. I walked in. The inside of the cabin was even darker than outside, pitch black. With my flashlight on, I hunted for the light switch, rubbing my hands all over the walls, looking and feeling for a switch across my fingers. I didn't feel anything except the smooth walls, smelling the scent of whatever type of wood the cabin was made of. I searched farther into the cabin by a few paces. Every step caused an echoing thud from the elevated cabin and thin wood under my feet. The flashlight only lit up one little circle on the wall, barely helping.

"There we go." I said as I felt the switch on a column near the kitchen.

I flicked it on, and with all sincerity, about three inches above my hand on the column was a spider bigger than my hand. It was larger than if my hand was as wide open as I could possibly make it with all my fingers spread wide. It was huge, I mean, a colossal-sized spider.

"Ahhhhhhhhhhhhhhhhhhh faaaaaaaaaaaaaaaaack!!!!!" I shrieked at the top of my lungs.

I pulled my hand away and startled it, either from my scream or the light, and it ran up the column. Every step it took with its eight long, tall, thick, hairy, buff legs, I felt and heard because of how powerful and large it was. I could hear its spidery footsteps echoing throughout the cabin! It looked like it was the face-sucker from the movie *Alien*.

I thought about my options for a couple of seconds while standing in the only room of the cabin, afraid to move, looking at that beast, now perched near the low ceiling. I looked down and saw that the cabin was supported by a few thick tree branches and trunks, but there were gaps in the floor of the cabin around the tree so large any animal could crawl right through it, like that spider.

"Where there's one, there's many." I thought.

I sized up its eight- or ten-inch wingspan.

"NOPE CAN'T DO IT!" I said very matter of fact.

I picked up my rucksack from the floor, threw it on my back and ran out. I threw my large twinkie-shaped rucksack on the front passenger seat through the driver door, jumped in, landing with the door already shut and engine started. I peeled out of there like a bat out of hell. I left the keys on the kitchen table and flew down the dirt road back to town. I had nowhere to go. It was 10 p.m., but I sure as hell wasn't staying there. The bed in the single room cabin was only feet away from that beast. I had visions of that creature in the middle of the night trying to plant eggs in my mouth like in the movie. I can't think about it, or I'll get nauseous. I sent an emergency "help me" text to the owner of the cheap, hip, surfer homestay in Péniche near Supertubos. Last time I stayed there, he told me to book directly next time instead of through the internet. I had his number, so I messaged him on WhatsApp.

"Sure, come on by!" He responded.

I headed twenty-five more minutes towards him, relieved.

I texted The Magic Cabin's host that I left her house and why. I told her I wasn't coming back, she could keep my money, but the keys were on the table in the kitchen. She was angry that I left her house unlocked, but I had no choice. I wasn't going back there. I'm also not sure why she bothered to lock her house with those monster sized gaps in her floor. Anyone like that spider could just squeeze their way in. Gross.

"Miss, I'm not like a city guy, I've lived in many cabins, I'm a camper, hiker, and outdoorsy guy, but your cabin isn't sealed from the outside, and that spider was otherworldly." I explained to her via text.

It would be like fighting with a large squirrel in your house. It was a furry animal, not an insect.

"Good luck getting that thing out, and you should really fix your house." I said.

"The Magic Cabin," I laughed saying the name out loud.

I really should have known better. I probably could have mustered up the courage to go to war with that thing and stayed there, but it was cheap, and I was on a surf holiday. After working during the busy hotel season back in Jersey, twelve hours a day for 120 days straight why should I have to have TWO horrible nights of sleep?! Sometimes I needed to voice my inner wimp to get a good night's rest. But, honestly, if anyone else in the world saw that massive spider, or creature, in their house, I guarantee they'd have something to say about it too. Like a heart attack. I made it to the hip surfer homestay. I told the owner the story and he had a good laugh. He gave me the keys, and I took my bag to my room. I laid down and sensed a mosquito hovering around me.

"Oh, I'll take you any day," I said to the mosquito and passed out.

Since I left Portugal, I looked at The Magic Cabin's accommodation listing again and read the reviews.

"DO NOT STAY HERE IF YOU ARE AFRAID OF SPIDERS" Other victims (guests) had written to warn others about these creatures in the cabin.

I laughed so hard when I read that review. It made me feel like I didn't over-exaggerate and wasn't alone in my experience.

I was leaving Portugal in two days! I surfed the north end of Baleal the next morning and found my spot again. I caught nice, larger shoulder-to-head-high lefthanders into the exposed rocks. I had my fast, last minute, pull-out-of-the-wave move, almost hitting the rock so many times. It was funny. I knew the rock was there, but no surfer wants their ride to end, so it became a game to stay on the wave as long as humanly possible and skirt around certain pain.

I surfed next to a girl out there who wasn't really doing much surfing, but she waved, and I waved back. I saw her after the session with her guy friends at their van, which my tiny Euro rig was parked right next to. We all started talking, and they were from Italy. They all drove that van down together from there. I love international places. It's so freaking fun talking to people doing the same thing as you, only from so many different countries around the world with different accents, languages, cultures, etc. They're after a similar experience but with their own unique flair.

I went back to the hip surf homestay after my surf and packed my things. I was heading down south of Ericeira for the last time to slowly make my way to the airport. I didn't have enough room in my bag anymore, and I destroyed my Australian Blundstone boots. The leather was completely off the sole, and they were on the chopping block. I bought them in Tasmania (where they were originally made) at a hardware store, far outside Hobart the city. I was in a little, hippy, hiker town and needed a pair of boots to hike in. They cost $30, and I didn't realize they were stylish until I wore them back in the USA and saw they cost $200-$300 there! Nevertheless, it was their time to go. I had too much attachment to them and couldn't throw them away in the garbage, I loved them too much. I left them outside in the back patio common area of the homestay, thinking maybe someone would take them and keep them alive on a different adventure somewhere else in the world.

The following day, it was time to start making moves, so I drove down to Lisbon and took a Covid test that was needed for my flight in a big outdoor drive-through tent. It cost €25. Some places in the USA charged $100, minimum. I drove back to Ericeira and called up the mom I met on the beach. I asked her if I could leave a board at her house for a while because I had nowhere to put it and couldn't take it back to the states with me. She didn't mind at all, and I drove it over and left it with her. Like I said earlier, I hate giving airlines more money, so instead I supported a fellow surfer buying the board in Ribamar rather than bringing my own. Even if I never saw that board again, my friend or her son could have a free board. That seemed like a better option than giving the airline (crooks!!) more of my money to check it. Or, I'll have a free board the next time me or my friends were in Portugal!

I found this local dive of a traditional Portuguese seafood restaurant in Ribamar's village, north of Ericeira, off the main road from the ocean. The owner of the restaurant kept pouring pints of beer for the old local men who would take the beers out into the street and hang out. I sat at a table in the back. The place had awesome murals of octopus and other oceanic creatures painted on the walls.

The owner came over to me and asked if I was a pro surfer in town.

"Na, I'm just a regular surfer in town." I said.

He laughed. I ordered a shrimp plate. He brought me bread and oil, and when my meal arrived, it was nothing more than a huge pile of shrimp on a plate. I had to de-head and de-shell all the shrimp myself, and after a while, I had shrimp all over me. It was one of the most fun meals I ever had. This restaurant was more expensive than most I had been to in Portugal, I think I paid $25 for my meal. Money was so easy here. It went way farther than in the states. This trip really made me think that I'm not interested in living my life in the USA. The USA is so much more complicated, expensive, and stressful than life should be, and for a lower quality of life than I'm after. What traveling does to open the mind is beautiful.

For my last night in Portugal, I drove down south of Ericeira. I had no surfboard and no purpose anymore. I was very sad to leave. I didn't want to detach from this place. I had grown to love Portugal after spending a month there. I had grown personally as well. Portugal's simple way of life, affordable prices, epic surf, relaxed lifestyle, and beautiful nature made me want to stay there forever.

I drove down to the Sintra area and stayed in a B&B, ate another traditional Portuguese meal, and passed out. The next morning, I returned my rental car and had to give the Portuguese man at the car rental place my handmade wool Portuguese blanket I finally bought for public surf-changing and car-camping. It was huge and wouldn't fit in my bag. It was bigger than my bag was.

"Hey dude, you want this handmade beautiful blanket?" I asked.

"My wife would love it!! Yes!!" I left it with him, caught a ride to the airport, and took off back to the USA. I had done what I came to do. And just like that, poof, I was gone.

Surfin' Dirty Jerz

"Surfing New Jersey is like eating at Denny's. It sounds awful, but once you're there, it's alright." I read in an article on Surfline, the surf forecasting app, about someone's opinion of the surf in Jersey.

XIX-Hurricane Swell, Ocean Grove, NJ. Digital.

It caught my eye, so I read it. I didn't get the name of the guy who wrote the article, but he was right. Well... Half right. *When* there was swell in Jersey, the surf was alright. And about three-quarters of the year, there was no swell pushing up the western Atlantic.

After Portugal, I went back to New Jersey, USA for three months to work the busy, summer, hotel season to re-up my adventure funds for the year. It's funny going back there year after year and applying newly acquired surf skills to the Jersey beach breaks.

Every year, for three years now, I took my surfing skills out to the average breaks in Jersey and noticed significant improvement since the last time I was there, nine months earlier.

This time, I got back after the off-season, and I was officially part of what my friends Chris and Brett on the North Shore of O'ahu called "the shortboard revolution." I had been surfing shorter and shorter boards for over three years now. After moving to Maui and surfing Costa Rica, where shortboards were more necessary, as the surf can be much bigger there, I finally preferred to ride shorter boards in bigger surf.

I got back to New Jersey, and after I got my first paycheck, I bought another shortboard. This one was THE ONE. I had been surfing a small fish and a Hypto Krypto high performance shortboard, but I was still looking for something a little smaller than the Hypto Krypto to continue my progress in surfing on smaller boards. Off Craigslist, I picked up an Al Merrick Channel Islands Neckbeard model. A lot of board companies use funny model names for their boards these days, including the Neckbeard.

The dude, who I bought the almost brand-new board from said he bought it new with fins and leash for around $1100. I bought it from him for $450 with fins and a leash included. What a deal! He said he couldn't ride it and needed a bigger board. His skill level wasn't good enough for it. I was hesitant because I was still sizing down from my 5'10" Hypto Krypto, a 33.5-liter board, to the Neckbeard, a 5' 9" 31.5-liter board. This was a big difference. Two liters less volume meant it was smaller and less buoyant. I was super anxious to get it in the water and see if I could ride it with ease, or if it was going to be very challenging for me.

Coincidentally, that night at sunset and the next morning, Jersey had a 2' @ 10 second SE swell with offshore winds. Waves that looked big enough to test out my new Neckbeard! This was like Christmas, or a birthday, for a surfer. Taking out a new board that was a new shape yet to be ridden was a ton of fun and exciting to test and advance my skill levels.

I waxed the freshly scraped smooth deck of the board with its first layers of wax. I was out of my usual Mr. Zog's Sex Wax and

212

used my bar of Sticky Bumps Wax. Both companies started in the early 1970s and have been making surf wax for over fifty years now. The bar of wax was hot from the sun and molded to my hands as I pressed it onto the board, so I grabbed a backup bar that was in the shade. This bar was hard, and I rubbed wax all over the fresh deck in crosshatch and circle patterns, so it stayed on the board for longer. I was ready.

I picked it up and walked to the beach, a tiny block away from my family's hotel. The board felt so nice under my arm, so light, and when holding the board on the rails, it felt like it still had some decent volume. This gave me hope that it would be easy to ride, even though the nose clearly was sharper with less volume and size than my Hypto Krypto that I was used to riding. I ran into the water and threw the board under me, gliding in the shallow surf. It felt light. I noticeably sank with the board a bit more. I duck dove under a few waves to get out, and duck diving with it was a pleasure. The board was smaller, lighter, and sharper making it much easier to sink and pierce through the incoming waves as I paddled out. After only waiting about a minute for a wave, I saw one coming in with a bit of steepness and a pitching lip. I paddled for it. I paddled hard, got into the wave, popped up, and took off frontside down the side of the wave. I pumped and made a few quick turns and popped over the back of the wave as it closed out. I was ecstatic! Yessssss!!! I could ride this board easily! No learning curve feeling like I can't surf! The rest of that two-hour sunset surf and the hour sunrise session the next morning, I caught over thirty beach break waves, frontside and backside. On a handful of them, I felt like I properly shredded, and the rest I surfed decently well. Only a handful did I feel like I surfed poorly, and some of which was because the waves were too small for that board. I found my new favorite board. Now I needed to find some larger surf around here. I would be there for two more months of the summer season, but hurricane season would be peaking in about a month. I'd have my chance before I left for some place with bigger, more consistent surf.

The surf in New Jersey was mostly all the same. Locals would disagree, I'm sure, as every peak along the shore has a different sandbar or jetty or sewer pipe (gross) that creates different characteristics in the waves, but the coastline is mostly the same. It's all the same type of surf. New Jersey has 127 miles of coastline on the Atlantic Ocean, and the majority of it, if not 99.999% of it, is beach breaks. It is all beach breaks. Beach break city. For the entire state. I am aware of two exceptions.

First, The Cove in Sandy Hook National Recreation Area. The coastline here in Jersey actually tapers! It runs northwest, instead of straight north and south, like the rest of northern Jerz. A straight east or southeast swell would cause the waves to peel to the northwest. Only how often do we get strong swells straight from those angles? Not that often. South swells are more common and don't hit with a perpendicular enough direction for them to produce nice point break waves. Then, all the way on the opposite southern tip, there is The Cove in Cape May. I have never even seen good conditions here, and I checked the live cam often, but on the map and cam, I can tell there's a potentially tapering coastline, offering a good left. It just must be rare. Besides those two, there are a few other spots in southern Jersey with river mouths or inlets that can create a decent wave off the corner of the inlet. But besides those, it is all sand bottom beach break with a jetty nearby.

Most beaches have man-made jetties every hundred or few hundred yards, which cause waves to break off them into the shallow water. That's basically most of Jersey waves. Then, September comes and for two months, hurricane swells tear up the east coast with strong 3'- 12' swells. Each storm can provide surf for a couple of days (if they're lucky), and there are maybe a handful of swells per season. After swells reach above the 7' range, it's hard to surf, especially at a strong interval. At least in Ocean Grove. The break becomes so powerful or sloppy that it isn't a very good time. It was great that my work season was at the beach, allowing me to surf sunrise and sunset, but every season I was there, I couldn't wait to leave and surf somewhere more consistent. My skills took a hit every summer. I needed to surf for a week or two straight, once I left to somewhere with more consistent surf, to feel dialed in again.

XX-"Down at the shore everything's alright." High tide lines. Ocean Grove, NJ. Digital.

I have one more Jersey rant I need to get off my chest. The life-guards. I have currently surfed in over thirteen countries in the world and surfed about six or seven states in the USA. New Jersey and New York are the only states or places I have ever been, to restrict where surfers are or are not allowed to surf. Surfers are corralled into one small area per town during the main part of the day, 9 a.m. to 5 p.m., every day in the summer tourist season. Everywhere else in the world that I have ever surfed, surfers have freedom and priority over the waves, and swimmers find somewhere else to swim, sit, soak, dip, play frisbee, or whatever. But not New Jersey and New York. These states do not respect the sport. The now Olympic sport, I might add. Lifeguards should be there for swimmers— by swimmer I mean summer vacation tourists, who stand in the water up to their shoulders and bob for a while, not actual long-distance swimmers— or if a surfer or anyone else happens to hurt themselves needing help, the lifeguards are there as first responders. They should not have any control over a surfer paddling out on a big day, or the ability to say what part of the beach a surfer can and cannot surf, based on some predetermined thought a board member of the town committee might think is best for tourism. The ability to close the beach if they think the surf is deemed too dangerous, or the right to kick surfers out of the water if it's during their tourist 9 a.m. to 5 p.m timetable, is unwarranted. Imagine if Hawaiian lifeguards closed Pipeline or Waimea to the pros because they deemed it as too big. They wouldn't. It's not in their culture. The bigger the wave the more challenging it is to navigate and surf it, and if you want to risk your life doing so, that's the surfers' freedom to choose. Many have lost their lives in this pursuit. Also, overall beach safety is not their primary concern because as soon as the tourist season and the beach stops making money, everyone packs up and the beach becomes free and unmanaged again. It's like organized crime.

It's a surfer's right to choose for themselves, not to be forced by a lifeguard who might not even surf or have a clue, like some of the lifeguards in Jersey. For most summer Jersey lifeguards, it's a high school or back from college summer job for kids who think it's a chill way to earn money while catching a tan. No kidding. Opposite of the respected position it is as a waterman in Hawai'i. This should change, New Jersey and New York. In my experience California State Beaches with restrooms and showers that also charge money to get on to (which is still crazy) don't restrict surfers, telling them what waves they can or cannot surf, and surfing is California's official state sport. What should happen is: the lifeguards need to create a sign called "swimming only beach" and corral all the tourist swimmers into one area of every town. Everywhere else signs should say "swim/surf at your own risk." As it's much safer to have heaps of people bobbing in the water near each other than loads of surfers trying to surf on top of each other. That is so much more dangerous! Surfing is only becoming more and more popular with loads more surfers every year. If anyone wants to spearhead this project, you have my support. Because surfing is freedom.

Pura Vida: Nosara

Nosara is another stylish, hip, surf town in Costa Rica like Santa Teresa, only smaller, sleepier, and with less hype. Nosara has one of my favorite beach breaks in the world! The waves there on decent swells tend to be gentle giants. The outside sets are always multiple feet overhead or more but not aggressive. The waves are slow and forgiving, making it a blast!

Many surfers in the world, including myself, have been trained or traumatized by waves that are extremely fast-breaking, and as soon as I see building energy, I assume the wave will aggressively throw its lip. This requires fast action from the surfer. In Nosara, the energy builds forever, and the waves seemingly never break. I found myself drifting deeper outside way too often thinking the wave would break sooner, only to then paddle back in (shallower) to catch waves in the correct position. Even on bigger days. The waves just didn't break, they stayed open for ages longer than many other spots. The rides that these waves offered, too, were some of the most fun I'd experienced in a beach break setting. This was also the first spot I ever felt the drop in my stomach from a taller drop, like I was on a rollercoaster. That free-fall feeling.

These waves are perfect for twin-fins. Larger waves with power, but mostly mellow banks that would wall-up and peel. This is great for twin-fins to make wide turns and glide effortlessly. I always rode my fish here. Nosara's waves are big, even on smaller swells. The waves are larger than other places. I have been there when it was too big with a shit wind a few times, but I started keeping notes about its best conditions. My favorite conditions occurred when the swell was a bit larger but clean and not out of control big that kept everyone out of the water. From what I saw, if the swell was over 4' it tended to be too big. Seemed like it loved a 2' or 3' up to 4' max swell height at higher intervals. Any more than that, and I never saw it clean and organized. I only surfed it in the dry season months, though, and the big swells came in wet season, May to November. I'm sure some 5'- 8' swells roll through and are epic as all hell, but I have never witnessed it. If you can score an offshore day, or day without wind with those 2'- 4' readings, GO!

One morning, while my buds Rick and Brett were in town visiting me, I decided to take them to Nosara. There are two ways to get to Nosara. The inland route, for nerds, and the coastal route, for people who want to get where they're going! The inland route took two and a half hours each way. The route went far inland and through Santa Cruz, the local small capital city, and all the way around. If you took the unpaved dirt road from just south of Tamarindo, it took about one hour and fifteen minutes. I have hauled ass and done it in an hour flat before. It just depended on how many slow cars or trucks you ran into along the way. Also, I had to get my shock mounts replaced already from how I drove in Costa Rica, so better off going slow. The boys were stoked to go check out somewhere new. We planned on leaving early in the morning.

The rest of that day before Nosara, we decided to go have a session in Tamarindo to sightsee and check the beach scene.

We also had a very important task at hand. Rick had to take out Kelly's board. We had a super close, dear friend recently pass away out of the blue for unknown reasons. His name was Kelly Clark. Brett and I knew Kelly for about ten years. Rick was closest to him and formed a friendship with Kelly a few years before us through the motorcycle chopper subculture. Kelly was the coolest dude I ever met. When we met him in our twenties, he was older, in his forties, and was the fully tattooed, jacked, pit bull-looking metal fabricator and motorcycle builder type. He smoked cigarettes and had short slicked-back hair. He rode his 1950s Harley-Davidson Panhead chopper around. He was tough and didn't let most people in. For one reason or another, when Brett and I moved to San Francisco and met Kelly, he opened up to us, and we all became great friends with him over the years. We called him our grandpa as a joke. He was a San Francisco staple. He had lived there forever and knew everyone. He helped my friends get motorcycle garages, apartments, motorcycles, jobs, etc. He was legendary to us like his father was legendary to the world – his father was the main member of The Byrds, one of the biggest bands in the world in the late 1960s. I didn't even find this out for years because he didn't want anyone to know. He was his own man, and man, was he.

After I got better at surfing and hung out with Kelly at his motorcycle shop, I found out that he spent a few years, decades ago, in Costa Rica surfing. I never knew he surfed, and he didn't surf around San Francisco, so I asked him about it.

"I had a good buddy who started a surf hostel thing down in Costa Rica, and I'd go down and visit and just stay there for months back in the 1990s." He told me.

"Why don't you surf anymore up here?" I asked him.

"Screw that, this water's freezing. You'll never see me in it. But, if I'm in water like Costa Rica, I'll surf with you." He responded toughly, like always.

He laughed, smoking his cigarette, wearing his thick, black frame glasses and skateboarding hat backwards. At the time, I laughed at his stubbornness.

When Kelly passed suddenly, everyone was devastated and a lot fell on Kelly's girlfriend and Rick, as they were the ones who were closest to him. Rick also shared a motorcycle shop/warehouse with Kelly and had to go through his things.

While digging deep through Kelly's things in his shop, Rick found Kelly's high performance shortboard sitting in its travel bag. He never got rid of it. He held onto that dream.

"Dave, you'll never believe what I found... Kelly's surfboard! I'm bringing it and leaving it with you in Costa Rica where it belongs." Rick said, after he bought his plane ticket in San Francisco and knew he was coming to Costa Rica to visit me.

I started to cry when he said this. It meant so much, and he was right. I was the only connection to Costa Rica the group of us had, and Kelly exclusively surfed that board there. When Rick and Brett arrived, we had our own paddle out with Kelly's spirit on Kelly's board in the place where he rode it and enjoyed life. We hung out with him out there, yelling, screaming, shredding, laughing, as if he was there with us, and telling him how much we missed him. We all took turns trading boards and we each caught waves on his board. Even Rick, who wasn't good at shortboarding and is a way bigger dude than Brett and me, still got up on the little sharp shortboard and dropped in. It was awesome. A seriously incredible moment with the best of friends there are. That board is still currently sitting in my house in Costa Rica to this day. It's at home.

After I fell into an exposed rockpile while surfing, my fish was dung up bad for a while. I was forced to use Kelly's board as my main board for a week while I repaired my fish. That helped me originally learn how to shortboard. It was my first time really trying, and after a week, I was catching waves! So, thanks, Kelly. Miss you, dude. Anytime you want to come down and take your board back, I'm just holding it for ya. Let's go surf that warm water together, buddy.

The next day, we were up early for a quick breakfast and hit the road for Nosara. Of course, I took the faster coastal road to get us there quicker. There was a bigger 4' swell, and I thought Nosara would be firing. I checked the live cam, before we left, and the waves looked great. I knew the road to Nosara now. I'd driven it over ten times. Along the drive, there was one looming obstacle I thought about for almost the entire drive. The only challenge, the river crossing.

I am from the USA, and in the USA, unless maybe you're in Alaska or deep in the mountains somewhere, there are no river crossings. Most Americans do not possess the skill set to negotiate a car through a river. It was not taught or tested to obtain your driver's license. No-one's dad taught them this. It was just unheard of. The first time I tried driving to Nosara, I got to this river crossing and turned around and went home. Not knowing it was in the cards to drive through it. I thought there was supposed to be a bridge, and the rainy season floods took it out of commission. Turned out, this river never had a bridge, only a janky walking bridge that motorbikes would ride over.

Everyone drives through this river for some reason. Maybe it wasn't deep enough to necessitate a bridge. The first time, or first few times I crossed it, I waited forever until I saw multiple other cars cross it and I mimicked their maneuvers. Seemed like there was an obvious shallow section far to one side, so I followed that way and got through it ok. After a few times of crossing this way, I thought it was no big deal. But this time, I had my friends in the car. The pressure was on.

Brett and Rick were going to see me cross this river, and it was going to be easy, I thought. After an hour, we arrived at my obstacle. I stopped, looking face to face with the river.

"Shit it's bigger than it used to be… It's wider and deeper." I said to the boys in the car.

It was early May, the beginning of the rainy season, and even though it wasn't the month of torrential monsoons (October), I think the extra rain in the recent days added to the river's size. There were no other cars in sight. We waited for ten minutes, then I just decided to go for it. I reversed and backed away from the muddy decline of the dirt road to the river, to get some more runway for speed. I was nervous and thought because the river was wider and deeper that I needed more speed for momentum to coast though it. I was wrong. Very wrong. As wrong as I could be. My friends are great at doing most things, but they also had no major experience in river crossings, so they just watched.

"Rock 'n' Roll" by Motörhead was playing off Rick's phone, I cranked the volume up for motivation, then pretty much floored it. I built enough speed that I shifted up into third gear and... BOOM!

We hit the water. Everything seemed ok at first when it was shallow, but what I couldn't see under the water was a trench that the current of the river created in the middle at the deepest point. This caused the car to buck from its speed. The water was up on my hood, but the force from the car's speed hitting the angle of the trench caused a tidal wave above the car's windshield to send water all over the car. All of us got rag-dolled in the car as if we were in a legitimate accident. Shit in the car went flying everywhere. Technically, my plan of "momentum will get us to the other side" worked, only as soon as we were back on land, the car puttered out and died. I killed the car!

"What the hell!! You're crazy!!!" I heard yells from both my mates.

I laughed hard, feeling stupid. We got out and popped the hood to check the damage of what I just did. The motor was steaming from water hitting the hot case. Every few minutes, I tried starting it, and it never worked. The dash gave me some engine light I had never seen before. I screwed us. We were now stranded about twenty minutes from Nosara in the middle of nowhere jungle. I took a pee on the side of the road that met the jungle. Rick and Brett are both more mechanically inclined than I, so they started troubleshooting without any tools.

One or two cars drove by after a while without tools or anything helpful. They miraculously crossed the river with no problem at all, doing 1mph through it, not 30mph. Like the tv show from the 80s where the main character used his unconventional problem-solving skills to get out of sticky situations, Rick "MacGyvered" the situation by turning his carabiner on his shorts holding his keys into a flat head screwdriver to open the airbox and take out the air filter. This was the culprit. There were bubbles and foam everywhere. Apparently, air filters are coated with a chemical that turns water into foam on contact to protect the motor from getting water inside, which would destroy the motor. We were all sitting there scooping handfuls after handfuls of foam out of the air intake manifold. Rick took off his shirt and used it as a towel, to dry out the intake area, and we left it baking in the sun for a while with the hood still open. Man, Kelly would have been yelling at us and laughing hysterically if he saw what a predicament we were in because of my stupid ass.

After a few minutes a Tama Cruiser (AKA Tamarindo piece of shit garbage car that barely ran and was probably missing doors, a hood, the trunk, mirrors, had mis-match paint, maybe it smoked, etc.) crossed the river just fine, and the guy stopped behind us on our side.

"Are you okay?" He asked with broken English, but we were thinking the same about him and his car.

He got out and looked at his own car after he crossed the river and noticed that he went from one license plate down to zero. He thought his rear plate fell off in the river. He asked if we saw it.

"Dude, no you just crossed the river, and parked behind us, how would we see your REAR license plate when we are parked in FRONT of you." We said laughing.

He rolled his pants up, which didn't matter in the slightest, took his shirt off, and went for a walk in the river. He was feeling with his bare feet for the license plate on the river floor. He spent a long time in there and came out drenched, head-to-toe with no plate. He was upset and went to take a pee near the jungle's edge. He walked back after his pee with a license plate in his hand. We watched him tack on a random license plate to the back of his car that was not his. He just found it on the ground while he peed at the beginning of the jungle. He got back in his Tama Cruiser and took off down the road.

"Helllllll yeah!!!" I yelled as we all laughed hysterically.

We put the airbox back on without the wet air filter. We thought it might be starving the motor of air. Sure enough, it started! It seemed like everything just needed a chance to dry out after we opened it up and took out the sopping wet air filter. I closed the hood and re-tacked the bumper back in place that had fallen off on one side. It was just hanging there. Then, we hopped in and took off.

I drove super slow just to make sure I wasn't killing the car any more than I already had. It seemed ok. Ten minutes down the road, we pulled into a gas station just outside Nosara town. The gas station was also a parts shop, but they didn't have the air filter for this Chinese car. We had an idea. They also had a repair shop next door that was open. We walked over and asked the guy if he could spray our soaking wet air filter dry with his air compressor. It took a few minutes of blowing bubbles out of it, but after a bit of time, we had ourselves a totally dry air filter! We threw it back in the airbox and once again took off down the road! We gave the dude a few bucks for helping us out.

We finally made it to Playa Guiones, the surf beach of Nosara! After all of that, we parked and checked the waves and... it wasn't good! The wind had turned, and it was too big and messy.

"Screw it, let's paddle out anyway." Brett and I said.

I couldn't make it out on my fish, but Brett managed to duck dive his way through on his shortboard and caught a few big dumps out there while Rick and I hung out on land and watched. He got out quickly and we took off. All that for bad surf... But what a crazy day it was. We easily could have stayed in Tamarindo for better waves.

"DON'T LEAVE WAVES FOR WAVES." My buddy Chris's words haunted me again.

I drove us slowly through the river on the way back... successfully!

<u>The correct way to drive through a river is:</u>
1. Never drive perpendicularly through a river.

2. Always drive with the current and make a gradual turn through the river.

3. Drive slowly and stay consistent in your speed until you get back out of the water on the other side.

4. Don't shift gears, break, or come to a complete stop while in a river.

I did almost all these things wrong. But you live and you learn. Right?

Pura Vida: "Ze Germans"

I was at my family's house in Playa Langosta, Costa Rica, and the afternoon was creeping toward sunset. In Costa Rica, the sun sets very quickly, so I needed to make plans for sunset before sunset. It was maybe 4 p.m., and I had about two hours left before dark. I grabbed my board, threw it in the car, and headed for Tamarindo beach. I waxed my board and paddled out. I caught a wave or two, then I saw this guy in the surf who I recognized from the gym. I said hi to him in the water. We chatted about a few things, including that we had both lived in Hawai'i.

After a few minutes, I noticed that there was a lingering girl who seemed like she wanted to join the conversation.

"Hi, I'm Dave," I said in her direction.

"Juliana," she said, starting our own conversation.

We caught waves and continued to talk for the entire session. At one point, she asked me where I liked to surf besides the Tamarindo river mouth.

"Nosara!" I told her "I am heading there tomorrow. The swell looks good! You want to go?" I asked.

I assumed that was an empty ask because we didn't know each other at all, and I'm not used to very spontaneous people.

"Yea for sure!" She responded, "As long as there's a seat for my friend Lisa. She's visiting me from Germany, and I can't leave her behind!" She said, super excited.

"I have four seats, so we're good." I responded.

We planned together while waiting for waves. We planned to meet at Pico Café in the morning. After surfing, I went home, cooked some fish, and passed out.

At sunrise the next morning, I got out of bed, checked my local Playa Langosta surf conditions with a coffee, which looked very good actually, then left to get the girls. On the way out of the house, I packed three boards. I wasn't sure if the girls had their own boards or not. I arrived at Pico Café, and they walked up a minute later. They threw their mid-length boards on the roof of my car, and I ratcheted them down with straps. We hopped in and took off for Nosara. I took the coastal route again, and the girls were stoked on being in the jungle. I arrived at the daunting river crossing and stopped. We got out and I told them the story of how I got my friends and I stuck because I blew through the river too fast and flooded my motor, or air intake.

"I wonder how deep it is? I can't really tell. It's too murky." I said.

I leaned over and was digging for my water bottle out of my back seat, and when I looked up, Juliana was standing barefoot, knee deep in the middle of the river.

"I'd say it's about knee high." She said and we all laughed.

These were my kind of people – spontaneous and not afraid of getting wet or dirty or bit by a croc in a murky river in Costa Rica. After seeing how deep the water was, I was confident to drive through.

"Oh, we got this, no problem." I said.

I crossed it slowly and steadily in first gear, making a big arc, mildly turning through it, and we were out.

"Alrighttttttt!!!!!" I screamed. I was so stoked to make it successfully and get some river crossing confidence back again!

About fifteen-minutes later, we pulled up to Playa Guiones, the main surfing cove in Nosara, got out, stretched the legs, and walked through the trail to check the surf. The conditions were awesome. It was one of those good sized Nosara days, organized with a light off-shore morning wind, so we ran for our boards.

Lisa was a little less experienced as a surfer than Juliana, but I told them if they needed, I could give them a few tips out there. Lisa was a little more reserved as it looked like bigger waves, but I reassured her it was fun and would be great. Playa Guiones, almost every day I have ever surfed it, went like this. The mornings were super glassy (meaning the texture of the water was smooth and ideal for surfing), clean, and fun. Then around 10 a.m. to noon, depending on the day, the wind shifted, and the surf got messy all afternoon until around 4:30 or 5 p.m. The wind continued to die until dark, glassing off again the longer I stayed out.

It seemed like whenever I went to Playa Guiones, I surfed a mid or higher tide around sunrise or sunset and the tide always went out in the afternoon, but obviously that changed daily. I just seemed to go when the tides lined up with the better wind conditions. We paddled out into great waves. They were about head high and thick; some set waves were larger out back. I was on my fish, and the girls were on their mid-length rental boards they got for free from the surf shop Juliana worked at in Tamarindo. I had to guide them out a bit, but eventually all three of us were out and in the lineup.

I caught a bunch of fun waves while the girls were a little more hesitant. After a little while, Juliana got up on a few, and Lisa was still unsure, paddling a little too doubtful for the waves. I could tell she was nervous. I gave her a few tips.

"Choke up on your board a bit, paddle harder, and sit inside a touch more. You're too deep to catch them there." I instructed.

After a while, she was going for waves properly and standing up on her board. After we surfed for three hours and the wind started to shift, we got out and had lunch at Rosi's, the best soda in town. A soda is a typical Costa Rican food restaurant that's cheaper compared to other restaurants around.

A few hours went by. We walked around town and decided to go back to the beach. We had no plans and were unsure if we should leave town or stay and surf another session. I told them that it was always shit in the afternoons there, but it would start cleaning up soon as the wind calms after the hottest part of the day. Guiones was also notoriously packed at sunset, the entire town paddled out when the surf was good. To strategize around this, I figured, if we paddled out around 3:30 or 4 p.m. and surfed until dark, our session would get cleaner and cleaner the longer we were out. And the first hour and a half would be a ghost town. I was right, and we scored some rides before the crowd came at 5 p.m. Juking the masses yet again.

This was the story of my life! Always juking the masses for a better quality of my life's experiences. The term used to be "quality of life." Now there are so many people in this world doing the same activities that the new term I use, "quality of life experiences" is appropriate. It's more specific to the experiences we are after than just an overall quality of life in general. Of course, I think everyone has a better quality of life living at the beach, surfing, but if everyone in the world is living this same lifestyle, everyone's "quality of life experiences" would be horrible. This is happening in the world due to the internet, social media, and the pandemic. If you were to go to a movie theater and the theater didn't cut off the ticket sales when the seats ran out and you had to cram in somewhere, sitting on people and on the floor like sardines, would you still go?

Knowing your "quality of life experience" would be less than what you remembered it being when doing this activity in the past?

Well... there are no surf regulators, generally speaking, and there better never be. Surfing is freedom! But without regulation and tons of people, where is the answer? The answer most people come up with is, "I'll still throw myself in the packed surf, and act meaner, nastier, and tougher to people in the lineup. Or making it seem like I have more clout to be there than them because I live closer or am more skilled than them. I deserve to have more fun than everyone else, catching all the waves, making the rest wait and watch. Because I am the center of the universe, not them." What a bunch of crap that is. Somehow, I am the only one this occurs to most of the time, and it blows my mind. Maybe it just upsets me more. Either way, people are like blind cattle. Everyone is rushing to this one thing, like lemmings jumping off cliffs.

They all seem to say, "I must have it exactly the same as I watch everyone else having it."

All that attitude does is provide a horrible time. If it was in the stock market, it would lose all your money. In fashion, it can camouflage you to look like everyone else and not the individual you really are. If it was in the housing market, it would raise prices to stupid levels. Don't let others think for you. Use that brain to think outside the box and score in surfing and life!

It was 3 p.m., and we got our boards and paddled out in choppy windy surf. I was right. The first thirty minutes or so we didn't catch much, but we were ready in the lineup for when the wind started to taper off. Guiones, for a beach break, has a super far paddle out. Especially going after the larger, outer set waves, which was right where I went.

This time, Juliana wanted a crack at one of my shorter boards and took out my 6'0", probably 38-liter thruster set up, meaning a shortboard but wide, thick and easier for someone trying to learn on a smaller board. I was on "Orangie," my 1970s burnt-orange color retro fish, and Lisa was still on her rented mid-length. This round, Juliana was on fire! I coached her into a few waves, yelling at her over and over.

"Paddle... Paddle harder!!! Go! Go! Go! Go! Go!!!" I yelled.

My enthusiasm gave her the extra push to go for some big ones. She would drop in and cruise down the open face of the wave. By the end of the night, Lisa also stood up on a few waves, too. Lisa got out early, but Juliana and I stayed, navigating around the crowd of people until the stars were out. As soon as the sun set, the lineup thinned out again, and gave us about thirty more minutes of less crowded surf. It was worth holding out until I couldn't see anything at all. We got out so tired and surf-stoned (like runner's high). It was intense.

We were exhausted. We probably surfed six hours in total that day between both sessions and we were absolutely starving. We dried off at the car and headed to a local restaurant in town for dinner. After a great Casado (a local Costa Rican dinner of fish, rice, beans, veggies, and salad) and ceviche (my favorite), we began heading back to Tamarindo on the dirt road in the dark. Shortly after, we reached the river crossing again.

I had never crossed the river at night! It was spooky and there was no one around. Besides my headlights, it was pitch black. I watched the river's current flow in the dim, confusing light that my headlights faintly laid onto it. I was nervous. I turned up the sweet grooves of the "Zam Rock," Rock 'n' Roll/psychedelic bands from the early 1970s from Zambia Africa, who were influenced by Jimi Hendrix and James Brown. Then, I was ready to go for it.

I chose the path to the right, which usually is one of the two shallow areas, but once again my nerves hit the pedal for me harder than I wanted to. We bounced around and got to the other side of the river. My car was going uphill in the mud, climbing the land to get out of the river, and once again my car stalled out and died. This time, the rear three-quarters of my car was still in the river. I pulled the emergency break up hard, but I remembered it was broken and didn't do a damn thing. I quickly made sure the car was in first gear. I didn't want the car to roll backward into the deepest part of the river or possibly have the river push us downstream away from the road into the jungle!

I opened my door and hopped into the shallow part of the river that was below the driver's door. I popped the hood. The German girls in the car were laughing so hard, but Lisa, the more reserved German, looked a bit uneasy and doubtful.

"This happened once before with my buddies. After a few hours the car was fine, and we drove away from this. The first time was much worse too as I definitely went faster through a deeper section that time. We should be able to get out of here soon," I told them while trying to ease their fears of being two women from another continent and country, broken down in a river, in the jungle, in Costa Rica, at night, with a strange tattooed man, they'd just met the day before.

I started searching around in the car for a screwdriver to take the airbox off with. I looked and looked.

"I DIDN'T PUT ONE IN THE CAR AFTER THE FIRST BREAKDOWN!!!" I yelled at myself. "I'm such an idiot, really," I said.

We waited for someone to drive by who hopefully had a tool.

We waited and waited. It was around 7:30 p.m. I kept trying to turn the key to see if I would have any luck, but no. The motor never started. My family's car was a Ssangyong brand car. It was relatively new, from 2017. It had the same unique dashboard light that was illuminated last time. If I had to guess, it was because it's a newer car with more sensors, and it sensed the moisture in the air intake heading to the motor and killed the car to protect the motor from water getting into it. I also turned off all the interior lights and headlights. I took the keys out of the ignition, too. I made sure that anything that could drain the car's battery was off. The last thing I needed was to get the car running and not be able to start it due to a dead battery.

We waited longer and longer in the dark, occasionally with our cell phone flashlights on. A car came and drove through the river toward us. As my car was on the far side of the river crossing with all my car lights off in the dark, I waved my cell phone light back and forth to let the other driver know I was there so they wouldn't cross the river into my car. It was a little hard to change trajectory after entering a river. And it was exceptionally dark in the jungle at night.

The car crossed and stopped.

"Están bien? Necesitan ayuda?" A man asked if we needed help in Spanish through his open window.

"Si!!!" I responded and laughed.

I don't know how to say tool or screwdriver in Spanish, so I mimed it with my hand turning and twisting my closed hand.

"Ah, no tengo, lo siento." (I don't have I'm sorry) He said and left.

We waited another twenty minutes. Another car came. This time, from our side of the river. It stopped before it got to the river. This kid opened the door and got out. He spoke some broken English and was maybe in his early twenties. He was cute, chubby, looked friendly with his baby face and asked us what the problem was.

We explained our predicament and asked him for tools.

"I have no tools and am not a mechanic, so I am no use to you, but I will wait here with you, so you are not alone," he told us.

The German girls and I looked at each other.

"Are you kidding me??? How sweet is that!!" All our eyes said to each other in agreement.

No one, I mean absolutely NO ONE would ever do that or behave that way in the countries we came from. It was incredibly sweet. We started chatting with him as we waited for more cars to pass. As it got later, we were wondering if cars would eventually stop coming. Who crosses a river in Costa Rica after 9 p.m. anyway?

After waiting another long while, a car drove through the river. Again, I signaled with my cell phone light that we existed there. This time it was a newer car, windows raised up, they drove through the river, around us. I signaled with my cell phone light in the air and asked them to stop, saying that we needed help, and they drove off.

"Tourist." The Costa Rican kid that was sitting and waiting with us said.

It happened two more times where our excitement rose as a car's headlights came close, and the approaching car was a newer rental. We waved our hands in the air with flashlights yelling for help.

"Please stop! We need help or a screwdriver!!" We all yelled in desperation.

The cars didn't stop and didn't even acknowledge that we were there.

"Tourist," the kid said once again.

We were starting to get discouraged after waiting a couple of hours, when another car came by. This one was a serious Tama Cruiser, lemon-junker of a Bronco from who knows how long ago. It crossed the river and pulled over. There was a Costa Rican couple inside. They asked if we needed help. The man parked his car and jumped out with his wife to come take a look. He didn't have a screwdriver either, but he was looking in his car, which was filled with crap, to see if he had anything else that would work. His wife started speaking broken English to the German girls while he looked. Another car pulled up, about to cross the river, parked, and they got out, too. They were also Costa Rican. They were two men who knew the Costa Rican couple and asked what the situation was. Now all the Costa Ricans including the kid, were all speaking Spanish together. They were laughing, probably at my lack of driving skills. It turned into a hangout on the side of the dirt road next to the river that my car was stuck in. At night. In the jungle. In Costa Rica.

The new guys had a screwdriver! I quickly opened my airbox again and removed my wet air filter. I towel-dried as much of the airbox and intake I could reach and stuffed the towel in to absorb any water. The husband called his brother who was a mechanic to ask if it was safe for me to drive the car again. The mechanic brother said it can be damaging to the motor, and I should let it dry overnight. Unfortunately, we were stranded in the jungle and didn't have that kind of time.

"I suck at this, and it happened once before. I drove it away last time, and it was ok. I will attempt to do the same now, but I appreciate you calling to find out!" I told them.

After a few minutes, I tried to turn the key in the ignition again. This time it half started. We were on the right track! All five Costa Ricans were there waiting with us. I waited another couple of minutes and tried it again. It was even closer to starting. I waited another couple of minutes, talking and laughing with the Costa Ricans. I finally turned the key and the car started up! Everyone yelled in celebration!

The Costa Ricans moved their car for me, and everyone stepped aside. I drove the car SLOWLY out of the river and up the bank of the dirt road and let it idle for a few minutes. I furiously thanked the Costa Ricans and asked if I could give them money to buy them dinner. Every single one of them refused my offer.

"We need nothing from you, but it was nice to meet you, and we are glad your car problems are over." The five Costa Ricans said.

The German girls and I thanked them again and again, then we got in the car and drove off down the dirt road for about an hour until we got back to Tamarindo around 11 p.m. All in, it took about three hours to figure out getting the car out of the river. Not too bad. Costa Ricans rule! Honestly, the way the kid said "tourist," when a car passed refusing to help us, made me think. It made me think if a Costa Rican was on a holiday in Costa Rica would they still have helped us? Or if I was in my hometown or on the side of a highway or in a remote part of the USA, would I receive the same treatment? I'm not sure. Either way, I am so thankful those people were so kind! They were true gold.

I dropped the German girls off and headed home. My dad had a spare air filter sitting in the shed. I swapped that in as soon as I got there to have a clean, dry filter in the car. I brought all my boards inside from the car and passed out hard from an epic surf day, and spontaneous river adventure.

Pura Vida: Pavones

The second longest lefthander in the world. That's one hell of a claim. A point break so long that surfers are on the same wave for almost a kilometer (a little more than half a mile). I couldn't believe this. It was too hard to fathom.

I only had a couple of weeks left in Costa Rica on this two month stay, the second winter living there. Besides surfing locally, I felt like I hadn't ventured out far enough yet. It was time. I had traveled on planes all over the world to surf. The second longest wave, that's also my frontside, was only an eight-hour drive away. It was time to go check it out.

Pavones has a lot of hype. When big swells come through, people come from all over to surf it. I hear lots of Brazilians fly over just to surf a swell at Pavones. It can be incredibly packed and busy. I hate surfing a busy wave more than anything. The art of surfing quickly disappears into an aggro competition of machismo with little respect given. Not cool. I watched Pavones forecast for weeks waiting for a window where there would be some swell but would not be large enough or impressive enough to alert the entire world and have everyone there. I found my window. It was coming in a few days. The swell was ramping up for three days to be around 4' @ 18 seconds, but the first day or two it was only 1.5'-2' @ 16 or 17 seconds. This was my window. Everyone would run to Pavones the day the swell height was 4', when the southwest swell brought its strongest energy, but I would try to sneak in beforehand, score a few empty waves, and leave before anyone even began driving there.

I prepared the day before. I hadn't camped in my car in Costa Rica yet, but I was about to change that! My Chinese Ssangyong car was a tiny SUV with a hatchback, so I folded the back seats down and was planning on sleeping in the back. I was just going to line the back with pillows to sleep on, when I remembered in our house there was a daybed in my bedroom with a soft mattress.

"I'll just throw the daybed mattress in the back," I thought.

I went upstairs to take it to the car and, no shit, it weighed one hundred pounds. I felt like I was dragging a dead body, not that I ever have, but it felt like dead weight! I hoisted it over my shoulder, staggered to the staircase, and from my bedroom, threw it down the stairs. I picked it up, hobbled it over to the car and chucked it in with all my might. I couldn't believe how heavy and awkward it was. I pushed it around until it was in a good place where I could close the hatchback.

Ok, the bed was finally done. I packed three boards – my fish, my Hypto Krypto, and my higher volume 6'0" thruster/egg. I packed a few pairs of board shorts and towels, too. I packed a few lunches with sandwiches, extra water, and some whey protein. I was ready. I passed out that night, excited for a solo Costa Rican road trip.

I woke up around sunrise, jumped out of bed, and made some coffee and breakfast. I ate my eggs and toast and took my coffee to the beach to check Langosta before I left. Even though I wouldn't surf it if conditions were good because I was leaving for Pavones... I just had to... It was my daily morning ritual. I walked the beach, drank my coffee, looked for puka shells, and watched the surf. I started walking back and was about to leave back up the trail, when something caught my eye moving in the reef. I couldn't tell what it was, but a little black thing was flailing in the crazy stone reef that sat above the waterline at the lower tide.

The reef was almost like a huge piece of concrete with holes in it the size of a hole on the green of a golf course. I walked up and crouched down for a better look. Stuck in a reef hole was the cutest thing I'd ever seen in my life. My heart melted. I watched a baby sea turtle stuck in a hole, flailing around trying to get itself out. Honestly, I wanted to help it badly. It was torture watching it, but I know people aren't supposed to intervene in things like this. With some animals, if a human touched it, that was it. The mother would never take them in again. I don't think that was the case with turtles because they hatch out of eggs, and I think they're on their own once

235

they hatch. But I'm no biologist! Secondly, if I helped it get to the ocean, it wouldn't use its tiny turtle muscles that would help it grow to be a strong turtle. It really looked like it needed a hand though. I thought about it hard for a second, and when I was thinking, a man and his dog came walking in my direction on the beach.

The dog was a large German Shepherd. It was not on a leash, and it was coming right for me. It would most definitely be interested in this flailing turtle. I had only a few seconds to think. If I was the little sea turtle, I would be so grateful if someone helped me. I picked it up as gently as possible with only two fingers that were touching the outside of its shell, as if I was picking up a fancy hors d'oeuvre off a silver tray that I've only seen in movies and wasn't planning to eat. As I ran the cutest turtle in the world over to the ocean, it was still trying to swim or crawl in the air. Its fins were slapping the sides of my fingers. After I walked a few paces with it, I quickly and gently introduced it to the water because I wasn't sure if it had ever been in the ocean in its life yet! The champ took off like a speed demon as if it had been swimming for years. I was so proud. I turned around and the German Sheppard was sniffing the hole I picked the turtle out of. I was so happy that I saved the turtle from almost guaranteed death or injury by the dog. I walked back to my house with a huge smile on my face for helping my fellow sea turtles out! In Hawai'i, we hung out all the time together while I was surfing, we were friends. They were the size of manhole covers. I loved seeing them! They would surface for a breath of air and scare the shit out of me every time.

I was ready to leave for Pavones. I had my bed, boards, and spare clothes in the car from the night before already, and just packed some water and food from the refrigerator before leaving. I was off. The first few hours of driving I recalled from other trips before and remembered some of the Nicoya Peninsula and around to Puntarenas. Puntarenas is technically the closest beach area to San José, the capital city of Costa Rica, but it's a pretty desolate place. After Puntarenas, I had only driven towards the city before, in which the directions turn east, but I was officially in new terrain heading south toward Jaco. I had never been to Jaco before, but I heard a bunch of terrible things about it from the locals in Tamarindo. That it was all drugs, prostitution, a party every night, dirty, and lots of crime. It was the closest real beach town and surf town to the big city, so it was much busier than Tamarindo, which is hours further away.

I was too excited to get to Pavones to stop in Jaco, so I kept driving past. From the main road, there were a few beautiful cliffs that looked out over the ocean, and many people were exercising, runners and cyclists were everywhere. Cycling in Costa Rica is huge. These cyclists have all the spandex gear, teardrop aerodynamic helmets, and fancy bikes.

I ate a few meals while driving. I had a protein powder drink, a sandwich, and a banana, all while trying to make good time. After I passed Manuel Antonio National Park and Uvita, I really felt like I was getting somewhere. The road down near Uvita hugs the coast, but there was often a row of jungle trees in the way of the view of the surf. A few times, I could see the ocean or surf for a brief second or two before it was hidden again.

I was on the last leg of the trip. The road had taken me inland to avoid the large Pavones Bay I needed to drive around. I was no longer on a main road (there are no highways outside of the city area in Costa Rica). I was driving over little rinky-dink bridges over creeks, through neighborhoods, and I ended up at a new river crossing. This one looked way sketchier than the one I had to cross to get to Nosara up north. The terrain was different, I had to go down a large mud hill, the river was much wider, and there were cattle everywhere.

"That's it, I can't make it. I need to find another way," I immediately thought, giving up quickly.

A few seconds later, I witnessed an Imperial beer delivery truck drive through the river and up the mud hill. I was so impressed how the truck navigated it.

"Hmmmm… Well, if that massive beer truck crossed it maybe I can too," I thought.

I waited a while and watched a handful of other cars cross the river. All were successful crossings, seemingly with ease, and not all cars were crazy jungle safari 4x4s.

"Ok, screw it." I said to myself.

I cranked the tunes – Spacemen 3. One of my favorite bands. Pioneers of original shoegaze. This space-psychedelic alternative garage rock band was exactly what I needed to get through this river. Some attitude.

XXI-River crossing. Road to Pavones. Costa Rica. Digital.

"Here we go," I said, hyping myself up.

I remembered to stay slow. I was in first gear, forcing myself to remain at a crawling speed. This river was wider than the Nosara River, but I stayed calm. After a few heightened moments of anxiety, I got through it and waited on the other side to see if my car was going to stall again. But it never did. It just kept right on idling.

"Owwwwwwwww!!!" I celebrated with excitement.

I continued through more empty neighborhoods and crazy beautiful palm tree farms. Seeing groves of large palm trees together was seriously incredible. I am from New Jersey, and I lived in California for a while. This type of scene was extreme and exotic to me, like nothing I had ever seen before. They looked so raw and mighty when there are many together without space singling them out. It was like they stood for something. Something wild, that only existed in those jungles there, holding their secrets, foreign to what I knew.

I finally made it to the turn for Pavones. This might be one of the shittiest roads in all of Costa Rica. I bounced around all over the place trying to avoid as many holes in the ground as I could. In some places, there were holes in holes. It didn't make any sense.

As I got closer to the beach, I passed some stores in town and this whole place looked beat-up and run-down. I had no expectations for the town, as I was there for the remoteness and the waves, but this town looked like it had been swallowed up by the jungle decades ago. For such a famous surf break, it surprised me. I guess since it was so remote, it was hard to get materials there for maintenance and upkeep.

I started seeing little snippets of the ocean through the trees. I kept driving, not really knowing exactly where the beach or surf was. I drove on this cute little dirt road, going only a few miles per hour stunned, staring at beauty. Both sides of the dirt road were lined with palm trees growing in every direction with other plants and vines with vibrant flowers, like huge hibiscus, popping color all over the lush green jungle. I really couldn't believe it. Tamarindo didn't look like this. Nosara didn't look like this. Santa Teresa didn't look like this. It was breathtaking.

I drove to a different little town only a few minutes and a bridge away. Its name was Punta Banco. I drove until the road ended. I managed to find another surf break that was in the Punta Banco area and saw a surfer out, but the wind wasn't cooperating, classic in the afternoon.

I was starved, so I found a soda. Sodas, again, are restaurants in Costa Rica that offer local, or they say "typical," Costa Rican food. All the food on the menu was the traditional meals that they source locally, like fish, chicken, rice, beans, salad, ceviche, and plantains. Sodas really are the way to go in Costa Rica. They're half the price of any other restaurant with gringo food. For those that don't know, gringo is a term for white Americans, but it's now generalized to all white English-speaking tourists. All Latin American countries use this term. It can be used offensively or non-offensively based on the tone and context of the person using it.

I stopped and ate. This soda was like everything else nearby, kind of dilapidated and extremely DIY, they seemed to not have proper materials, so they used what they had to build their restaurant on the beach. Everything was outside – the kitchen and all the tables. There was a roof structure blocking the sun or rain from entering the kitchen. Sticks were used instead of wood 2x4s in places. A large wooden spool that looked like some electric company had professional-grade wire wrapped around it was impersonating a restaurant chair. I used it, sitting down in front of my table. Driftwood was used as shelving and wood for a little bar, but not in a hip, beach-vibes, chic way but in a developing country, remote kind of way. I liked it. It was real. No frills, great food, and for cheap. It was packed with surfers and locals, too.

After I ate an insane amount of ceviche and Casado, I went to find the Pavones wave. It was late afternoon, and the wind was still strong, but soon it would calm, and I wanted to be prepared to surf as soon as it did.

I drove back to Pavones from Punta Banco and found the beach. I parked and looked out. It was empty. No one was surfing, only a few people were on the beach, and there was somewhat of a wave. Even with the not ideal wind, I could see the potential of the break-ing wave, peeling from left to right on the beach. The tide was lower, and it exposed the rock reef mixed with sand.

I decided to paddle out right there and be in the water for the last two hours of daylight. I grabbed my orange fish from the car, put my keys in my lockbox attached to the handle of the car door, waxed my board, and ran to the beach. I paddled out and so did one other guy a minute before me, which I took as a good sign that others were pad-dling out expecting the conditions to get better, too.

Out of nowhere, a set came through that was head high and I wasn't ready for it! I duck dove one, paddled out farther, duck dove a second, and was in a better position for the third. I turned around and started paddling. I saw the sweet spot on the shoulder, where I want-ed to be, and went for it. I popped up and caught my first Pavones wave! I was gliding my fish on my frontside, pumping until a section closed out in front of me that I couldn't make it around. I dove off my board into the breaking wave piercing through it, to safety on the backside. It was amazing. What a long powerful lefthander! I under-stood why this wave was so unique. Its power and fast-peeling point break qualities were not something I had surfed before. The swell was small yet head high! I paddled back for more.

When the conditions are perfect, all the different sections along the beach connect for the ultra-long wave, but between the swell not being very big and the wind not great, I was only surfing a section of the full wave. Still, the quality of the left was amazing compared to the beach breaks in Tamarindo I had surfed often. No comparison. I surfed that night until dark, catching wave after wave with only a couple of other surfers who were nowhere near me. I had every wave I wanted and had some long rides! I scored.

240

This break would be littered with hundreds of surfers in two days when the swell reached 4' @ 18 seconds. I may not have had the best conditions imaginable, but I caught tons of waves at Pavones with no one around. It was sick. On my way out of the ocean, my shin caught a boulder underwater and gave me a big bloody scratch. I still have scars on my shin today from that boulder. I got back to the car, poured water on it, and put some antibiotic cream on it to try to keep the cut from getting infected. I dried off, changed, put my board in the car, and drove around looking for a place to park the car and sleep until sunrise.

I headed back toward Punta Banco, from Pavones proper, on the dirt road. I was looking for a natural jungle spot where I could pull the car in and pass out. Somewhere I wouldn't be bothered or bother anyone else. As I continued down the tropical flower and palm tree-lined dirt road, it was dark, and I searched for a place to crash by my headlights alone. I found a small pull-off that was big enough for a car, about the size of a small driveway meant for only one car. I decided right there, this was it. There were palm trees everywhere. I backed in and had to wedge the car in between about five different smaller, skinnier jungle trees on every side. I wouldn't be able to open one of the rear passenger doors because I was about three inches away from a jungle tree on one side, but the rest worked great.

XXII-Car camping Punta Banco, next to Pavones. My car is behind the thickest palm. Digital.

I turned my headlights off and took out the keys from the ignition. Here was home. I turned on my flashlight and saw that I was parked only six feet away from the sand on the beach to my bumper. The beach level was a foot or two lower than the palm tree-lined area I was in.

There was an ominous ambient noise that was happening all day and night, that sounded like a massive transformer from an electrical plant was right next to me humming in some strange melodic pattern. I noticed it on and off all day. Like a dark, analogue Moog synth sound from Brian Eno, back from the 1960s -70s or something. It was an unnatural, ubiquitous, eerie melodic hum through the trees. I think there were some very strange birds or flying insects in the trees. Maybe some sort of cicada that made a hum, but it sounded like there were millions of them, collectively making the hum very intense. It was spooky at night. I opened my hatchback and took out one board that didn't fit in my sleeping arrangement. I put the board underneath my car, hidden from the eye in case someone had sticky fingers overnight and saw me parked there.

The other two boards I stacked on top of each other, taking up half of my bed in the back. The other half was for me. I ate a snack and brushed my teeth. It was so early, like 6:45 p.m., but I had nothing else to do except sleep, so I got into bed. I attempted to close the hatchback and all doors and windows to keep the mosquitos out. In about two minutes, I was sweating so badly from the humidity and still air that it was impossible to sleep in this sauna I created. I got up, put the keys in the ignition, rolled the windows down halfway, and opened the hatchback. I would rather get chewed up by mosquitos than sweat to death.

I got back in and felt the ocean breeze sweep through the car.

"Ohhhhh yessss," I said in sweet relief.

I expected the mosquitos to be barreling down on me in any second with an entire army. I put in earplugs so I wouldn't hear them kamikaze my ears like they tend to do. I really wanted to sleep to the ocean sounds, but it was more important to get sleep.

I awoke in the middle of the night to the sounds of the ocean and water being very close, it sounded like I was in water. Had I been dreaming? It was loud! I sat up and took my earplugs out. It sounded like water was right beneath me! I turned on my flashlight and got up. The tide had come up so high, the ocean water was hitting the lip of the dirt area I parked on, flooding feet higher than the beach below. Even cresting the lip and soaking the dirt that was a few feet away from me. I was spooked! The water startled me, and I thought I was going to be consumed by the tide in my half-awake dream state. Once I saw it was there and not actually under me, I got up, peed on the dirt ground, and laid back down. I thought if it got worse, I would move, but I did quick math and figured this was the top of high tide. It was such an extreme change from when I went to sleep. The entire beach was visible, even to the reef after the sand, like a football field length! Costa Rica's tide swings really are impressive.

In California, Hawai'i, and other places I have lived or spent time surfing, the tide swings (difference in water level from high to low tide or vice versa) are not nearly as significant. I could surf mostly throughout the whole tide cycle and still have waves. In Costa Rica, there is no wave or water at all at low tide.

I awoke at first light, 4:45 a.m., and got up. I brushed my teeth and spit onto the dirt ground. I ate a banana and drank my leftover coffee, from the drive down the day before, that was sitting in my cup holder in a cardboard cup with a lid. The tide was lower again, and I walked alone onto the beach for a Zen early morning walk. Not a sole around, just like sunset. A few minutes later and after a few stretches, I packed up my board from under the car and took off to go check the Pavones wave again. I arrived back in the little dirt car park in front of Pavones and watched. I didn't see any waves as fun as yesterday, even though the swell was supposed to be increasing. I packed up and drove out. I had a few other spots I wanted to check on the way back up north.

I left and drove out the same way I came in, I think it was the only way. I drove on the worst dirt road in Costa Rica, through pothole land, bouncing around everywhere in the car, trying not to pop a tire. I drove over the bridges, next to the palm tree farm, through the abandoned neighborhoods, and back to the main road that headed north up the coast. I drove for about three hours and pulled off into Uvita.

I always wanted to check this town out. Uvita is a surf, hippie, traveler town in southern Costa Rica, where the coastline looks identical to the shape of a whale's tale, as a peninsula sticking off the coast. There are three sides to the peninsula, the flat bottom of the whale's tale and its two sides. I really wanted to check out the surf there, and the town in general. I drove through all the streets, some were cute with cafés, accommodations, and street vendors. I tried going to three different beach access points, and every time the road was closed, or I was forced to change my route. There must have been one major beach where everyone was forced to park. I couldn't find it. After a little while of searching, I headed back to the main road and took off to head farther north, it wasn't meant to be.

Not far after Uvita is the TRUE Playa Hermosa (beautiful beach). I say "true" because there are at least six different Playa Hermosas in Costa Rica, but the Hermosa near Uvita has the best surf and the most epic landscape.

I didn't know it was THEE Playa Hermosa I had heard others talk about around Tamarindo. On the way down to Pavones, I had seen surfers in the water through the trees from the main road and thought on the way back up north I could pull off and surf check.

I parked between the mangroves in the sand and walked out onto the beach. I was blown away, stunned by beauty. Playa Hermosa is a large cove. I decided to stretch my legs and walk to the northern end. The beach ended at a few tall, rugged cliffs with vines hanging off them like an *Indiana Jones* movie. On the walk, I looked up and saw two huge Macaws, flying majestically and effortlessly, gliding through the air.

A Macaw is the largest parrot in the world. These were bright red with huge beaks, and they were about three feet from beak to tail with a wingspan of up to four feet wide. They were incredible looking birds, surreal, and the definition of exotic. Nothing like I had ever seen before. When I used to live in San Francisco, California, I would get woken up every morning by little green parrots that would perch on the fire escape outside my window. I thought those were much more exotic birds compared to the ones I grew up with in New Jersey. Doves, Robins, Cardinals, Chickadees, and Canadian Geese were the birds I was used to. Macaws were in a league of their own. Like some sort of mythical Phoenix in the sky on fire.

Everywhere I looked, my mind melted further into bliss. I watched the surf on my walk and there was a wave. It was low tide, and this place was beach break city. It was possible there was some reef under there as I walked on some stone slab exposed near the waterline on the shore, but the waves were behaving in beach break fashion. Very organized A-frame waves would come in and peel right and left away from the peak. It was a fast wave, how beach breaks tend to be.

"Screw it, there's one surfer out on the whole beach, let me take out my Hypto Krypto and see if I can ride a few of these on my shorter board!" I told myself.

I paddled out and hunted for a left. When surfing beach breaks, I've learned I need to always be hunting around for the peak. They move around and are not exactly consistent, especially compared to a classic point break. Point breaks consistently break in the same area. Once I found a peak I was in the general area for, I tried to position myself just to the left (surfer's perspective) of it to drop in on the edge of the pitching peak, then ride the shoulder of the wave as it developed and it's transition walled-up steeper, beating the lip that eventually broke to more open transition ahead.

It was a quick, hollow wave. My first few ride attempts were unsuccessful. Just a drop-in or a drop-in and one pump down the left side at best before the rest of the wave closed out on me, cutting off the open ridable real estate to zero. Or I would drop in too late, and the wave would pitch on me. I kept moving around the beach paddling farther north. I wasn't about to give up. Even if the surf wasn't great or was too difficult for me, I still was in one of the most beautiful places I'd ever been. Where else was I going to go? This is the correct positive attitude a surfer should have. If you're frustrated that you aren't catching waves and that puts you in a bad mood, maybe surfing isn't for you. The people who are stoked to be in the ocean, regardless of their successfully ridden wave count are the ones that fill the lineup with good energy. They're always the ones having the most fun!

After a while, the tide started filling in, and the waves got better and better. The size grew, and the thickness of the waves grew, providing longer rides. This is why in places like Costa Rica, with significant tide swings, it's important to do research!

I finally started dialing them in and had some unbelievable beach break rides! There were now three other guys out there besides me, but it was still empty, and I caught a few more.

I had never ridden the Hypto Krypto so well before. I think I was getting the hang of the shortboard and riding it in the conditions it was made for. My timing got better, my pop-up got quicker, and my legs got more used to landing on the board already in a balanced and activated way. I started maneuvering the board quicker than before, or quicker than other boards with more volume and size.

It was genuinely fun. I had a blast. I loved shortboarding! It was more grueling for sure. I tended to catch less waves per session than if I rode a longer board, not that it mattered. Fun is fun. Shortboarding was way more work to paddle into waves for a shorter ride than a longboard, as a longboard can catch mellower waves much deeper. I have longboarded for many years and wanted to continue developing my surfing skills to the next level!

"There's a shortboard revolution happening, Dave." My buddy Chris on O'ahu always said, pushing me to take a shortboard into the surf.

He would say it in reference to my old ways of exclusively long-boarding, never willing to size down to a shortboard. I had finally committed to this revolution and was trying to actively rip harder each time I surfed. Every day I was in the surf, I was learning new shortboard techniques and maneuvers. How to bottom turn, top turn, snap, cut back. I was also buying (used but new to me) smaller and smaller boards, downsizing and getting better at riding shorter, less volume, higher performance, shortboards in bigger surf. I was always making mental notes and adjusting/correcting from my last ride. This allowed me to continue to grow and be a better surfer. By the end of the session in Playa Hermosa, I was catching long, steep, A-frames, pumping down the line and riding the Hypto Krypto better than I had yet. I got out and walked the long sandy beach back to my car.

While I was next to my car drying off, a dude pulled up in a tiny safari Jeep-thing with no doors or roof. He pulled his board out and started talking to me while he waxed his board. He was a local. Not a native Costa Rican but lived nearby and was from Brazil. He made it sound like the tide conditions here were just getting good now and I should go back out.

"You're probably right, but I had a fun session and caught a bunch!" I told him.

"What about Pavones!?" He asked, then said, "You see the forecast? It's going to be firing tomorrow. Are you headed there?"

This is when I knew I won.

"No, I'm headed back up to Tamarindo, but I was there yesterday, and I was one of the only dudes in the water for the smaller swell," I responded.

He was having difficulty comprehending that I was the only one out there catching waves. He had clearly only gone when the larger swells were hitting, and that was when everyone and their mother went. This was exactly what I tried to avoid and did. I could tell that I opened his mind to find opportunities to score under the radar. We said goodbye, he paddled out with a few more guys now in the lineup, and I packed up and took off north.

I pulled off at Quepos and Manuel Antonio for lunch. I knew nothing about Quepos and just drove through the town on the way to the Manuel Antonio area. I had been to Manuel Antonio before, the first time I was in Costa Rica, when I was eighteen on a family vacation.

Manuel Antonio is a town with accommodations all along the extremely tall cliffside with a National Park below. As soon as I drove in, I regretted it. This was one of the heaviest trafficked areas in all of Costa Rica for tourists. Manuel Antonio is a Costa Rican experience that many people go for. I was in gridlock traffic. Locals were trying to force me to park and pay high parking prices. I managed to sneak out without paying and pulled into a free café parking spot right near the entrance to the National Park. I ate a delicious tuna steak and rushed out of the hectic tourist zone as fast as I could to head back onto the main road.

Jaco was next after another hour of driving. I had never been to Jaco officially, and like I said, I had all the Tamarindo locals' words in my head about how sketchy and dirty Jaco was. I wanted to see for myself. I knew it had surf and was a surf town like Tamarindo. I figured I would check out the beach and get a coffee for the last four hours of the drive still in front of me.

I pulled off the main road to the south side of town and drove near the beach to check the waves. I didn't even have to get out of the car to see that the waves were complete garbage. Close outs. Not a good shape or ride existed out there that day, that was for sure. I left and found a coffee shop close to the north end of town. I drove on the main road in Jaco where all the bars and restaurants were on both sides of the street. This looked like THEE party strip if I ever saw one. It was gross, honestly. It reminded me of Las Vegas. There was even a Harley-Davidson-themed bar. It looked like Vegas if Vegas had an even dirtier, older, shittier cousin. Maybe the place came to life at night with all the drugs and alcohol that were supposedly there. That scene wasn't for me. It looked like the biggest tourist trap in the world for drinking and party culture with some super lame-looking bars. It screamed sketchy, and not my vibe! I quickly got my espresso for takeaway and took off down the road back to Tamarindo.

It was ridiculous how Tamarindo was ever compared to Jaco. Tamarindo is significantly smaller, like one-fifth of the size, and Tamarindo is known for its nightlife scene, too, only there are about enough bars in Tamarindo to fill the fingers on one hand. Jaco has enough to fill a ten-gallon bucket. Also, the Tamarindo area is beautiful, the beaches are beautiful, and the culture is very friendly. I found Jaco to be more aggressive and less friendly in the couple of interactions I had in town. And the area wasn't nearly as pretty. Easy to check off the list as having been there and never needing to go back!

I finally got back to my house in the Playa Langosta area of Tamarindo around 9 p.m. I unpacked my car, took out my boards, brought them one by one into my house, and drug the dead-body-day-mattress back into the house and up the flight of stairs. I hoofed it into my bedroom and onto its frame, and I was done for the day. Tapped out. No more energy for me. I turned around, keeled over into my bed, and passed out.

From Pura Vida To Nica

Witches Rock is the most famous surf break in Costa Rica. I feel like I can't talk about surfing in Costa Rica without at least mentioning it. Witches Rock was made famous by the surf film *Endless Summer II*. *Endless Summer*, the original, is the most famous surf film ever made. It's a classic. It took surfing to a completely different platform back in the mid-1960s when it came out. Its premise: to travel around the world from surfing location to different location, always in the on-season for surfing swell, constantly scoring amazing waves. In the film, they surfed California, Senegal, Ghana, Nigeria, South Africa, Australia, New Zealand, Tahiti, and Hawai'i. One of the two main character surfers in the film moved to Tamarindo and is still there surfing and shaping boards. *Endless Summer II* had a different cast, but they surfed Witches Rock in Costa Rica. This sequel was released in the mid-1990s and put Costa Rica on the surf mecca map.

I have never surfed Witches Rock. It's not easy to get to. I'm the type of person or traveler or surfer that prefers doing things myself, DIY-style. I don't like fancy, expensive accommodations, I don't like eating out constantly, and I don't like services doing everything for me. I prefer to live modestly, save money, do things myself, and enjoy the little things in life.

The way that most surfers, or tourists, would access Witches Rock is by paying quite a bit of money to a company to drive them there though the sketchy jaguar-filled jungle in the National Park or driving you to a boat and taking a longer boat ride to the surf break.

It's remote and difficult to get to. I love difficult adventures, but in Costa Rica, I do not have a 4x4 vehicle and I get stuck sometimes in crossing the little river to Nosara, so I don't think it's wise to try in my rig.

I almost went with a few local buddies once. We were trying to rent a boat to split the price which might lessen the cost to around $50 a person. Still, I would be driving past every other surf break along the way that was free.

"Never leave waves for waves!!" Again, Chris's saying popped into my head.

Especially free waves! There are other places in the world where I needed to take a boat to an outer reef spot or a boat crossing a croc-infested river that was really the only way to surf. They were quick and super cheap too.

Technically, Witches Rock was a break that I could drive to my-self, it was just sketchy. It wasn't in a National Park, like National Parks in the USA. Costa Rica's National Parks are jungles that are not monitored the same way as National Parks in the USA. They are pure and wild. Whenever I have been in exotic natural places, surf-ing, hiking, or adventuring, it never failed that I always manage to get significantly more injured than back home. I didn't know the lay of the land or the flora and fauna that were dangerous. I constantly had infected reef cuts or tons of mosquito bites or sea lice (not the same thing as regular lice), making my entire body itch, or stomach issues or injuries more severe than that. I have learned by experience when to inject myself into wild situations more strategically as I put some years under my belt with this lifestyle. This has kept me from driving myself to Witches Rock, thus far. Maybe one day that will change… Mostly, it was just that I didn't need to pay over $100 and burn an entire day when I could access beautiful, warm water waves across the street for free.

I had made a friend named Kim, who was my neighbor in Playa Langosta, who helped me get into my house one night when I flew back into town late. I was stranded without keys, and she invited me in while we got in touch with the management company together to toss me some extra keys. I walked in and her son Matt was sitting on the couch. He was a long brown-haired, jam-band following, open sandal-wearing, Colorado mountain hippie from Tulsa, Oklahoma. We met, and he asked me to let him know whenever I paddled out. He wanted to learn how to surf. He seemed nice enough and came from a cool mom, so I figured sure why not. I also usually surfed and lived alone in Costa Rica, so a new buddy sounded cool.

I took him out the next day. We surfed one of my many local spots almost daily together for a few weeks. Even during the first session, he stood up on his log, catching his own waves, and the more sessions we had together, the noticeably better he got. He was also a hiker/mountaineer/climber in Colorado where he lived in his van that he built out himself. It made sense that he would pick up surfing quickly. He was athletic and always down to throw himself into waves that were above his pay grade, or beyond his skill level. I really enjoyed the motivation he had. He was fearless.

The longer I surf, the more I understand the potential dangers that can be present on certain days, and I try to navigate around them with the surfing skills I have developed. He was such a rookie that he hadn't been through any negative situations to give him any real reason to doubt anything. He was super gung-ho. I loved it. He jumped right into the fire. After sessions of us surfing together and me giving him pointers in the water, I started letting him borrow my shorter, higher-volume boards to try out shortboarding. We pulled up to Playa Avellana one evening at sunset, but it looked like the conditions were bad. We decided to just hang on the beach, but then in the blink of an eye, the conditions switched, as if just for us, becoming clean shoulder-high glassy waves. We ran into the water for forty-five minutes before dark and caught wave after wave. Matt was on my thicker 6'0" thruster shortboard. It was his first feeling of shredding. I watched him catch and surf this lefthander (his backside), and I knew it was all over. He was officially a real surfer.

There was a lull in the swell for a few days after Matt and I had been surfing together tons. We decided to give our arms a rest and took a little trip to hike around Monteverde. I hadn't done virtually any hiking in Costa Rica. The beaches and surf were like a vortex for me. It took Matt to mention an interest in something different for me to realize there was way more out there than surfing and beach life in the world, and in Costa Rica especially!

We booked a little cabin high up in the mountains up a crazy steep road. It was so steep that my car had trouble getting up, and the road was paved! Monteverde is a super-sick hippie town mostly in the mountains of Puntarenas, spilling a tiny bit into the Guanacaste province about four hours east of Tamarindo. We booked a single-room cabin for one night and planned to do a few hikes between two days and drive back to Tamarindo the second night. We arrived and ate at an artsy café off the main street in town, parked our car, and decided to just walk around.

We walked a mile or two checking out the town when we saw signs for a waterfall trail. We paid a couple dollar entrance fee, supporting the locals, and started the hike. It was a short thirty minutes of being thrown into incredibly lush jungle scenery. We followed a river for a while until we made it to the falls. The tree roots grew down all the cliff faces into the river below. It was a unique spider web of root systems that were thick and old. It was evidence of how life always found a way to survive. We jumped into the lagoon surrounding the waterfalls. We really had no plan or expectation, which made this little mission so worth it. We walked back toward the car around the time the sun was setting. We passed a lookout point that half the town stopped at to watch the sunset. Buses were stopping to let people off for it. We were on foot anyway, so we stayed and watched as the sun set into the western mountains over the high lakes. It wasn't an ocean sunset, but it was epic.

We made it back to the car and cabin. The wind picked up significantly. We could hear it howling outside our door. We went back into town for some food and ended up at a fish taco restaurant sitting on a second-story outdoor patio. I was frozen. I didn't think that I was going into the cold mountains! I only had board shorts and t-shirts! We got back to the cabin, and I dove into my bed under the covers for the rest of the night.

The next morning, our plan was to hike the Monteverde cloud-forest trail. We were up and coffee'd early in excitement of the cloud forest! I remember being in temperate rainforests in California and Oregon. It was one of my favorite places. I grew up in New Jersey, a more average place, without temperate rainforests anywhere near me! We got in and hiked around to the top of the mountain. We were trying to find little side trails that would allow us to leave the tourists behind. We hiked up for hours, looking out at views of jungle-covered mountains and fog everywhere. It was an interesting dynamic to see an area in Costa Rica so cold. From the top on clear days, you can see the Pacific Ocean and Caribbean looking right and left! So cool!

Shortly after the Monteverde trip, I decided to plan a trip to the San Juan Del Sur area in Nicaragua. Specifically, to surf Playa Maderas with a gym friend named Pri. She didn't surf, but we were hanging out on the beach one day and she asked if I wanted to go.

"Hell yes I do!" I replied instantly.

Technically, San Juan Del Sur is only about a three-hour drive from Tamarindo. Most people don't travel between these surf towns very much because the countries and borders don't exactly make it easy. I don't know how accurate this was, but I asked my Costa Rican friend why.

"Nicaragua does not like the USA, and we (Costa Rica) like the USA, so they are very different countries with different ideals." Pri, explained to me.

The process of going through customs wasn't very easy or straightforward, like how in Europe, for example, I can travel freely between countries without needing to go through ANY customs or border crossings.

We planned out our trip for two nights and three days and booked accommodations in Playa Madera, just up the hill from the beach. Playa Madera is about twenty minutes north of San Juan Del Sur and was the first surf break I ever paddled out in, about eleven years earlier. I was super pumped to be an international traveler in Central America again! And in just a few short hours of driving!

Once Pri arrived at my house, we took off early one morning and started driving north. After about an hour, we got out of Tamarindo's beach area and were in empty nowhere. Just big semi-trucks blowing by or the same trucks creeping up steep hills. We took my car, and the plan was to leave it in someone's yard at the border, then walk across the border and rent a car on the other side. This was how the locals did it. Apparently, I couldn't cross the border with a car if my name was not on the title of the vehicle. In my case, my dad bought the car so his name was on the title, meaning I couldn't take it over the border. Instead, we needed to park in this guy's dirt yard for five bucks a day.

As we drove in the middle of nowhere getting closer to the border, I got pulled over by Costa Rican police. I asked what the problem was, but Pri told me to let her do the talking. I can speak caveman or five-year-old-kid-Spanish, but she was a local. Apparently, I

253

needed a license plate on the front and back of my car, and I was missing one in the front. It either got stolen, fell off in the river I went too fast in, or fell off on a bouncy dirt road somewhere. This was a serious offense, too. They could choose to not let me continue to drive with only one plate (such bullshit). Side note, my old Toyota Tacoma truck is plated to my family's house in Arizona, and the DMV only issued me one plate for the rear of the vehicle there. Totally unnecessary to have two. Anyway, Pri used a bit of her Costa Rican charm and the police let us go after checking our passports. If I was alone in the car, I would not have gotten away with that.

We continued driving to the border. We reached the border traffic that was exclusively tractor-trailers in gridlock at a dead stop for miles and miles. There was a little shoulder in the road the cars were sneaking forward in, and I jumped into that makeshift lane, following the moving cars. We made it to the point where Pri told me to turn right into this guy's yard. It was a house with a family sort of living outside. Their kitchen was in the backyard, and their oven or range was a stack of cinder blocks with fire in it, cooking something on top in a pot. I parked next to another car in the dirt yard. It looked like he could fit roughly ten cars on his property, maybe a few more if he squeezed it. Pri talked with him again and agreed on the terms. We were planning to be back in three days to pay and pick up the car.

I had no idea what I had gotten myself into, and I had no idea the logistical nightmare I was about to have to jump through in order to cross this border. It was always wrong to assume anything. Especially while traveling in countries that are not your own. I assumed this was like a ten-second walk, so I grabbed my rucksack on my back and stacked my two boards together. I carried them freely under my arm without a travel bag of any sort. I thought after this ten-second walk we would be in our rental car in Nica, but we had to walk well over a mile, and we did not know how far it was the entire time.

I kept switching my boards under different arms back and forth, on my head, and every other way I could think to carry them. I got tired of those positions, too, and tried inventing more. We finally arrived at a military man in uniform with a gun.

254

IV-Confused traveler border crossing. Digital.

"Which way to Nicaragua?" Pri asked in Spanish.

He pointed, waving us farther down the road. We continued to walk. I was in agony from holding the boards for so long. I started to feel uncomfortable where we were. I wasn't scared, per se, but I felt like this land between the countries was like a war zone. It had a post-apocalyptic vibe with cement walls, barbed wire, and garbage. It seemed like there should've been an unattended fire burning in the distance. I felt like I was in Russia during the Cold War or something. Even the architecture of the government buildings had a cold, eastern-European, stand-off-ish energy to them. There was no one around either. How was there no one here at a border crossing!? How are we in the empty corridor between countries when there were about three miles of semi-trucks at a dead stop waiting to cross? Nothing about this place made any sense, and I couldn't wait to be at the beach.

About another fifteen-minute walk (or about a mile) there was a man sitting in an old chair that looked like it was from an old elementary school library in the USA. The man didn't have a military uniform on or didn't seem to have a gun. He was just a guy. He asked to see our passports and stamps. We didn't know what he was talking about and inquired.

"You can't go through because you have not gotten stamps yet. You must go get stamps." Pri translated what he said for me.

He pointed at a building that we needed to go to for stamps on our passports to enter Nicaragua. We turned around and walked the distance of a few city blocks over to this stamp building. We walked in and waited in line.

"We need stamps please." Pri asked the border officer.

They took our passports and looked through them.

"You do not have exit stamps from Costa Rica, you must go get those first." The officer said.

I was at a breaking point. I had no more patience for this insane system they had.

"So how did we get this far then?? How are we here if we are not supposed to be here? I'm a man holding two surfboards. I'm not exactly sneaking around!!" I told Pri. "I want to go back to Tamarindo, screw this."

She calmed me down and insisted we try one more time. We walked farther to the Costa Rican building, back the way we came from, still carrying my boards and rucksack. There were no signs or greeters or attendants to ask for help or direct on where to go. The street was vacant. Once we found the place, we finally got stamped out of Costa Rica and walked back to the unnoticeable, without signage, Nicaragua Welcome Building, that sat a fifteen-minute walk from the Costa Rican border building.

I had no arm strength left. These surf boards were not light anymore. They were large, awkward, and heavy. In the Nicaragua stamp office, we had to pay to get a stamp. This was the only country I have ever been to that required you to pay to get a stamp. $20 per person! Not for a visa. There is no visa for Americans or Costa Ricans. I can stay for ninety days, like in Costa Rica, visa free. It was like we were being extorted at the customs office.

"I think they were just pocketing our money. We should not have to pay anything here." Pri even said.

We finally got through with Nicaraguan stamps. Now we walked back to the plain man in the old 1980s library chair on wheels that looked like it had been in a city dump for twenty years.

"Passports and stamps please," he said in Spanish.

We showed him and he looked at the passports for too long, finally allowing us to pass. We were so excited to get the hell out of there. We still had to walk a significant amount farther but finally got out of the government military zone. We walked over to the rental car tent where we had a reservation for a car.

Pri ran in and got the car for us while I hung outside with my surfboards on the ground. I really needed a travel bag. I have multiple travel bags! I didn't think to bring one because I had no idea it was going to be like this! I honestly thought that we would park at one edge of the border, then walk fifteen feet to the other side of the imaginary line where a car would be waiting for us. I am such an idiot sometimes.

We got the rental car with relative ease, even though they were very anal about every tiny pin-sized nick that was already on the vehicle, meaning they planned to try to charge us for any extra scratch they saw. I was terrified of this because I beat up vehicles more than the average adult. I threw my soft rack on the rental car's roof, threw the ratchet straps through the car doors and secured my boards to it. We took off and I tried to drive extra carefully. I figured we were only in Nica for three days and we shouldn't be driving that much, really.

After we were on the road, it took a little over an hour to get to San Juan Del Sur. The border crossing took about three hours, which was the amount of time it was supposed to take from Tamarindo to Madera, but we had nothing to do except surf.

We were starving but wanted to get to the hotel to drop off our bags and my boards.

I hung out in San Juan Del Sur for about a month, over ten years ago, when I was backpacking through Central America with my ex-girlfriend. I remembered liking San Juan Del Sur, but looking at it now, it was a shit hole. It looked like Jaco. Just a dirty place without good surf. Only a place to drink, do drugs, and party all hours of the day. Tons of riffraff on the streets and bars were everywhere. Funny how I saw similar things that affected me differently at different periods in my life. We blew through San Juan Del Sur and continued to Playa Madera. The paved road ended, and we were driving on a dirt road from here on out. Playa Madera seemed to be a little more my style. Empty. Every now and then a house, then nothing but more desert jungle again.

The climate and environment we were in was funny. Costa Rica is a very tropical place, but northern Costa Rica where Tamarindo is located is tropical desert. Southern Nicaragua, in terms of geography, is super close and in the same region. Northern Costa Rica actually used to be Nicaragua, and the Costa Ricans took it from the Nicaraguans at one point in history (maybe another reason why the countries are not super friendly). The climate is the same in both.

There were palm trees and jungle plants, but there were also cacti everywhere, and this region doesn't receive any rain for six months out of the year. In most tropical places with a wet and dry season, it rains less in the dry season, but here, it rained zero. A Tamarindo native once told me that there was only one other place on earth with the same climate, and it was somewhere in Africa.

Places with dirt roads and no rain are incredibly dusty. All the trees that lined the road were caked with dirt so thick we couldn't see the lush green color of the leaves.

We got to a massive hill or small steep mountain, however you want to call it. The directions told us our accommodation was on top. Our car was small. It was a Euro compact with manual transmission. I made it up some of the hill with a struggle and had to go slower and slower, dropping the gears lower and lower to continue forward.

I was in first gear and stopped. I tried giving it gas and letting the clutch out to go forward, only we started rolling backward downhill. I slammed on the brakes, but that just made the car's wheels lock up and continue to slide backward in the dirt and gravel. I looked through the rearview mirror behind us and there was no one coming up the hill and nothing for us to hit. I kept the steering wheel straight, keeping us on the road avoiding falling into the ditches on either side. We came to a stop back at the bottom of the hill. We were screaming the whole time.

"Ok, let's try that again. This is the only way, right?" I said, laughing.

"Yep," Pri responded.

I reversed farther down to get some good speed for momentum to take us up farther than the first time. I stayed in lower gear and shifted down quicker when I needed to. There was one hump that looked like a drainage pipe was buried under the dirt road, which I got stuck on initially. I drove up fast and negotiated the hump in a way that took us more sideways on it, like an S-turn, and made it over. I kept it in first gear for another minute, and we made it back to the top! Holy shit that was hard. We pulled up to what looked like a chic hotel and café, which was where we were staying. I was surprised because the price was only around $35 per night for each of our rooms.

We walked in with our bags and checked in. The café in the lobby was super stylish. We were too hungry to look elsewhere, so we ordered food at the hotel, and I ate three plates worth, a normal quantity for me. It was mid-afternoon and I wanted to go check the surf at Madera. The hotel had a ridiculously spectacular view from the clifftop over the Pacific Ocean, but with the way it was angled, we were facing just a little too south and couldn't see Madera or any waves from there. The staff saw me bring my boards in and told me about the path I could take from their hotel to Playa Madera. It was about a ten-minute walk. I was stoked to not drive again, so we took the path to the beach. Without knowing the conditions or which board to bring, I took my fish that's easier to ride in most conditions.

We snuck next to a different hotel and walked down the hiking path in the trees. The trail spat us out at a DIY café on the main dirt road near the beach, then we arrived. Finally, Madera!

Now, normally, if this was anywhere else in the world, even Costa Rica most of the time, the winds would not be great in mid-afternoon, but Madera... Madera was special. Southern Nicaragua has a unique natural wind phenomenon, where the huge great lake, Lake Nicaragua, generates lots of wind and consistently blows strong trade winds to the west. The narrow strip of land where Madera is located sit in between the lake and the Pacific Ocean, and the land is thin enough that the wind from the lake blows all the way to the ocean. Lastly, Madera sits mostly hidden from those strong winds, as the big hills and cliffs that our accommodation was on, and a few others, block the surf from being blown too hard by these trade winds. Giving Madera phenomenal offshore conditions ALL THE TIME! All... day... long. All it needed was swell.

Sure enough, we walked out and there were super fun A-frames with perfect offshore wind. I couldn't contain myself. I ran to the surf and paddled out. Pri hung out on the sand reading and walking around. I caught wave after wave while the tide was still a little low. As the tide came in, more and more locals paddled out. I found a nice left and surfed it over and over on the south end of the beach. It wasn't the longest point break in the world, but the fast transition was just asking to be shredded. It wasn't huge, but it was supposed to get bigger in the following days. I surfed for a couple hours until it got busy closer to sunset. I got out after catching my fair share of waves, and chilled on the beach watching the magnificent colors in the sky and the sun sneak behind the ocean.

We walked back up to our hotel the same way we walked down the mountain on the hiking trail. Only this time, going up was loads harder and we ended up getting lost. We walked around the long way and had to hike up the steep backside road that the rental car had a hard time getting up on our initial drive in. We finally made it, so tired, and we ate dinner at the café in the hotel again before passing out in our rooms. What a wild day, but in the end, totally worth it. It always is.

The next morning, I woke up and had a sunrise session before the café was open and before Pri was up. This time, I took my short-board down to the beach via the hiking trail and paddled out. The region of the world I was in, sometimes defined how crowded the lineups were, at sunrise and early morning times. Some places in the world were packed, like Bali, where hundreds of people were in the water by 6 a.m., but other places, like Northern California, people don't really start existing outside for a few hours after sunrise. This place was the latter. At sunrise, I was the only one standing on the beach watching bigger waves than the day before, held open by the beautiful offshore wind. I took it all in before paddling out. The cliffs to the left of me against the beach, the sheer-rock reef jetting up out of the ocean also on the south side, all the rock formations, the steep hills behind me, and more outcropping rock formations to the north. It was spectacular. Really, an exotic place with a lot of natural ener-gy happening in all directions.

I paddled out. I went after this peak on the north side of the cove this time, as I saw a lefthander breaking over there. This place was a little confusing. I wanted to make sure I knew if there were rocks or just sand below the break for my safety, and for the level of risk I put myself through in the barrels and such. Like I said, there were huge slab rocks on both ends of the beach jetting out of the sand, but the shallow walk out was all sandy bottom. Sandy bottom surf breaks are always safer as there's nothing to potentially impact or impale me. Also, the waves behaved more like a beach break, always shifting, never consistently in the same spot. So, I deduced it was all sand and started going for some waves. I caught a killer head-high fast barrel-ing left, then paddled back out for a set of righthanders breaking in the same spot. I tried to catch whatever was dealt to me.

After a while, another guy paddled out, someone was doing yoga on the beach, and there was another person jogging by. I still could not believe that these conditions were sitting here for the taking. The sun was up and no one in town seemed to care. The other surfer and I took turns catching two different peaks that would end in a similar place, breaking toward each other. The swell was much stronger than the day before. I was amazed by the size, force, and hard pitching lip from these waves. It was beautiful to watch. No wonder it's a famous spot. I was almost in a position a few times to get barreled, but it was intimidating early in the morning, when I wasn't awake yet, and I missed the opportunities. I still had some great rides on open waves, and it was time for me to hike back up the steep hill for some coffee and breakfast.

I met Pri and we ate again at the cool hotel café. This hotel was a vortex because of its unique style. It was a mix between chic and old barn/farmer antiques with bull skulls painted crazy colors and old, rustic, wooden furniture. The place had the best view of the ocean I had ever seen from a hotel, plus a good coffee shop/café for food. Besides surfing, there was no reason to leave! I didn't like this though as I'm an adventurer not a lounger. I usually couldn't afford places like this, so I never got the experience. Here in Nicaragua, it was affordable, so I tried to enjoy it as best I could as it was only for a couple of days. Still, I tend to boycott too much decadence and luxury.

I wanted to check out other surf spots around. After we ate breakfast and hung out on the patio for a while with our coffees, I tossed my boards on the soft travel roof rack I installed on the rental car, and we headed south. For the better part of the afternoon, we checked El Remanso, Tamarind, Hermosa, and El Yanke surf spots. Every other spot was not as good as Madera, if not completely flat or a complete close out, like El Yanke. Still, it was fun to get out, see some new things, and get to see all these spots in person.

"Don't leave waves for waves," Chris said in my mind, again, haunting me all the way from O'ahu.

I didn't surf again until we got back to Madera later that afternoon, which was fine, because having three surf sessions in one day is gnarly, and it would make the next day much more difficult from soreness. I paddled out for a long sunset session and navigated around the crowd. Now the entire town was out, unlike my sunrise session. I still managed to catch a bunch of waves.

I really liked a lefthander that was on the south side of Madera's beach. There was also a wave I did not investigate that was even farther to the south, breaking off a rock point offering a beautiful lefthander. It was sketchier in the sense that the wave broke off a big outcropping boulder, jetting out of the ocean. Ideally, I would sit inside or just next to that rock and catch the wave as it peeled off the rock. Still, it seemed there were more rocks under there. I was too nervous to go over alone to investigate…

I got a few bad vibes from the local barrel-hunting shredders, but besides a couple of looks, it was all good. I just moved over to a different peak. I got out just before the sun went down. Pri and I went for a swim, duck diving through some waves near a bunch of different outcropping rocks, which in hindsight was sketchy, but fun in the moment! We hiked back to the hotel the right way this time, showered off, and had dinner at the café overlooking the ocean again. We planned on hanging out at the beach the next morning, and after lunch, we would drive back to Costa Rica.

The next morning, I didn't wake up as early to surf, just because I knew it was my last session and wanted to have some coffee and chill first. I preferred not to rush and have one more solid session for two or three hours before lunch. I took a coffee down to the beach and checked what Mother Ocean was providing us.

It was by far the biggest day out of the three I was there. This was the real deal Madera. I'm sure it potentially got even bigger, but this was no joke, well overhead, powerful waves. I walked back up, had breakfast, and was planning to charge it. We packed up our stuff into the car and drove to the break this time, instead of hiking the trail, and would leave for Costa Rica from there.

I paddled out and was trying to decide where I wanted to be and where I was trying to avoid. I saw a set come in, a total powerhouse. It was breaking much deeper than the previous days. I paddled back to get into the right area to try and time one of them. I waited a while. Another set came and I hopped on the first one, popping up on my Hypto Krypto as it was still developing. It walled up fast, and I pumped like hell to stay in front of it. I was hauling-ass until the section in front of me was closing out toward me. I launched myself off the pitching lip, landing behind the wave, airing off my board at least six feet in the air. My adrenalin was pumping, and I paddled back for more. I caught a handful of these beefy overhead set waves before I called it a day and got out to meet up with Pri and head out of Nicaragua.

An hour and a half later, we were returning the rental car, and they didn't see anything they could charge us extra for. Win! I took my soft roof rack off the car and stuck it in my rucksack. Once again, we walked through the post-apocalyptic no man's land between both countries. Costa Rica didn't require an exit stamp from Nicaragua like Nicaragua does, and Costa Rica's entrance stamp was free. Go figure.

We walked all the way back while holding my boards, struggling, until we got back through to where we parked. We had to walk up to an armed military toll booth that was meant for the mile-long line of grid-locked semi-trucks entering Costa Rica. We snaked on foot in between the semitrucks to show our passports in the middle of the road.

We got through and got back to my car. I tossed my boards and rucksack through the hatchback into the car. Finally. I was sweating so bad. We paid the man $15 for three days we parked on the crazy property with chained up Chihuahuas everywhere and drove off. We had to go through another Costa Rican toll booth checkpoint, and they stopped us again for my license plate. They told us it was illegal, and we could not enter the country without two plates. I wasn't sure my car had even left their country, but they stopped us regardless. In Spanish, Pri politely explained how one fell off in a river, and we were going to replace it promptly, and they let us through. Once again, only because she was Costa Rican. The trip was her idea, but it was only successful because of her and her ability to talk to the local police. If it was just me on this trip alone or with other gringos, I would have been screwed. We got back to Tamarindo early that night. A success!

Juking The Masses

This is one topic I don't really want to talk about as it's one of my secrets in life, bettering the quality of my life experiences, but it needs to happen. Average people in this world need to stop existing unaware and start thinking for themselves. I lived in Brooklyn, Chicago, Phoenix, Denver, San Francisco, Oakland, and Los Angeles. I lived in places that weren't cities too, but my focus is that after living in so many densely populated areas, I started noticing my quality of life going down the toilet. Everything I ever did took SO long, sometimes ten times the amount of time it should, because of the number of people trying to do the exact same thing at the exact same time.

Driving to work during rush hour in Los Angeles, or in San Francisco over the Bay Bridge. Good luck with that. Or going to the grocery store at 6 p.m. after work to pick up food for dinner at the Trader Joes in Eagle Rock, Los Angeles. Good luck with that. You'll never even find a parking spot, let alone make it out of that packed store. In San Francisco, there would be a line wrapping around the entire store's perimeter to check out at the Safeway on Mission St. It would take two hours to buy a single banana. The same thing goes with dinner on a Friday night, brunch on Sunday, or surfing.

If you are trying to get better at surfing DO NOT GO SURFING WHEN THE REST OF THE WORLD GOES SURFING. Or if you are a decent surfer, then get better by being crafty, and if the world knows the local break is awesome at mid-to-high-tide, paddle out just after low, and surf it into mid-tide, getting better waves throughout your session until it gets too crowded, then get the hell out of there. Let the people without brains fight and compete for the thing they are supposed to love that gives them happiness. They sure don't look happy at busy times. Surf sunrise. If you can't get out of bed by 5 a.m., change something in your life. The early bird catches the worm, but the smart bird knows where the worms are and when they're out.

I've surfed breaks that are packed at sunrise and dead by 9 or 10 a.m. Switch it up and go then. There are too many people in this world today all doing the same thing you wish to do, making us all very not special. So, get off your high horse, like you invented the sport and are the only one doing it. Will you head to a surf break expecting to catch waves when there are one hundred other not special people all there with the same expectations of catching all the waves? If there are only three waves every five minutes, what do you expect to happen? Too many average surfers look at the forecast, look at the current conditions, look at the tide, and see when it's going to be best that day or best in their free time that day, and go. There needs to be another layer of wherewithal in planning. Where you ask yourself, "what will ninety percent of other surfers do when they see these conditions and tides, today?"

Drive farther, research harder, wake up earlier, surf non-ideal tides and conditions, etc... These are ways to score. My definition of scoring is catching waves on a day when the conditions are decent, good, or great, and the most important part being when there is close to no one else there. The less the better. Giving me pick of almost any wave I want. This is truly scoring waves. Not being aggro and talking smack to people in order to intimidate them to catch waves. Or having a dozen surfers drop in on the same wave expecting the best ride of their lives. I'd rather be surfing shitty, windblown, off-tide, or smaller waves, still catching whatever I wanted, than sitting in a lineup of fifty people, watching the most angry, aggressive, yelling, asshole, macho dudes be the only ones catching waves, ruining everyone else's stoke.

Even better, I left California and surf the east coast every summer now for the last three years while working, and it has been a pleasure, surfing miles and miles of empty beach breaks with some decent swells and often offshore or glassy days. I still love the other places, of course, but people in them don't appreciate what they have on a communal scale. Entitlement is the worst thing in the world, and it's fake. Surfers have entitlement issues and false clout because they work at the local grocery store in a surf town and think that means they deserve more waves than someone else, for example. This is gross, fake, and a problem with the world. George Greenough in the *Crystal Voyager* surf film from 1973 talks about this and how he prefers to surf crazy spots alone to get away from everyone. I completely understand.

Surfing in these modern days takes surf skills plus navigation skills to navigate the masses. Juking the masses. If you possess both skill sets, you're on your way to a much more stoked, fulfilled surfing future. If there are a hundred surfers out at your favorite spot, and you have your board in the car checking spots, go to the grocery store. It'll probably be empty. I learned this behavior in San Francisco when I had a bartender's schedule. I started connecting the dots between the past cities and the punishment I had put myself through. A bartender's schedule is generally off during the day and working at night. I started work anytime between 5 p.m. and 10 p.m., and I would surf during the day. I went grocery shopping with the beautiful, retired grandmas at 1 p.m. I would cross the Golden Gate Bridge at 2 p.m. and cross it again at 3 a.m. after work, headed home. It was always a ghost town. I lived in a city and never saw traffic or crowds, only from behind the bar. It was bliss. My point is, the nine to five job commitment is forcing people to get trapped in their everyday lives. Trapped even outside of their job. In lines, traffic, busy everything from the majority, all living within the same time commitments. Since I quit my last full-time job over five years ago and started hustling more entrepreneurially, I never felt freer and happier. If you're not stoked on your job, go make some bread from scratch and sell it on the corner metaphorically. You'll be stoked.

The moment I quit my last regular job was one of the best days of my life. I worked for a lighting/audio/video/staging/power/decor company in San Francisco. I was their technical producer, producing their events for clients. I worked in the office for about a year after being a freelance audio, video, and lighting engineer for a few years. I hated my life. I didn't realize my level of upset-ness, as I, and most other people out there, bury these work/freedom-less feelings deep down, trying to justify them or temporarily cover them with spending money or drinking.

I took a trip for a few days, which required me to request days off. I needed to acquire permission to live my life for a few days, and my request was granted by the all-powerful, gracious boss. I went on a motorcycle camping trip in California with friends and after, went back to work. I had all this accrued paid time off that was part of my compensation package. I still had a bunch of days leftover, after I took the motorcycle trip, as I had not taken a day off the entire year.

The week I got back to work, from my short motorcycle trip, I put in another request to take a few days off a couple of weeks later. After I sent this email request to ask for permission to go live my life again, I got a denied response and a request for a meeting with my superiors. They called me into their office for a talk.

"Dave, you know this is our busy season, and you're one of our only four producers, and you just took a trip. You can't keep taking time off whenever you want... We need our producers to be here," the all-powerful bosses told me as if I was in trouble for asking to go live my life again.

"Ok, then I quit. I don't want to do this anymore." I said nonchalantly without much thought or emotion.

I got up and walked out of their office. I sat back down at my desk in the communal producer office. They immediately called me back in.

"We're sorry, we meant you actually can take off as much time as you want. Take more if you need, and we'll pay you a higher salary, too," the all-powerful bosses said, backpedaling.

I called their bluff. But the seed was planted. I was done. I saw my freedom flash right before my eyes and I took it.

"Na, I'm not interested in doing this anymore and you just made me realize it right now," I told them as if I were a simple child telling them I didn't like playing with a particular toy anymore.

"We'll double your salary," the all-powerful bosses said in desperation.

"Thanks anyway, I'll stay till the end of the month for you." I told them.

They tried everything to keep me there because my position had about a six-month training period until the employee would be completely proficient in the role. That was a difficult thing to replace during "a busy season." I just woke up.

"This sucks," I realized. "Why am I doing this? This is my life."

267

I dove into bartending and bar managing full-time and didn't look back. I also made my own schedule. I took off any shift I didn't want to work and went on living MY life again. Working to live, not living to work. But what sounds more prestigious? An audiovisual technical producer and designer for filthy rich tech companies in Silicon Valley, or a bartender? These are the things I had to let go to truly be happy.

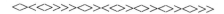

Whenever I was on a flight back to the USA, I tried remembering everything I had experienced in the unique country I visited and told myself I would try to implement this traveler-mindset back in the states. It was this type of behavior – always reaching out to people, being more extroverted, asking questions, being inquisitive, being outgoing and spontaneous – that kept my happiness up and mind growing. I wanted to continue the search, to be "after it" – after new experiences, growth, and excitement, in all aspects of my life. Even when I was not actively traveling. Or are we always traveling forever in our lives?

For a healthy mind, I think it's important to have this spontaneity and outwardness, otherwise, we can become stagnant and introverted, which can lead to doubt, insecurity, depression, etc. I want to push myself to be better at this every day. Happiness is not free. It's as organic and sensitive as your physical body, which always needs fuel and maintenance. Positive attitudes, healthy lifestyles, and pushing my own boundaries are all ways of keeping my stoked tank full and happiness levels up.

Unfortunately, the real-world modern-day rat race strips everyone of their positive energy. I defend myself daily by doing everything I can to simplify, resist society's judgements, and feed my stoke. What I practice are active strategies to help happiness grow from within. Inward happiness exudes outward happiness, but outward happiness without the spark or seed from within is only temporary.

PMA! Positive Mental Attitude

These are the activities that I have found make me the happiest person I have ever been in my life. Learning is everything. Be a student forever. The moment you think you know everything, your life is over. Modesty is key.

I was in two motorcycle accidents in my life on Harley-Davidsons. Both had a very high potential to be deadly, but I luckily managed to get out alive with nothing more than road rash and a boxer's hand fracture. One accident was in Tempe, Arizona when I was riding to my production job one morning. A college kid, texting behind the wheel of an SUV doing 50 mph (80 kph), didn't see me sitting at a four-way stop sign. Without even breaking, he hit my bike from behind catapulting me off superman-style.

I had no helmet on. Arizona does not require it by law, and I was young and dumb. I did a flying front flip in the air from the force of the car crashing into my rear wheel. I flew over my little, tight-grip chopper handlebars that my friend made for me and had the force and trajectory same as being shot from a cannon. An off-duty EMT witnessed the entire thing and documented that after my summer-salt, flying through the air, I landed on my head and shoulders and slid for over one-hundred feet. I never lost consciousness. I don't remember being hit, but I do remember flying through the air. I remember the feeling of grinding my head, shoulder, back, and body on the asphalt until I came to a dead stop.

"Shit." I remember thinking.

But for some reason, it was with a smile. Like a masochistic stunt man, enjoying the trauma, or enjoying that my ordinary day just got tossed an exciting curve ball. The off duty jogging EMT man called an ambulance immediately. He thought he had just witnessed a death. Or at least a spinal injury bad enough to cause paralysis or head trauma bad enough to not wake up from.

The ambulance arrived and the EMTs threw me on a stretcher and tossed me into the ambulance. From there, they poked and prodded me the whole way to the hospital asking if I was losing my feeling. I had been joking with them and making them laugh. I felt fine, but they told me it was impossible for me to be fine after what I just went through.

After five minutes in the ambulance, I told them my feet were tingling. They freaked out and thought I was going paralyzed in front of them. It turned out I bought a new pair of Vans skate shoes the day before and always bought them a half size too small. I would put them in the oven or microwave, heat them up and wear them around to fit my feet perfectly for optimal skateboarding performance. Also, because my feet are a half size different from each other, it was impossible to buy shoes that fit correctly, and this helped. I forgot that I bought new shoes and didn't have time to heat them to fit right yet, so my feet were losing circulation from them being too tight, not from paralysis. I sure gave those ambulance workers a scare. Once they rushed me into the emergency room, thinking I had internal bleeding and was going to die or be paralyzed, I had all the attention from every doctor in the whole hospital the second I was pushed through the front doors. This is how you beat the wait at the emergency room. Make them think you're dying.

After every minute, more doctors peeled off and went back to what they were doing previously until only one remained.

"Well, I can't find anything wrong with you, so I guess you can get up and go if you'd like..." He said as if annoyed I wasn't in worse shape.

Like I waisted his time as a doctor.

I hopped up off the tall gurney onto the floor. I jogged in place throwing celebratory dancing air punches like Rocky Balboa beating an impossible opponent. I was victorious.

This accident woke me up. It told me that, at any given moment, my life can and will be over. That's it. That quickly. That's all the time we get.

In my second motorcycle accident, I was forced to drop my Harley on its side doing forty-five miles per hour (72 kph) because an old woman cut me off. She tried making a left from the fast lane in the opposite direction, not the turn lane. I had to lay down the bike to avoid T-boning right into the side of her car. This time, I had to watch my now ex-girlfriend bouncing on the asphalt while I slid backward down the street tearing our skin to shreds. Again, in the end, it turned out we were both fine, but it woke me up for a second time in my life. It woke me up to realize that I could be and should be dead from these situations.

Due to my adventurous behaviors and activities, I have managed to almost kill myself or skirt around death a handful of other times as well, including my almost drowning and out-of-body experience at Ocean Beach, San Francisco. After every experience was a wake-up call. The message: "Enjoy every moment where you are now because it will sooner than later be gone."

If you have a dream, live it. If you have a bucket list, start it. If you are unhappy in your life, change it. Now. We all inherently won't have later forever. Let this serve as a wake-up call for anyone in search of it. THIS IS THE SIGN. You don't need to go to a funeral or have something horrible happen to you for you to wake up and start smelling the roses in your life daily. Ignore the rat race. Ignore negatives from society and people putting you down. It's all about a positive outlook, and a positive mental attitude. I'm here to be stoked.

Live. See. Exist. Experience. Be true to what you are, a soul in this temporary vessel, here to live, learn, and love.

Time to go shred.

About The Author

Dave Boss is a 35-year-old nomad who was born and raised in central New Jersey. After high school, for the last 17 years, Dave has bounced around western America, eventually living internationally. After decades of skateboarding, snowboarding, surfing, playing music, and traveling in all atmospheres, he has found a balance between being active and creative as his yin and yang in a healthy, sober, adventuring lifestyle.

Dave received a bachelor's degree in art from Columbia College Chicago in his early 20s on his path west. He has lived in New Jersey, New York City, Chicago, Denver, Phoenix, San Francisco, Los Angeles, Hawai'i and Costa Rica. He can now be found traveling, learning new cultures, surfing, at the gym weight training, playing music, shooting photography, or hiking with his Australian Cattle Dog, Rodeo.

Dave finds inspiration through genuine experiences, nature and people who live authentically in the moment. A spiritual connection with nature is most important, which is why he will continue to explore, always seeking more. *Juking The Masses* is Dave's first book. He was inspired to write it by how many hotel guests he spoke with over the three years of managing his family's hotel, who were interested in his life, and repeatedly told him to write a book. He still doesn't think his life is that unique.

His upcoming adventures are to explore more surf destinations in places less traveled as *Juking The Masses* is partially about navigating the overpopulated world. He continues to seek out locations in the world with epic beauty that are still pure and empty.

Coming soon…Bali Bound

Bali, Indonesia. The Island of The Gods. The most sought-after destination this year by people all around the world. Bali opened its doors April 1, 2022, after being closed for over two years from the pandemic. Surfers, yogis, digital nomads, remote workers, influencers, backpackers, vacationers, political refugees, and everyone else curious, all trying to move to Bali to exist in Bali's incredible energy.

This adventure starts with Dave Boss spontaneously visiting Bali five years earlier, on a month-long solo-traveling surf trip, as a less advanced surfer. He visited Bali two more times since then in 2022, spending three months there after the country's reopening. Dave spent time adventuring, surfing, and living as a local. He noticed the island and surf towns in it had changed drastically from his first trip, five years earlier, and even between his two separate trips this year. Between May and October. The difference between Bali in May compared to October was unbelievable. He had experienced Bali in May, only 30 days after its reopening, before the masses had arrived. Then experiencing Bali in October, after the masses had come from all over the world, once everyone knew it was open to visit, live, and work remotely. The demand turned Bali and its surf towns upside down into a hectic, futuristic zoo with all walks of life.

As a world-traveling surfer of over twelve years, Dave explains and explores Bali's world-famous surf breaks and other surf breaks that are lesser known, but just as epic. He writes for the beginner surfer to understand, the intermediate surfer to take his advice, the advanced surfer to connect with, or someone who doesn't surf but is interested in the hype of Bali and surfing for a vicarious read. *Bali Bound* also incorporates the unique traveling friendships he made while on this journey.

Dave describes Bali's vastly different cultural dichotomy between its Hindu, Muslim, and western influenced zones. He breaks down Bali's cheap economy, which is very enticing for Americans and the world, currently dealing with inflation and difficult living in modern day. *Bali Bound* allows the world to see Bali through Dave's surf-adventuring eyes during the most popular time Bali has ever seen.

Made in the USA
Middletown, DE
29 May 2023